THE GOTHIC KING

By the same author and published by Peter Owen

Robin Hood: The Unknown Templar
Pity for the Guy: A Biography of Guy Fawkes

THE GOTHIC KING

A BIOGRAPHY OF HENRY III

PETER OWEN PUBLISHERS
London and Chicago

PETER OWEN PUBLISHERS
31 Ridge Road, London N8 9NP

Peter Owen books are distributed in the USA and Canada by
Independent Publishers Group
814 North Franklin Street, Chicago, IL, 60610, USA

First published in 2013 by Peter Owen Publishers

ISBN 978-07206-1480-0

A catalogue record for this book is available
from the British Library

Printed and bound in Great Britain by
CPI Group (UK) Ltd, Croydon CR0 4YY

DEDICATION

For my parents

ACKNOWLEDGEMENTS

Writing a biography of Henry III has been an enormous pleasure for many reasons and greatly enhanced by the past efforts of others. Before the nineteenth century it would have been nearly impossible to complete a book of this magnitude without decades of painstaking research of the original paper records. Thanks to the work of people such as Henry Richards Luard and John Allen Giles in the mid-1800s the work of the original chroniclers are today accessible to all and are undoubtedly the most important sources for this work. Similarly over the past century our knowledge of the period is indebted to the work of a number of historians. Among the most relevant to this investigation are the works of Sir Maurice Powicke, David Carpenter, J.R. Maddicott and Sir James Holt, all of which have added greatly to my understanding, and enjoyment, of the subject. Obviously any errors in the text are my own responsibility.

Since embarking on my research I have been led on the most unexpected journey, not only through history but across England and Wales. It has been both entertaining and enlightening. My visits to Winchester, Canterbury, Lewes and Evesham were especially memorable. On these occasions I owe a debt of gratitude not to a single eminent historian but to the organizations that care for their buildings' preservation. Over the past three years I have been aided by all types of people, including librarians, clergy, and, perhaps most important of all, volunteer guides, every single one of which took the time to answer my questions with genuine enthusiasm. Thanks to the tireless commitment of bodies such as the Simon de Montfort Society, the Lewes Priory Trust, the Sussex Archaeological Society, the Churches Conservation Trust, Cadw, English Heritage and the National Trust not only do the physical sites continue to stand long after those who once occupied them but each decade seems to bring new discoveries that continue to shape our understanding of history.

As usual I extend my gratitude to all at Peter Owen Publishers for commissioning the book and for their support throughout the writing of my three historical biographies.

My most heartfelt gratitude must be reserved for my friends and family, in particular my wonderful parents Mike and Kay Davis whose support and enthusiasm has shaped the creation of this book. Separate thanks are also due to my father and my uncle, Pat Sayles, for contributing the photographs credited to them in the plates section and, in some cases, travelling specifically to take them.

My last acknowledgement I reserve for little Adam. Welcome to the family!

CONTENTS

PREFACE

History is strange in many ways. Whatever the time, place or country, its tales are often subject to different interpretations based on our environment and perceptions.

For no period is this more true than the Middle Ages. For many people, particularly Europeans, this is the period that symbolizes history most completely. When visiting one of the great castles or cathedrals it is easy to let our imagination run wild, allowing us to connect with the way things were, at least according to the way we have been brought up to see them. Yet the possibilities are endless. When writing a history book or essay, be it a broad investigation or a historical biography, it is common to start out with one set of beliefs and end with another. The Middle Ages are like that.

It was a similar experience that set me on my way to writing the book you are about to read. Few people in England will have heard of the village of Beaudesert. Located eight miles from Stratford-upon-Avon, adjacent to Henley-in-Arden in the heart of Warwickshire, it is easily missed if you do not know it is there. Even less well known is that Beaudesert once had a castle. In its prime this had been a glorious motte-and-bailey structure, typical of early Plantagenet England, overlooking the village. Researching the matter, I learnt that its owners had been a family called the de Montforts. Like most English people I had heard the name before. Many will be vaguely familiar with the exploits of Simon de Montfort, 6th Earl of Leicester, who brought about reform during the thirteenth century. The discovery at Beaudesert intrigued me. Could it be that Simon had a castle that history had forgotten?

Two surprises awaited. The Angevin pedigree of the Earls of Leicester was sufficiently removed from the Norman-bred de Montforts of Beaudesert to confirm that there were no blood ties, but the families did have a different connection. The lord of Beaudesert at the time of Simon's rise to power was Peter de Montfort, himself instrumental in the reforms of 1258–65. Incredibly, the lord of the disappeared Beaudesert Castle was the man who oversaw Simon's famous Parliament of 1258. In a way he was the first speaker of the House of Commons.

At the time I was writing another book, later to be published as *Robin Hood: The Unknown Templar*. According to one medieval chronicler, the legendary outlaw had lived during the thirteenth century and been in league with the de Montforts. My quest for Robin Hood took me to Simon de Montfort's head-quarters, the mighty Kenilworth Castle, not far from Beaudesert. If this chronicler was correct, the historical Robin Hood had been part of a major rebellion. In searching for the legendary outlaw I found myself wondering what exactly happened during the thirteenth century to encourage Simon and Peter de Montfort to pursue their political reforms.

The signs at Kenilworth pointed to rebellion against King Henry III.

Though my search for Robin Hood moved on, the enigmatic king was starting to capture my interest. I wanted to discover what happened to the de Montforts during their rebellion of 1258–65. For over 700 years the most commonly held view was

that the King of England's misgovernment and wastefulness had
brought about the rebellion. Simon's success was a challenge to
the absolute authority of the Plantagenet dynasty and sowed the
seeds of later democracy. Indeed, as recently as the nineteenth
century he was mistakenly viewed as the founder of Parliament.

Strange that the king was so little known.

It was somewhat ironic to me to learn that Henry III had been
the eldest son of King John – the king, alongside Richard I, most
closely associated with Robin Hood and also famous as the king
who signed the Magna Carta at Runnymede. Contrary to popular belief, it was Henry, not John, who dealt with the fall-out
from the Magna Carta. John died within two years of the events
at Runnymede, and it was Henry who had to deal with its implications. He was still a child when he succeeded his father, and
the implications of the charter were untested. A new thought
came to my mind. Was it possible that Henry III's largely forced
acceptance of the Magna Carta was at least partly responsible
for the rise of Simon de Montfort?

Though I no longer believed Henry III to be the king mentioned in the tales of Robin Hood, the Middle Ages were a strange
period. Yet again what began as one thing developed into something different. Without question Henry III's connection with
Kenilworth was significant, and over the next few months it
became clear that this king, so seldom mentioned in the history
books, was responsible for the construction or development of
many of the great ruined castles that still mark the landscapes
of England and Wales. We have all heard of Edward I, and his
'Iron Ring' of castles that dominates the Welsh landscape is
legendary. It now became less surprising that Henry III was
Edward's father.

By early 2011 I had decided that my third historical biography had to be of King Henry III. When I made this choice

known, most of my friends and family reacted in a similar way. They asked, first of all, who was he? The second I found altogether more amusing.

Henry III? Don't you mean Henry VIII?

I dare say this is something that all of the previous seven Henrys have in common, at least outside the academic community. While many reading this will undoubtedly recall the activities of Henry VIII's father, Henry VII, and his triumph over Richard III in the Wars of the Roses, the long and important reign of Henry II, later infamous for his feud with that 'turbulent priest' St Thomas Becket, or the active yet at times distorted achievements of Henry V, few kings have quite captured the imagination like the man who married six times. It is strange how some kings are so much better known than others. The more I thought about this, the less sense it made. What makes a king great? Does he have to be victorious in battle? Did he serve his people conspicuously well? In every century there is a new readership and a different group of historians, all looking to judge a king or queen by the values and expectations of their time. How else could a king like John be viewed as a monster between the thirteenth and sixteenth centuries, an English patriot in the seventeenth, only to be consigned to ignominy again within a hundred years?

What struck me most was that many of the most favoured kings were not particularly outstanding. When I was researching my biography of Guy Fawkes I was intrigued to learn that the man famed for attempting to destroy the government was also voted in one poll as the thirtieth greatest Briton who ever lived. Did Fawkes really deserve that accolade? Writing the Guy Fawkes book provided me with an answer. It isn't about the man's achievements or even his personal qualities. It is simply about how successfully he has been presented to the public.

At that moment I came to a new realization. Not once has Henry III been featured as the central character on film or television or in the theatre. There have been no historical epics, no dramatized television series about the antics and activities of the man or his court. Nor are there any quotes from Shakespeare. This was the impetus I needed to inspire my research.

The challenges of each historical investigation are unique. With Henry III they certainly differed from those of my previous research. The purpose of this book is not necessarily to answer specific questions. Unlike Robin Hood, there is no doubt that Henry III existed; unlike Guy Fawkes, the life of Henry III is not overshadowed by a single event. Certainly there are parallels – between the Magna Carta and Robin Hood's alleged battle for justice, for instance – but, while Guy Fawkes fought against a king he viewed as a tyrant, Henry's story was much more complex.

The biggest challenge with any biography is finding solid evidence. In the case of Robin Hood it is very limited; with Guy Fawkes it is largely confined to one event and location. With Henry III there is a different problem: there is so much of it. Since the twelfth century practically every aspect of government in England has been set down on paper. Many of these records survive, and over the past two centuries a good number have been translated from the original Latin or French into English. In addition to royal accounts letters, documents and other written accounts have been tremendously useful. Perhaps most importantly, and certainly at the heart of this investigation, I am grateful for the tireless efforts of the medieval chroniclers to record the events of their times.

In the case of Henry III there is certainly no shortage of information, nor should there be for a man who lived for sixty-five years, reigning for fifty-six. What surprised me is how little of it is currently in the public consciousness – again at least outside the academic community. During the past century only two eminent historians covered the subject at length. Sir Maurice Powicke did so twice, first with his 1947 two-volume work, *King Henry III and the Lord Edward*, and again with his *Oxford History* of 1963. The second was David Carpenter, author of the 1996 publication *The Reign of Henry III*. Both are unique and invaluable. Since that day in Beaudesert I have regularly turned to their work, often finding myself struck by their thinking – even if at times they disagree with one another or I with them.

My greatest disappointment was how few historians have attempted to approach Henry's long reign chronologically. The thematic approach of Powicke and Carpenter was appropriate because their aim was to target areas that needed particular examination. Similarly, in the nineteenth century, both Henry Richards Luard and Francis Gasquet devoted books to Henry's relations with the papacy. But not since the days of William Hunt and Thomas Frederic Tout in the late nineteenth century has there been an endeavour similar to the one I have undertaken.

The objective of this book is threefold. First, it has been my attempt to present the reign of Henry III in the most straightforward way possible.

Second, I wanted to paint a portrait of the man. While many historians have focused on the events of Henry's reign, his personality and achievements have been regarded as of secondary importance. This book is not, therefore, about a battle, uncovering an identity or even the culmination of a set of circumstances. In many ways Henry III's anonymity has helped me. Unlike some of his predecessors and successors, only a handful of stereotypes needed to be addressed. Better still, unlike monarchs such as Richard and John, perceptions of Henry III have not been conditioned by any deeply entrenched beliefs in popular mythology or indeed my own views.

Third, the reforms championed by de Montfort in 1258–65 have long been viewed as the key feature of Henry's long reign. That they were the most important is fair, but it cannot reasonably be argued that his reign can be defined simply by one event. For that reason I have tried to offer a balanced representation of every year of Henry's reign, rather than concentrating on a particular area. My aim has been to understand what he did and who he was. I have attempted to provide a solid account of all his military activities, particularly his conflicts with Wales and France. Also of significance are his religious endeavours, his relations with his family and, perhaps most enthrallingly, an insight into his mind and personal tastes, which helped produce the famous Gothic architecture that we still see around us today.

As mentioned, the structure of this book is grounded in chronology rather than themes. On a few occasions I found it necessary to segment some areas to avoid confusion – for instance, it would be difficult to follow the events of Henry's visit to Gascony and France in 1253–4 while simultaneously attempting to understand the concurrent events in Sicily – but even here I have proceeded with care. By presenting a chronological commentary I believe it is possible to see the reign of Henry III as a progressive evolution. During the thirteenth century England went through a process of transition. During his fifty-six years on the throne his country advanced, arguably every bit as far and perhaps further than at any other time in history.

In bringing the events of this often troublesome period to life, the biggest problem I found was how deep to dig. This book could have been at least ten times longer than it is. I have decided to present the key events accurately and objectively, leaving critical evaluation to the final chapter. This book is about a man and his time. I hope you will find it enjoyable and enlightening.

PRELUDE

From Rouen to Runnymede

Plagued by fatigue and illness, King John of England ended his days at Newark on 19 October 1216, some time in the early hours of the morning. He had reigned for seventeen years, five months.

His last week had been one of the most difficult. England was at war at home and under attack from abroad. A substantial body of French troops had reportedly landed in England five days earlier, strengthening the cause of the rebellious English barons and their new leader, Prince Louis of France. In the eyes of much of England Louis was now the rightful king and potentially just days away from completing his conquest.[1]

It was written by an anonymous Barnwell annalist that John was a busy prince but seldom a contented one. As the fifth and youngest son of Henry II and Eleanor of Aquitaine, he was never likely to become a king. The first in line had been William, who died in infancy. Following him was Henry, who was crowned as joint king alongside his father. Had Henry the Young survived, he would have reigned as Henry III, but death in 1183 prevented him from inheriting the throne.[2]

Henry II's death on 6 July 1189 marked the end of an industrious reign that had seen the empire of the King of England extend across much of modern-day France.[3] He had failed to live long enough to take his revenge on his rebellious son Richard but just long enough for John, the son he cherished, to desert him. With Henry's passing and burial at Fontevraud the Crown of England passed to Richard, along with the Angevin Empire that included Ireland, the duchies of Normandy and Aquitaine and the counties of Poitou and Anjou.[4] He reigned for ten years before dying without a legitimate heir. As Richard lay on his deathbed he announced that John would reign as his successor.[5]

On hearing the news John left Normandy, arriving at Shoreham on 25 May 1199, and hurried to Westminster two days later for his coronation. Like his predecessor he knelt before the high altar and swore in the presence of the barons and clerics to observe peace with God and the Church, to administer justice to those in his care and put an end to any evil laws or customs in his realm. Once he had sworn his oath he was undressed down to his undergarments and anointed with oil on his head, chest and hands by Hubert, Archbishop of Canterbury. For the clergy the anointing with oil was the heart of the ceremony, even more than the crowning. Only through that rite was the king of England bestowed with the authority of God to rule as monarch.[6]

In France John's long-time antagonist, King Philip II, prepared a long-awaited invasion of Normandy. Loyalty to John in Normandy was finely balanced, despite the recommendation of both Richard and their mother, Eleanor of Aquitaine, that the nobles should swear fealty to John. In nearby Anjou, Maine and Touraine the nobles rebuked John for past treachery against his father and brother and declared their intention to follow the custom that the right of succession belonged first to the eldest son of an elder brother in preference to a younger brother of the current king. Thus their backing went to John's nephew, Arthur, Duke of Brittany, the twelve-year-old son of John's late brother, Geoffrey.[7]

Less than a month after he was crowned, John returned to Normandy. He held an assembly at Rouen in August and managed to consolidate both military support from Normandy and England and the allegiance of at least fifteen French counts, in addition to his nephew, the King of the Germans. His prudence in taking advantage of his brother's past diplomacy and his mother's shrewdness allowed him to secure Normandy peacefully. Arthur and his mother paid homage to John on 22 September, though less than twenty-four hours passed before rumour of a plot against him saw Arthur enter into an alliance with Philip of France. However, the latter was reluctant to go to war. John's resources in England and the Angevin empire were still formidable, even though much weaker than his father's. The temporary stalemate forced Philip to agree to the Treaty of Le Goulet on 22 May 1200, confirming John as Richard's heir, with Arthur ruling Brittany on John's behalf. The following day cordial relations reached their height at the celebration of the wedding of John's niece, Blanche, daughter of Alphonso of Castile, and Philip's son, Louis (later Louis VIII).[8]

Within eighteen months of his coronation John remarried. His first marriage to Isabella, the granddaughter of the Earl of Gloucester, himself an illegitimate son of Henry I, had been condemned by the Pope owing to their close family ties (they were second cousins), and even after ten years of marriage John was still to father a legitimate heir.[9] On his accession he sought the assistance of some of the bishops, and the Church eagerly approved the annulment of the marriage. His new wife, also named Isabella, was daughter and heiress of Angoulême, part of Poitou, and aged somewhere between nine and fifteen. They married on 24 August 1200 in Bordeaux, and within two months both were crowned at Westminster Abbey on 8 October.[10]

Despite its advantages for John, the marriage created at least one problem. At the time Isabella was already betrothed to the powerful Hugh de Lusignan, a lord of Poitou, whose anger at John saw his allegiance pass to the King of France.[11] Philip was equally mystified by John's behaviour. So great were Hugh's complaints that Philip summoned John to appear before him. As Duke of Normandy and Aquitaine and Count of Poitou and Anjou, John was a vassal of the King of France and ruled the lands as a fief of the Kingdom of France.[12] When John failed to attend, Philip's anger boiled over. By April 1202 he had knighted Arthur and announced confiscation of all of John's territories in France in favour of the prince and began preparations for Arthur to marry his daughter, Mary.[13]

As Philip and the Count of Boulogne continued into Normandy prepared for war, Arthur and the Lusignans captured Eleanor and held her prisoner at Mirebeau in Poitou. John's reaction was unsurprisingly heated. Despite his frosty relationship with Eleanor in his youth, whatever bad blood once existed had faded following the death of Eleanor's other children, and during his absence from Normandy John placed the duchy under her capable supervision. While still at Le Mans John put plans in place to rescue his mother, and forty-eight hours later Mirebeau was taken by surprise attack. The victory was commendable, comparing even with the triumphs of Richard, but John's lust for revenge was to prove costly. His lack of mercy for his prisoners, many of whom were knights of Anjou, lost him the respect of his key followers, William des Roches and Aimeri of Thouars, leading to their defection. By early 1203 John had lost the key city of Angers in Anjou, and his withdrawal into Normandy left Philip unopposed to take Anjou, Touraine and Maine.[14]

In the course of the hostilities Arthur disappeared, almost certainly murdered. The young duke's appalling treatment of Eleanor was perhaps John's one justification, but rumours of his fate won

John little favour among his supporters. His inability to keep the lords onside saw him return to England with Normandy all but doomed. By April 1204 Eleanor was dead, losing him another key ally in Poitou, and by June Normandy was lost. As his position continued to weaken the King of Castile invaded Gascony.[15]

Two years passed before John launched a defence of his realms. His army had assembled at Portsmouth in numbers in 1205, but the barons' refusal to support him forced the expedition to be cancelled.[16] When he finally managed to get a force to La Rochelle by July the following year he was at last able to consolidate his hold on Isabella's birthright before driving the Castilians from Gascony. His march took him to Anjou, at which point the warring kings came to terms. John had succeeded in salvaging Gascony and much of Poitou, but he was unable to reclaim anything else. In the context of English history the event marked a significant turning point. For the first time since the conquest the King of England was now ruling territory primarily in England and Ireland alone.[17]

While problems overseas had proved a challenge to John throughout his reign, an even greater one was his difficult relationship with the papacy. Following the death of Hugh, Bishop of Lincoln, in 1200 John kept the see vacant for two years, enabling him to profit by over £2,000.[18] A similar situation occurred after the death of his key adviser Hubert, Archbishop of Canterbury, in 1205. The monks and bishops of the province each appealed for the right to participate in a free election for his successor.[19] While John argued for a postponement, hoping to profit once more from a vacant see, some of the monks elected Reginald, sub-prior of Canterbury, and immediately looked for validation from Rome. But shortly afterwards, rather than arouse the wrath of the king, the election was forgone in favour of John's favourite, John, Bishop of Norwich.

Back in Rome Pope Innocent III quashed both elections and invited the monks, though not the bishops, to hold another. After further deadlock Innocent put forward a new candidate, Stephen Langton. Despite approval from the monks John refused. In the feud that followed Innocent consecrated Cardinal Langton as archbishop in 1207 while John seized Canterbury's assets and refused Langton entry into England.[20]

These events continued to dictate much of England's future. In response to John's refusal to inaugurate Langton, the realm was placed under an interdict – forbidding certain rites – on 23 March 1208.[21] All Sunday services were banned, and no Christian could be buried in consecrated ground. For a country that was fervently Christian the result was disastrous. Stories began to circulate of large numbers of corpses going unburied, some placed in coffins hanging from trees until permission was granted for burial. The following year Innocent relaxed his demands, allowing monasteries and nunneries to celebrate Mass on a weekly basis, but by January 1209 he threatened John with excommunication within three months unless he accepted his demands. Instead, John used the interdict to confiscate the property of departed clergy; in October Langton left England and placed an excommunication order on John from across the sea, though for now it was published only in France. With the exception of the Bishop of Winchester, Peter des Roches, all the bishops left England under instruction from the Pope.[22]

For the next four years things were delicately poised. John did allow the Pope's messenger, Pandulf, to enter the country in 1211 to present Innocent's terms, but the king still refused to sanction Langton's appointment. In 1212 Innocent issued a bull, finally declaring John excommunicate by name and dethroned.[23] The threat was serious. Nevertheless any hopes the barons had that the king would make peace with Innocent and finally leave the Angevin territories to the French were not to be. Three years of success over the Welsh, Irish and Scots had once again consolidated John's position, while six years of carefully amassing his fortune enabled him to put plans in place for another Poitou expedition in July 1212. An uprising by the Welsh forced a change of tactic, leading him to move his army from Portsmouth to Chester. Then, while he was in Nottingham on 14 August, a messenger from the King of Scotland informed John of a plot against him. Around the same time word reached him from his daughter, the wife of Llewellyn, of a second plot by the Welsh and two rebel barons.[24]

The complications of 1212 were compounded in 1213 when Philip finally made ready an invasion of England. On 13 May the papal nuncio, Pandulf, met John in Dover and threatened him with immediate invasion by the French army. On a memorable 15 May, just outside Dover, John agreed to Innocent's demands and also formally submitted England as a fiefdom of the papacy in a ceremony witnessed by the entire baronage. The royal charter confirmed that John gave these things with the common consent of the barons; the same day the Bishop of Norwich and several of the nobility attested the act in a second document.[25] Innocent III would receive an annual tribute of 1,000 marks (700 for England, 300 for Ireland), and the disgraced Robert Fitzwalter and Eustace de Vesci, who had fled following the conspiracy at Nottingham the previous year, would be allowed to return.[26]

At no point in the history of England, either before or after the conquest, had a king of England surrendered so much authority to the papacy. Though John's decision astounded the people of England, Innocent was no longer pressing Pandulf to rally the French for an invasion. For the King of France the news of John's submission was devastating. Over £60,000 had been spent on preparations for the invasion, and had it not been for issues with the Count of Flanders it would most likely have gone ahead any-way.[27] Within a month John attempted another voyage to Poitou, but again the lords refused to accompany him. The lords of the north, in particular, adamantly stated that they were not required to perform service overseas and returned home. John received absolution from the Bishop of Winchester before he finally crossed to La Rochelle in February 1214, and within a short space of time won the submission of the Lusignans at the cost of giving away Saintonge and the Isle of Oleron. Had John continued his early progress success might have been his, but the presence of Prince Louis in Anjou obliged him to retreat. He managed to keep his forces united until he suffered a great defeat at Bouvines in July. As Philip's position continued to strengthen, John argued for terms, and a five-year truce was agreed in September.[28]

Failure in France in 1214 brought John's policy at home further under scrutiny. With the king away, the barons met at St Edmunds, resolving to take to arms unless the king agreed to grant a Char-ter of Liberties.[29] When the barons met the king on 6 January 1215 at a conference in London they came armed and unwilling to com-promise. While John was well aware that discontent was spread-ing, leading him to order the royal castellans to alert his castles in case of war, he did not cease his demand for scutage (payment in lieu of military service) for the recent war in Poitou, and he also sent agents to Rome asking for the Pope's backing.[30]

In England rebellion against the monarch was not unusual. Every ruler since the conquest had been forced to defend him-self from potential usurpers. Yet the situation differed from the reigns of John's predecessors, as there was no heir apparent or alternative candidate to take his place. The heir to the throne, Prince Henry of Winchester, was only seven years old and in no position to lead an uprising against his father. The suspicious disappearance of Arthur put an end to a threat from the male offspring of Henry II, while any claim by Prince Louis, husband of Blanche of Castile and daughter of Henry II's daughter Eleanor, was weak.[31]

In the absence of a plausible alternative to John the barons drew up a plan of reform. The idea was not entirely new, nor was it uncommon for a king to grant a charter at the end of a war.[32] On his coronation in 1100 Henry I had voluntarily granted a charter to abolish all evil customs, though this was mainly a publicity stunt rather than a genuine attempt at furthering the liberties of his subjects. Stephen also issued vaguely similar charters at the beginning of his reign in 1135 and again the following year. Inspired by these events, the barons created what would later be known as the Charter of Liberties. The assembly in January endorsed the charter, the barons swearing an oath that they would stand together for the 'liberty of the Church and Realm' and demanding that John either confirm the coronation charter of Henry I and agree to further reforms or he would be made to do so by force.[33] John responded that he would deliberate at an assembly near Northampton on 26 April. The rebel barons petitioned the Pope for support, but their behaviour was largely condemned, though Innocent did ask John to try to work with his barons. John strengthened his own cause by taking up the cross as a crusader on 4 March and distributing white crosses among his entourage.[34]

He was unwilling to agree to any charter. Rather than give in, he devised a new oath, not only of loyalty to him but against any such charter. While he strengthened his army with mercenaries from the continent the barons of the north assembled at Stamford and brought their forces to Northamptonshire for the assembly on 26 April. On hearing of the gathering John stayed away, fearing capture. In his absence the barons renounced their fealty, and the army, led by the enigmatic Robert Fitzwalter, prepared for war. Risings began in Devonshire and Northamptonshire, the northerners took Lincoln, and, on 17 May, only ten days after the City of London had been honoured by John with a new charter that included the right to elect a mayor, its citizens opened London's gates to the barons.[35]

Talks between the parties brought initial progress.[36] Rather than risk war John agreed to uphold a Charter of Liberties. A conference scheduled for 9 June was put off until the 15th, when the barons met the king at Runnymede to discuss their final terms. Four days later John confirmed his agreement. For John it had brought a fragile peace; for his opponents, to be significant and lasting, its clauses required effective implementation. A committee of twenty-five barons, established in response to clause 52 of the charter, met in London and busily set to work to ensure that its terms were upheld.[37]

The harsh clauses of the agreement, if implemented, gave the king so little power that the twenty-five barons effectively took power while John became a figurehead. John wrote to the Pope in mid-July, seeking his influence in escaping from his predicament. He argued that the barons had no right to put a papal vassal under such control and that his agreement to the charter had been given under duress. By early September the Pope had replied. According to Innocent, the Charter of Liberties was not only 'shameful' but 'illegal and unjust' and should therefore be annulled.[38] Writing on 24 August 1215, Innocent recorded the penitence of John for his past misdeeds, praised him for taking up the cross and criticized the rebel barons for preventing John from carrying out his crusader vow.[39]

The threats from the Holy See had little effect on the barons. Innocent's letter to the Bishop of Winchester, Pandulf and other bishops ordering the excommunication of the barons none the less induced a sense of urgency for peace among the clergy, and Innocent also went on to excommunicate all disturbers of the peace and place their lands and possessions under interdict. In addition, he gave warning to any bishop who failed to publish the document. On receiving this letter Langton refused to publish it until he had seen the Pope. Winchester and Pandulf published it, and Langton was suspended.[40]

Buoyed by papal backing, the king marched his army towards London. His intention had been to unite with France in his fight against the barons, but the barons had similar ideas. Despite the issues in his claim upon the Crown, a potential usurper had presented himself in Prince Louis.[41]

The rival forces clashed at Rochester. This city had traditionally been a royalist stronghold, but the barons had requisitioned it during the brief rule of the twenty-five barons. A seven-week siege of the castle severely depleted the resources of both parties, but John eventually captured the city. Almost immediately he sent word to Canterbury to help strengthen his siege of the castle, and by November all that was left was the keep. Despite the damage the barons continued their resistance until 30 November when finally their food ran low.[42]

John's preoccupation with Rochester had given his enemies an opening. In Wales his other nemesis, Llewellyn ap Iorwerth, who was also involved in the conspiracy of 1212, captured seven castles in just three weeks. In Scotland Alexander II benefited from the support of the twenty-five barons in enforcing the Scots' claim for Westmorland, Cumberland and Northumberland as part of the Queen of Scotland's dowry from John.[43] The severity of the situation forced John to divide his forces, sending some to London and others north. As John travelled north he wrought pillage and destruction across the countryside, achieving some surrenders but more from fear than genuine homage. In early 1216 he invaded Scotland, taking Berwick, and caused further widespread destruction to the lowlands before heading to East Anglia in March. Colchester was retaken, but a lack of funds and clear direction of government led to a loss of initiative.[44]

Back in Rome Innocent ordered further excommunications of rebels in December 1215. The papal demands brought some to peace with the king, including the powerful John de Lacy, but it did not end the rebellion.[45] Around this time the papal legate, Gualo, was dispatched to France, ordering Prince Louis to refrain from invading England. As the Pope's representative, including being empowered on both matters of faith and settlement of ecclesiastical matters, the role of the legate was vital to John and would continue to be so throughout the remainder of his reign. Philip responded by arguing that England was not a vassal of Rome and John was not the rightful king because of his treason against Richard the Lionheart. Rumours of John's role in the disappearance of Arthur continued to intensify, while the French king argued that no king could give away his own kingdom without the assent of the barons.[46]

Despite extensive defence of the coast on land and at sea, John failed to prevent Prince Louis and his fleet from disembarking at Sandwich in Kent on 22 May 1216. Rather than face his enemy, John returned to Winchester, helpless to stop Louis's force from advancing to London. On 2 June, in a ceremony in London, Robert Fitzwalter and the citizens of London swore allegiance to the French prince.[47]

Four days after his arrival Louis was on his way to Winchester. John, meanwhile, had moved on to the West Country, settling at Corfe Castle, his favourite residence. Later in June he gave permission for Winchester to surrender to the prince and in doing so many of his loyalists defected, leaving him with less than a third of the baronage. The short-lived submission of five of the barons and gentry also ended with the arrival of the Frenchman.[48] Louis's position was now very strong. Within three months of his arrival he commanded Winchester, London and practically the entire east of England, including all of the Cinque Ports apart from Dover. After his success at Winchester the King of Scotland came to pay homage to Louis, and he agreed to honour the recent concession of Northumberland, Westmorland and Cumberland.[49]

In July 1216 Innocent died.[50] He had been one of the Church's most able popes. His election in 1198 at the age of thirty-seven, the nephew of Clement III, saw the beginning of a new era in the role of the papacy. Its power as a political entity became vested in moral rather than temporal authority. Innocent's capability as a student of law and theology under the guidance of some of the most impressive scholars of the day became the springboard to a distinguished career, and papal authority spread to Scandinavia, Spain and the Balkans and, of course, led to greater influence in England. But significant though this was for the papacy, his crowning achievement was reform. In 1215 he had presided over the fourth Lateran Council, an event still famed for its impact on both the history and the structure of the Church, as well as the influence the Church had on the countries of Europe.[51]

Taking Innocent's place was Cencio Savelli, known from that moment as Honorius III. Honorius wrote to Gualo on 25 July 1216, announcing his election as Pope and confirming Gualo as legate of England. He highlighted the importance of a Christian Holy Land and John's need as a papal son to contribute. He also took advantage of the war to fill the vacant see at Hereford, for which John had refused to give his assent to the elected candidate, while ordering the Archbishop of Bordeaux, the most important city in Gascony, to support John against the barons.[52]

The rebels' progress none the less continued. In the north the Yorkshire barons were recovering what John had previously regained, while the King of Scotland was attacking Carlisle. The northerners had pledged fealty to Louis in September, giving him the obedience of all the key barons.[53]

John now attempted to regain some ground. Marching north, he reinforced the garrison at Lincoln which was currently under siege and did significant damage to the county in retribution for its loyalty to Louis.

More worryingly for John was his physical state. On the evening of 9 October he suffered a bout of dysentery. He left King's Lynn on the 11th and continued to Swineshead Abbey. What happened on the journey would prove disastrous for the king and a turning point in the direction of the war. While he was taking a short cut to Lincolnshire across the Wash at low tide, an unexpected tide came in. The whole of his baggage train, accumulated from the spoils of ransacked castles recovered from the barons, was lost.

John's condition had worsened. On 14 October he wrote to Honorius informing him that he was nearing death. He commended the future of the kingdom into papal hands, including his natural children. Bedridden by dysentery and fever, he died on the night of the 18th and was formally pronounced dead on the morning of the 19th.[54] His intention had been to be interred at Beaulieu Abbey, but that was not possible owing to the enemy's presence there. In accordance with his wishes, his body was taken from Newark to Worcester Cathedral. He had been a great admirer of St Wulfstan and requested that his body be interred between the tombs of St Wulfstan and St Oswald.

The king was dead. His followers proceeded to Gloucester, where they drew up plans for the crowning of his successor.[55]

I

ARISE, SIR HENRY

At the time of John's death the fate of the war remained uncertain. The arrival of Louis had aided the rebels greatly, and their position had been further enhanced by recent reinforcements from France. In the north of England the barons had augmented their control of the important counties, consolidated by the support of Alexander II of Scotland thanks to the submission of the three northern counties. In the south and east the barons were as dedicated to rebellion as the northerners. Cities as far apart as Winchester, London, Carlisle and Lincoln were all in the hands of the rebels, as were the Cinque Ports, the keys to the kingdom, apart from Dover.[1] Across the border in Wales, Llewellyn ap Iorwerth was also in league with the opposition while continuing to enhance his position in his own country.

Yet despite the rebels' dominance the attitude of the general population to the war was not of overwhelming sympathy with the rebels. Sentimentally the Runnymede Charter may be regarded as the cornerstone of English law, but the idea that it brought about a significant change in the rights of the common man belongs more to myth than history. As the war continued, many people saw their livelihoods destroyed by acts of violence, and there were murmurings of dissent against the barons who were now being seen as aiding a French invasion rather than fighting for liberties.

King John was buried at Worcester Cathedral in a ceremony of necessity as much as reverence. Those who remained closest to the king oversaw the transfer of his body from Newark to Worcester and its interment in the Norman choir. Following the king's funeral, the legate, in counsel with John's key supporter, William Marshal, the Earl of Pembroke, called a meeting that would go on to decide the future of the kingdom. With the King of England dead, it was time to carry out his will and crown a successor.[2]

The heir to the throne was John's eldest son, Henricus of Winchester. Aged just nine years, Henry had enjoyed a relatively good relationship with his father and a peaceful upbringing away from the turbulence. Though he was young in years there were no question-marks over his right to reign, as there had been with his father. In 1209 John had demanded that an oath of fealty be taken to him by the people of England, while a similar instruction was made on his deathbed.[3] No one in John's presence at Newark refused to take the oath granting the accession of Prince Henry.

At the time of his death John's wife and most of his children were in the south-west of England, almost certainly at Corfe Castle. On hearing of the legate's intention, Henry was taken to the castle at Devizes, then under the command of the Justiciar, while John's executors went on to the royal castle at Gloucester to prepare for the coronation.[4] Under instruction from William Marshal, Henry was collected from Devizes by Thomas of Samford, along with those who had cared for him. A few days later Henry met Marshal on a plain outside Malmesbury. The young man was said to be of princely stock, possessing a fine figure, a kind and handsome face and a kingly manner. He was carried into the earl's presence by his governor, Ralph de St

Sanson, and on greeting him said, 'I entrust myself to God and to you.' On hearing the prince's words, the Earl of Pembroke took him in hand and swore to do his duty to him. Whether overwhelmed by the occasion or still distraught from the death of his father, the soon-to-be king could not hold back tears.[5]

The setting for the coronation was Gloucester, an ancient royal borough that was still under royalist control. In past years the city had become famous for the tradition in which the Norman kings visited once a year for a procession wearing the crown.

The day was 28 October, the vigil of Simon and Jude. Though some of the lords argued that the event should be delayed until the arrival of Ranulph, Earl of Chester, the greatest of the nobles, those in control decided there was not a moment to lose. A small number of bishops and barons gathered in St Peter's Abbey awaiting the prince's arrival. When the moment arrived, the prince was carried inside and taken before the main altar. He was dressed in royal robes, made to his size, and appeared in every way a child of destiny. The occasion was marked with tears among those in attendance, not of sorrow but of love for the innocent boy about to be crowned – and perhaps of hope for a better future.

In the absence of the Archbishops of Canterbury and York and the Bishop of London, the responsibility for crowning the king was handed to the Bishop of Winchester, Peter des Roches – the only bishop to stand by John during the papal interdict. It is possible that Gualo was also involved in the event, though the sources are unclear. Unlike his predecessors, the king was crowned with a plain hoop of gold provided by his mother. The original crown was missing, perhaps lost on the way to Newark or located somewhere in the south, out of reach of the desperate royalists. Jocelin, Bishop of Bath, administered the coronation oath that Henry swore to uphold as his father had before him.[6]

Henricus of Winchester was crowned King of England. He was

the third Henry of England, named after his grandfather, Henry II.[7] In the presence of the legate Henry swore fealty to Rome as his father had done three years earlier and undertook to make the annual payment of the 1,000-mark tithe. After reciting the usual oaths, the Earl of Pembroke was given the honour of knighting the king. Forty-three years before he had done the same to Henry the Younger, son of Henry II.

Once the event was over Henry was carried out of the abbey and taken to his chamber. Such was the occasion that many strove for the honour of carrying the young king. His assembly robes were replaced by lighter ones, more comfortable for the challenges the evening had in store.

No king of England came to the throne in more difficult circumstances than Henry III. No longer did the Plantagenet kings of England hold dominance over the Angevin territories, and, as a result of the ongoing war, no longer was the authority of the king enough to guarantee the allegiance of his subjects. Despite John's death more than half of England still sided with the rebels, while Louis maintained the allegiance of some two-thirds of the barons.

Though the situation looked grim, all was not lost. In William Marshal and Ranulph, Earl of Chester, the king had the support of the two most powerful earls in the kingdom. Also on his side was William Brewer, based mainly in Devon; Walter Lacy, the Lord of Ludlow; John of Monmouth, a lord of the South Welsh Marches, along with the other powerful marcher lords: the Mortimers, the Cantilupes, the Cliffords and the Braoses. The Midlands and the west remained staunchly royalist and counted support from the powerful Earls of Derby and Warwick and the majority of the barons of the West Midlands. To the south, the Justiciar Hubert de Burgh still occupied Dover Castle, while the royal castles at Oxford, Wallingford, Windsor, Scarborough, Durham, Nottingham, Lincoln, Bedford, Kenilworth, Peak,

Knaresborough and Newark, given by John to his favourites, also remained in safe hands.[8]

However, this was not the royalists' greatest strength. As a papal vassal Henry had the support of the papacy. Prior to Louis's invasion the Pope had declared any attempt to usurp John's throne illegal, while explicitly declaring Henry innocent of his father's offences. Support from the prelates was firmly with the king, and any who refused did so under threat of excommunication.

While some of the rebel barons are known to have viewed John's death as a sign to renew fealty to the king, his death did not end the war. On the evening of the coronation barely had discussions commenced when news reached the royalists that the Earl Marshal's castle at Goodrich, only eighteen miles away, was under attack from the Welsh. Wasting no time, Marshal dispatched a party of knights, sergeants and crossbowmen to relieve the castle.[9] Goodrich was saved, but evidence of a new rising made forthcoming decisions even more urgent. Administration of the kingdom had lapsed in the recent war, particularly as the Justiciar was prevented from leaving Dover Castle. For those at Gloucester another matter of importance needed to be clarified. Henry III was the first king since the Norman invasion to ascend to the throne as a minor. Owing to his youth it was necessary that a regent be appointed until he reached the age of majority. The general view among those present was that William Marshal was the best candidate. Though Marshal received the immediate backing of the legate he protested that his age was against him. He suggested that the Earl of Chester was a more meritorious candidate, as well as more youthful.[10]

The day after Henry III's coronation many of the king's leading supporters, including Ranulph, Earl of Chester, arrived in Gloucester and pledged allegiance to him. At the time of the earl's arrival discussion was taking place in the Great Hall. For the second time in two days criticisms were voiced that the coronation had taken place in the Earl of Chester's absence. On greeting the lords Ranulph was quick to voice his support for the legate and dismissed the argument.

Discussion returned to the subject of regency. Once again William Marshal demurred, again on the grounds of old age and the good character of the Earl of Chester. To this Chester replied with equal humility. He boldly announced his support for William Marshal, vowing to serve him as best he could.

After the discussion had continued for some time Gualo took Marshal, Ranulph, Peter des Roches and some of the other lords into a private room. For the first time the legate requested that William take on the responsibility, in exchange for the absolution of his sins. Eventually Marshal relented, stating, 'If at this price I am absolved of my sins, this office suits me, and I will take it, though it weighs heavily upon me.' As on previous days, the occasion produced visible emotion among the royalists.[11]

Seldom in history have the achievements of a knight compared with those of William Marshal. Once described by his contemporary, Archbishop Langton, as 'the greatest knight in the world', Marshal's rise to regent marked the pinnacle of an exceptional career. Marshal's father, John, had been only a minor nobleman, whose allegiance alternated between Stephen and Matilda. According to a story told by his biographer, Stephen caught William while he was besieging his father's Newbury Castle in 1152; Stephen threatened to hang William in order to ensure that John honour his vow to surrender the castle. John used the opportunity to reinforce his garrison and informed the king that he was capable of producing even greater sons. Fortunately for the young William, Stephen could not bring himself to carry out the threat.

William's dramatic rise to prominence began at the age of twelve, when he started training as a knight at the household of William de Tancarville in Normandy. He was knighted around 1166 and the following year participated in his first tournament. As a competitor and jouster he had few equals. If his deathbed recollection is to be trusted, he conquered over 500 knights in tournament.

William was unique in the sense that he served four kings, five if his time in the household of Henry the Young is included. His valour in tournaments and battle is generally assumed to have had a profound effect on Henry the Young; William had also been a close guide in the prince's rebellion of 1173–4. Marshal was reconciled with Henry II and served him admirably during the last five years of his reign, before doing the same for Richard. His loyalty won him, among other things, the Earldom of Pembroke, and, despite enduring a turbulent relationship with John, he was one of the few noblemen who remained loyal to him throughout his reign.[12]

Within two weeks of Henry III's coronation Gualo held a council at Bristol. Only four earls attended, among them the Earl of Aumale whose allegiance had recently been won. Of more importance was the attendance of eleven bishops, confirming the support of the Church, while the lay barons were represented by a large following from the Marches.

The day was St Martin's day, 11 November. William Marshal was officially confirmed as regent. Marshal assigned des Roches as the king's personal tutor, in addition to being made a councillor. The third key appointment was for Hubert de Burgh to continue as Justiciar. This was the first time he had joined up with them, having negotiated a truce with Louis, who continued to besiege him at Dover Castle.[13] All three were experienced men of state, and each had formed a group of executors appointed by King John.[14]

Among the business conducted at Bristol was the reissue of the Charter of Liberties, viewed by the royalist magnates as essential given John's inability to win the war.[15] Unlike the Runnymede Charter, the Bristol one was backed by the legate and hence issued with the blessing of the papacy. The second charter was confirmed at Bristol on 12 November with some clauses from the Runnymede Charter omitted. In reality the charter at Bristol was more important than that of Runnymede could ever have been. Gone were the contentious clauses concerning constitutional reform, including the appointment of the twenty-five and the clauses regarding extraordinary taxation. Though time was of the essence, the new charter had been carefully revised and outlined a clear policy, with certain aspects to be reviewed at a later date.[16]

Throughout England there seems little doubt that the end of King John's reign saw a dramatic change in the nature of the war. The merciless treatment of enemies, coupled with the widespread destruction of towns and villages, had largely come to an end.[17] As usual, warfare died down in winter. From October on the conflict that occurred was mainly confined to castle warfare.[18] Hoping to take advantage of the complications in the forming of the new government, Louis worked steadily at completing his conquest of the south-east. In November he acquired the Tower of London, and within a short period he conquered the castle at Hertford.[19] A truce was mooted as Christmas approached, subject to the royalist surrender of Berkhamsted, but talk of peace was still some way off.

Reconciliation between royalists and rebels was also the key aim of the papacy. In early December Honorius demanded that the rebel barons swear fealty to Henry, once again insisting that Henry's coronation had established the beginning of his legitimate rule.[20] On 3 December Honorius also wrote to Gualo, assigning him the task of watching over both the kingdom and the young children of John.[21] Henry remained in Bristol for Christmas, celebrating with the legate and his new regent. The New Year began with councils in Oxford and Cambridge where the royalists and the barons respectively met. While Marshal and the legate took centre stage, Henry's early reign was largely sheltered. He continued his learning under the guidance of a tutor, one Philip of Albini, also warden of the Channel Islands, who was said to have performed his duty admirably.[22]

While Marshal and his council attempted to restore order, Louis was making progress. He gained the castles at Berkhamsted, Colchester, Orford, Norwich and Cambridge in addition to the baronial castles at Pleshey and Hedingham, though his conquests were largely through negotiated surrender rather than out-and-out siege. Louis's drive consolidated his hold on much of the south-east, but he had still to achieve any progress in the West of England or the Midlands.[23]

The end of 1216 culminated in a dramatic slowdown in the prince's progress. Not only was he running short of supplies; for the first time the barons were beginning to voice their discontent about his harsh taxation policy. Even more pressingly, many of the barons who had opposed John had done so because of his tendency to favour foreigners – a practice the French prince unsurprisingly shared. When the rebels gained occupation of Hertford, Robert Fitzwalter demanded the castle be returned to him. Louis flatly refused, stating that no Englishman who betrayed his natural land could be trusted with such responsibility.[24]

Elsewhere the prince encountered other problems. Prior to the siege of Dover, his viceroy, Enguerrand de Coucy, already threatened with excommunication for inciting violence against John, had entered an alliance with Henry. Gualo placed Wales under interdict because of its connection with the rebel barons, in addition to issuing further excommunication orders against the rebels themselves.[25] In England there was less threat of punishment. Instead, Marshal and the legate attempted to win support through diplomacy rather than conflict. Marshal promised that no inquiries would be made into past offences and that those who pledged fealty to Henry III would have their rights reinstated when the war was over. His approach was decisive and secured the allegiance of some of the barons, including several of those in control of the Cinque Ports. For Louis this was the worst possible outcome. For the first time in the war his position had gone from that of liberator to usurper.

The role of Gualo and the papacy was of vital importance during the first year of Henry's reign. While Honorius used his influence with the abbots of Cîteaux and Clairvaux to try to persuade the King of France to discourage Louis from proceeding with the war, the Pope also wrote personally to Henry, highlighting his hopes for the future and seeking his devotion to the Apostolic See.[26] Honorius and Gualo were particularly active in January. On 17 January 1217 Honorius ordered that letters be sent to the Archbishops of Dublin and Bordeaux, urging fealty to the king, while letters were also written to the Bishops of Winchester and Chichester and the legate outlining the importance of the king's supervision. The legate's position was further strengthened with the granting of powers against all ecclesiastics currently swearing loyalty to Louis, following which Honorius used the opportunity to attempt to fill vacant sees with his own choices.[27] Despite Henry's youth, the Pope also wrote to England on the subject of possible marriage with a princess whose position might benefit him.[28]

On the rebels' side, Louis's deteriorating position led to him request a brief truce. His intention was to return home to gather extra forces, but the loss of the Cinque Ports prohibited his departure from England without military action. To add to his problems, a revolt had broken out in the Weald, led by a squire named William of Cassingham, later dubbed Wilkin of the Weald. Wilkin captured two nephews of the Count of Nevers as Louis approached Lewes, and as the rebel forces continued to

Winchelsea Louis suffered a further setback as the men of the Weald broke down the bridges once they had passed.

Further trouble was to come. When they reached Winchelsea the people of the town destroyed their mills before taking to their ships as supporters of the king. As a result Louis and his men were forced to fend for themselves in a near-empty town with inadequate food supplies. When support arrived from London and Boulogne Louis and his troops had already spent two torturous weeks in Winchelsea, narrowly escaping starvation.[29] Eventually Louis returned to France. There is evidence to suggest that Marshal had attempted to capture him at this point, but Louis was assisted by his ally, the famous outlaw and pirate Eustace the Monk – a capable, yet notorious, mercenary who had served both England and France.[30]

Louis's absence was the break Henry needed. Marshal was able to raise the funds needed to restore order by raising a hidage (tax paid to the king for every hide of land, a hide being an average family's allocation) or carucage (tax placed on every plough or area of ploughland) in the shires Henry still ruled.[31] As spring progressed, Marshal focused on consolidating the royalist position. Several barons changed sides at this stage, while the heroic Wilkin was made Warden of the Seven Hundreds of the Weald.[32] As the year progressed, Henry's royalists recovered many castles, including Marlborough, Farnham, Odiham, Winchester and Chichester. King John's loyal ally, Falkes de Breauté, imposed his authority over the rebel-controlled Isle of Ely, while the Earl of Chester busily laid siege to the castle at Mountsorrel, near Loughborough.[33]

In Paris Philip refused to support his son's ambitions to conquer England. It seems probable that Louis's invasion of England initially had the blessing of his father, who had attempted a similar endeavour before 1213, but, from a diplomatic perspective, invasion of England by Philip was now highly controversial.

The war that had begun with John's refusal to abide by the Charter of Liberties was now an invasion of the realm of a child king. Waging such a war, particularly on one under papal protection, would have been a disaster for Philip, who at the time was planning a crusade and had no wish to damage any chance of reconciliation with the papacy.

While Honorius continued to use his influence with the bishops of Henry's lands in France and Ireland to aid the king, in April he once again demanded that Philip recall his son from England.[34] Louis endured a lukewarm reception at a Royal Council at Laon on 5 March and returned to England on 22 April with just limited reinforcements.[35] Though he had gathered only 120 extra knights, he was back in England in time for the expiry of the truce.[36]

After failing to make any impact in Dover Louis headed towards Winchester and joined with the Earl of Winchester outside Farnham Castle. On hearing that Mountsorrel was under siege from the Earls of Chester and Derby, he returned to Winchester and conquered it before sending forces to both Dover and Mountsorrel.[37]

Learning that Louis was on his way, the royalist forces retired from Mountsorrel to Nottingham. After securing Mountsorrel the French continued to Lincoln, hoping finally to gain the castle, which had been under siege since February.[38] Marshal heard news of events at Lincoln on 12 May while celebrating Pentecost at Northampton. After Pentecost the legate moved from Newark to Nottingham, while the royalists went to Lincoln via Torksey and Stow.

Marshal raised his army by conscripting the garrisons of various castles. What followed was a masterstroke. Despite his forces numbering just 400 knights and 300 crossbowmen, compared to the 600 knights besieging the town, the route chosen allowed them to progress to Lincoln largely unobserved. After resting on the night of 19 May, they approached the city and set about protecting the castle.[39]

The strategy of the day was devised by the Bishop of Winchester, a man of greater military than ecclesiastical skill. After Marshal had opened up communications with the castle, crossbowmen under the guidance of Falkes de Breauté joined with the garrison and ventured from the east gate into the street, leaving the earl's ascent on the poorly defended north gate to go practically unnoticed. The rebel forces were chased through the steep lanes that connected the upper town to the lower, and, after failing to revive their attack, they attempted to flee. Those who succeeded continued to London.[40]

The battle, though significant, was surprisingly bloodless – in total just three lives were lost. Following the victory, the legate excommunicated Louis publicly and offered an indulgence to Henry's soldiers.[41] For Louis defeat at Lincoln was an unthinkable setback. Marshal's intention was to finish the war in one final blow, but having raised the army from separate garrisons it was difficult to keep them together as one unit. The royalists' momentum none the less brought them the submission of the Earl of Salisbury and a further 150 or more rebel barons between May and August. Marshal restored order through the holding of two great councils at Oxford and Chertsey, while Louis returned to his base at London, having failed to take Dover.[42]

By June Louis's position looked increasingly desperate. On 12 June the Archbishop of Tyre, in England to preach the crusade, put forward provisional articles of peace for both parties.[43] Four members of Louis's council and twenty knights met Henry's council for peace talks at a location between Brentford and Hounslow, though this attempt broke down through Louis's excessive demands.

Nevertheless the tide had turned. No longer were the rebel forces capable of conquering England without further aid. Though the royalist victory on the battlefield was largely due to Marshal, evidence of the Pope's hold on England was further demonstrated during the summer of 1217. On 8 July Honorius wrote to the prelates of England requesting financial aid for Gualo to provide for the governance of the kingdom, while suggesting that the Earl of Chester be made joint regent alongside Marshal. Five days later Honorius wrote again to Gualo ordering the removal of the canons of Carlisle and their replacement with candidates loyal to the papacy.[44]

In London, Louis attempted one final push. Thanks to his wife, reinforcements came in the form of a hundred knights and hundreds of men at arms, including William des Barres, the Count of Blois and the famous pirate Eustace the Monk. On the eve of St Bartholomew, 23 August 1217, Eustace sailed from Calais, heading towards the mouth of the Thames. The entire coast was back in royalist hands, leaving Eustace only one way of approaching Louis in London. After allowing Eustace to pass Sandwich, Hubert de Burgh set out on the water and tracked the French up the river. The heavy French command ship was low in the water and difficult to manoeuvre, allowing Hubert's ship to get alongside it. The ships containing the soldiers were able to escape, but Eustace and many of the French lords were killed in the resulting action.[45]

The young king must have felt that God was favouring him. Greatly encouraged by his recent victories, he accompanied the regent to the siege of London. They met Louis at the gates of the city on 29 August, and on 5 September a general amnesty was agreed at Kingston. Peace was finalized at the house of the Archbishop of Canterbury at Lambeth on 11 or 12 September 1217, signed by the legate.[46]

For Louis the peace terms were generous. All of his castles were surrendered and his supporters released from their oath to him without threat of punishment. The king's regent also agreed that those imprisoned should be released without further ransom. To confirm peace Louis was also awarded 10,000 marks on condition that he would attempt to persuade his father to restore to Henry the territories lost during the reign of John.[47]

Eight days after the agreement Louis and his barons appeared barefoot and dressed in white before the legate to receive absolution. Louis departed on 29 September, taking a safe escort from Dover.[48]

The departure of Louis ended the first barons' war. With John dead and the future of the realm in the hands of the new king, who had agreed to uphold the charter, the reasons to wage war had been lost. Marshal and the legate were prudent in their readiness to dismiss any charges against rebel barons in exchange for peaceful submission. London was hoping to come to terms, and the clause in the settlement that allowed those reconciled with the king to receive their land back saw this happen. Of those who opposed the king, only the clergy suffered; their cases were sent before the Pope.

As for the young king, the war that he had played no part in starting was over. He had played his own role admirably, yet while his first military test had passed successfully the problems of government were only just beginning. As the young boy would soon learn, the war had been fought because of the way the Charter of Liberties had been enforced, not necessarily because of what it contained.[49]

2

WINCHESTER THE UNREADY

Henry III was still only ten years old when the war ended. During his first year on the throne he had been forced to face the challenges of losing a father, being taken away from his home and overseeing the nation's third major civil war, a challenge that had never before befallen a king of England.

Little is known of Henry's earliest years. He was born in Winchester on 1 October 1207, the eldest son of John and his second wife Isabella. This county town of Hampshire, famous for its impressive cathedral and attractive centre, was once the capital of England. The original site can be dated back to the Iron Age, and after the Roman invasion the area named Venta Belgarum became the fifth largest Roman settlement in England. Three centuries later it replaced Dorchester-on-Thames as the capital of Wessex, and by the reign of King Egbert it was arguably the most important city in England. Later in the ninth century King Alfred the Great was responsible for new street plans, replacing the original Roman outline that had been damaged when the Danes sacked the city in 860.[1]

It seems probable that Henry enjoyed his early years in Winchester. His affinity with the city lasted most of his life, and he often celebrated Christmas there. He was somewhat awed by stories of past kings, notably the Saxon martyrs, and such stories influenced his youth. He was born at Winchester Castle, an impressive Norman structure that survived almost unscathed until the days of Oliver Cromwell. The Great Hall that remains dates from 1222–35 and was added by Henry III.

Little else is known of his earliest years. Most probably he lived a quiet life under the supervision of a personal tutor, a wet nurse and the usual entourage of a member of the royal family. Among John's countless bastard offspring Henry had four legitimate siblings: Richard, born 5 January 1209; Joan, 22 July 1210; Isabella, some time in 1214; and Eleanor in 1215. All lived their early life in the South of England, away from the turbulence of John's court. One of the brief mentions of Henry's early life comes in 1212, when John placed him safely inside one of the royal castles in order to escape the rebellion of Llewellyn.[2]

Louis's submission at the Treaty of Lambeth not only ended the war but brought an end to any threat to Henry's right to rule. Louis's departure in September, along with many of his countrymen, eased fears of future insurrection, though the royalist government was cautious about inciting violence during the latter months of the year. A tournament at Blyth was cancelled in October through fears that the event might rekindle rivalries and ambitions among the participants, even though the nobles of both sides were largely reconciled after the agreement at Lambeth.[3] When the Earls of Chester and Derby went on crusade they fought without quarrel alongside Winchester and Fitzwalter.

In November 1217, almost a year after the revision of the Charter of Liberties, the new government reissued it a second time with several more clauses, including those concerned with forest law, removed. To combat this the magnates issued a second more detailed Charter of the Forest.[4] At the beginning of Henry's reign nearly a third of England was forest. Though this may sound idyllic, the woodlands of thirteenth-century England were often desolate places, havens of hermits and outlaws and home to fearsome animals such as wild boar and wolves.

Moreover, the word 'forest' carried a significant legal connotation because an area designated as such was placed under the monopoly of the king. Disafforesting older forests (reducing them to the state of ordinary ground) was a quick way of raising money for a king; John disafforested all of Cornwall for 2,200 marks and Devon for 5,000. Among the barons' demands at Runnymede was that the classification of forests should return to the position before the accession of Henry II. In clause 47 John agreed that all the forests created during his reign should be disafforested, but this changed the landscape little. The future of the forests was of great importance, so much so that even those who had fought for John were keen to keep the clause in the charter at Bristol. The Forest Charter issued the following year made further concessions, including legislation providing that all forests created since the reign of Henry II would be disafforested, that any freeman should have the right to develop his land within the forest and that no man should lose his life for taking venison as ordered by Richard I.[5]

On the same day that the charters were issued a letter was written to the Pope in Henry's name, almost certainly under the guidance of Marshal. Henry offered his gratitude for the support of the papacy and requested exemption from the payment of the annual tribute of 1,000 marks in view of his payment to Louis under the peace settlement.[6] He also praised Gualo for his invaluable help in overcoming recent troubles.[7]

Order had been restored, thanks largely to the efforts of Hubert de Burgh, Marshal and Gualo. The Exchequer reopened on 12 November 1217, after which a brief attempt was made to draw up accounts for the previous two years.[8] The shortage of funds was now the country's greatest concern. The king's own financial difficulties became clear when Henry spent Christmas at Northampton at the expense of Falkes de Breauté.[9]

Peace between Henry and Louis was again confirmed on 13 January 1218, while most of the lords owing allegiance to Alexander II of Scotland, including the king himself, paid homage to Henry and his advisers at Northampton.[10] Skirmishes with the Welsh, however, proved an unwanted distraction. In Gwent the tenacity of one chieftain, Morgan of Caerleon, caused Marshal to take up arms, and during the conflict Llewellyn conquered the royal castles of Cardigan and Carmarthen. The situation was defused when Llewellyn received assurances from the king's advisers that his right to rule his provinces would not be challenged, following which he paid homage to Henry at Worcester in March.[11]

Henry had successfully restored the castle at Newark to the Bishop of Lincoln after an eight-day siege, and by autumn 1218 his government was starting to make good progress.[12] A council was held, probably in September, at which it was announced that any charter created during the king's minority, including the recent Charter of Liberties and Forest Charter, would need to be confirmed at the beginning of the king's majority. It is also likely that the king's seal was used here for the first time.[13]

Gualo's time as legate was now up. The Pope wrote to Pandulf on 12 September announcing that he would take over the duties of legate. Pandulf was no stranger to England – he had been present, as a subdeacon in 1213, to receive John's submission and had been rewarded by being made Bishop Elect of Norwich. On his promotion to legate, however, it was decided that his consecration would be indefinitely postponed. Should Pandulf have become Bishop of Norwich he would have been a subordinate of the Archbishop of Canterbury.[14]

It is possible that Pandulf was in England as early as June, attending the rededication of the recently repaired Worcester Cathedral with Henry.[15] Honorius wrote to Pandulf again on 10 November, ordering that the recent treaty between England and Scotland be either confirmed or annulled.[16] Gualo had probably left by mid-November. His last act as legate was to write to Marshal, stating that Louis was still to release the hostages of the barons of the Cinque Ports.[17] Pandulf set to work readily, and the rest of the year passed by without incident. While the judges began to travel the country hearing criminal and civil pleas Henry spent Christmas at Winchester with his tutor, Bishop des Roches.[18]

The smooth passage of events in 1218 was followed by a series of problems in 1219. With Marshal ill at Caversham, a council was held at Reading around 12 April. His health failing, Marshal resigned the regency and made preparations for the future of the kingdom. He declared unequivocally that the regency must end with him. His last days had been blighted by requests from des Roches to be his successor and from various clerics to leave money to their churches. He claimed that no land in the world was divided like England, and it was perhaps through fear that an appointment would fuel ambitious plotting and intrigue that he decided he would have no successor. Evidently the next best candidate, the Earl of Chester, was on crusade at the time.[19] William Marshal died on 14 May 1219. He was interred at the Temple church in London, buried in the habit of the Templars. He died peacefully, and his death was widely mourned.

Clearly it was not Marshal's intention that a young boy of eleven should govern by himself. Having lived through the events of 1213–16 he understood the importance of the papal legate and that it was a matter for the papacy to choose the king's advisers. After his death control of the realm effectively rested with Pandulf – a controversial figure who was suspected of being responsible for Stephen Langton's suspension. Pandulf's rise to power brought with it increased control for des Roches, still Henry's tutor, with Hubert remaining as Justiciar. Pandulf himself took an active interest in the running of the realm. Within days of Marshal's death the legate wrote to des Roches and Hubert regarding the collection of revenue.[20] True to his nature, he interfered with practically every affair of state and offered his opinions on the appointment of royal officials, policy with respect to France and Wales and implementation of the recent papal edict that the barons could hold no more than one royal castle at a time.[21]

It was important to Henry and the regency to maintain peace with France. By May 1219 the five-year truce made between John and Philip, arranged after John's defeat at Bouvines, had come to an end. In a letter dated 10 May Honorius thanked Philip for his part in keeping the peace and requested a continuation.[22] Peace with France was renewed in July 1219 for another year, following which Philip condemned Louis's invasion in 1216. By January 1220 Honorius and Hubert were already in secret discussions about further extension of the peace, and on 3 March 1220 it was extended for four more years.[23]

With the government of the realm secure, Pope Honorius III wrote to Archbishop Langton, recently returned from his long exile, stating his desire that Henry be crowned a second time. Langton was delighted and immediately set about planning the occasion.

Henry celebrated Christmas at Marlborough with des Roches, following which arrangements were put in place for his second crowning.[24] The second coronation took place on 17 May 1220 at Westminster Abbey under the supervision of Langton. A day earlier the young king had personally laid the foundation stone of the new Lady Chapel which the monks had planned to construct in the style of the new 'Gothic' architecture.[25] Unlike the first ceremony at Gloucester, a large number of prelates and barons were present on this occasion to see Henry recite the coronation oath, the Archbishop of York being the only notable absentee. Replacing the simple crown used at Gloucester, the king was crowned with the diadem of St Edward the Confessor.[26] It was noted by witnesses that the event was wonderfully harmonious.[27] The king's government was now fully established. There also seems to have been a suggestion at this point that Henry should be declared of age, though this was not taken up.[28]

Honorius now wrote to Pandulf ordering that any bishop in possession of royal castles should surrender them to the king. On 28 May he wrote again to Pandulf emphasizing that no one was to be in possession of more than two royal castles at any one time.[29] The order was met with mixed reactions. While Hubert and Langton favoured the castles being placed in the hands of Englishmen, des Roches preferred further enrichment of the Poitevin faction, many of whom had been enriched by John (himself brought up in Poitou) and who still occupied royal castles. Around this time Henry's mother announced news of her marriage to Hugh of Lusignan, the Count of la Marche. The union was particularly ironic as her new husband was none other than the son of the man to whom she had previously been engaged.

The marriage brought conflict from the start. No sooner had the union been announced than Henry clashed with his new stepfather over demands by Isabella regarding her dower from John.[30] As the year went by Honorius grew increasingly impatient with their behaviour. In September he wrote to Isabella demanding that she end her harassment of her son and, on the same day, issued a warning to her husband about his attempts on Henry's land in Poitou. At the time Isabella's daughter, Joan, was also present at Hugh's court, having been promised in marriage to Hugh by John, prior to Isabella marrying him instead. Honorius also demanded the return of Joan to England. A truce was finally settled in the autumn.[31]

Back in England relations between the Justiciar and the Bishop of Winchester were becoming increasingly strained. Despite being two of the more consistent members of John's government, their relationship had threatened to break down when Hubert replaced des Roches as Justiciar in 1215. The main source of their differences was policy. While Hubert favoured giving key appointments to Englishmen, the Poitevin bishop preferred the upgrading of the positions of his countrymen. Evidently Hubert found Langton something of a supporter of his views, while Honorius remained unwavering in his demands that the king's castles, given by John mostly to foreigners, be surrendered.

Henry spent much of the summer of 1220 accompanied by his governors in attempting to reclaim his castles. On 11 June he met Alexander of Scotland, and while at York the two kings reached an agreement for Alexander to marry Henry's sister, Joan.[32] Recovery of the royal castles met with mixed success. William of Aumale refused to surrender his castles, resulting in the king having to take them by force. The first, Rockingham, was surrendered by late June and another, Sanney, fell on 28 June.[33] A few days later Henry was back in Canterbury for the long-awaited translation of the remains of St Thomas Becket into the cathedral. On 7 July he attended the ceremony which witnessed the relics being enclosed in a shrine behind the high altar. Extensive preparations had been made for the event, coinciding with the fiftieth anniversary of the former archbishop's murder. At the request of the prior of Christ Church the Pope granted an indulgence for all those who visited Becket's shrine.[34]

Christmas was again celebrated at Oxford, marred by further tensions with William of Aumale. Still aggrieved at the loss of his castles, William left the Christmas court abruptly and began a revolt in Lincolnshire. The catalyst this time was Hubert's intention of carrying out an order, initially promulgated in 1217, for the submission of Bytham Castle. In retaliation William plundered the neighbouring towns and churches and held many prisoners captive in the Bytham dungeons. When summoned to a council at Westminster, he marched with a large force towards the city, before changing direction, heading to Fotheringhay Castle.

His success was short lived. A council met to discuss a scutage for the conflict with Aumale, and before the month was over Pandulf officially excommunicated him. In the company of Pandulf and the Earl of Chester, Henry travelled to Bytham, arriving on 2 February 1221. Aumale sought sanctuary at Fountains Abbey in Yorkshire, and in his absence his followers abandoned Fotheringhay. After a six-day siege Bytham was recovered.[35] The earl came out of sanctuary and was pardoned on taking up the cross. Within a month he was back in favour at court, his rebellion against the king unpunished. It was, wrote the chronicler Roger of Wendover, 'the worst of examples, and encouraged future rebellions'.[36]

Though criticized by the chroniclers, the presence of the legate had been influential in putting down the revolt. On 19 March 1221 another legate, James of Ireland, settled a dispute between Henry and the Archbishop of Cashel, while on 29 April the Pope ordered the Bishop of Winchester, Hubert, the Earl of Chester and William Brewer to restore certain wards and escheats (transfers to the Crown of the property of persons who have died without issue) to the king.[37] The day before, the legate had laid the first stone of Salisbury Cathedral.

While Pandulf's duties as legate had been largely effective, relations between him and Langton had seriously deteriorated by the middle of 1221. Langton went to Rome around this time, complaining of the legate's constant interference. This brought to an end Pandulf's time in England. He returned to Rome, while Langton received the Pope's word that no more legates would be sent to England during Langton's lifetime.[38]

In May 1221 Henry sent representatives to France for the coronation of Prince Louis, who became joint king alongside his father. Since leaving England over three years earlier Louis had still not relinquished some English territories, as required under the terms agreed at Lambeth.[39] As the year progressed plans were also in place to secure the alliance with Scotland. Henry spent four days at York at midsummer where he presided over the marriage of the Scottish king and his sister, Joan, at York Minster. Peace with Scotland was further enhanced with the marriage of the widowed Hubert to Alexander's eldest sister.[40]

In Winchester outbursts of anger at the Christmas court of 1221 proved something of a portent for the year ahead. The strong influence of the government had largely succeeded in keeping the peace since the end of the war, but its record was blemished by a series of minor insurrections by the citizens of London. The reason was a lack of affinity with the person of the king – so great was the influence of his advisers, in particular Hubert.

A wrestling match between the citizens of the city and those of the suburbs on 25 July became the catalyst for a potential uprising. After the defeated tenants of the Abbot of Westminster asked for a rematch on 1 August, the outcome was unprovoked violence against the Londoners. While the mayor did his best to ensure calm, many took the advice of the troublesome Constantine FitzAthulf, once sheriff of London, who led an attack on the precincts of Westminster. The sheriff had been a vigorous supporter of Louis, and reports abounded that FitzAthulf's men cried, 'Montjoie! May the Lord assist us and our Lord Louis!' heightening rumours of continued support for the French prince. Hubert secured the assistance of former royal favourite Falkes de Breauté, following which Constantine was brought before them. The next day Falkes and a large force took the former sheriff and his two key supporters to Southwark, and all three were hanged without trial. Falkes forced the surrender of the Londoners while Henry seized the property of the former sheriff. The mayor was later deposed, and Henry took control of the city for the first time.[41]

Langton was back from Rome early in 1222. In April he held a provincial synod at Oseney Abbey, near Oxford, where the bishops published a constitution comprising some fifty chapters, concerning the roles and responsibilities of the clerics in society in addition to religious and monastic observance. The rising influence of Langton, coupled with his friendship with Hubert, had left des Roches isolated, so much so that he welcomed the opportunity to take up the cross with Falkes de Breauté.[42] When Henry held a council in London in early January 1223 Langton was successful in persuading him to comply with the terms of the Great Charter, resulting in disagreement between Langton and William Brewer as a result of Brewer's claim that the rights were extorted by force. Following his agreement to abide by the charter, Henry wrote to the sheriffs on the subject. News of Henry's actions was pleasing to the Pope. In April Honorius issued a papal bull declaring that Henry, though still in minority, should be allowed to assume full government. On 13 April the Pope wrote personally to the chancellor, Ralph Neville, also Bishop Elect of Chichester, confirming the decision.[43]

Five days later the Pope wrote to Philip about preparations to extend the peace that was again due to expire the following year. He also wrote to Henry on the subject of joining Frederick II, the Holy Roman Emperor, in freeing the Holy Land. Henry was requested to exempt anyone who made a crusader vow from paying tolls in order to help fund their passage to the Holy Land.[44]

While Henry backed the idea of crusade, the situation was complicated when war broke out with Wales. Though conflict occurred largely on the Welsh side of the border, the presence of Llewellyn was proving troublesome for Henry as it had for his father. Any hopes King John might have had of appeasing Llewellyn through marriage to Henry's illegitimate half-sister Joan had a limited effect on the ambitious Prince of Gwynedd, who was lacking in neither ability nor the support of rebel barons. Since paying homage to Henry in March 1218 Llewellyn had endured hostilities on the part of the eldest son of William Marshal, also named William and heir to his father's estate, which had plagued the south-west of Wales since 1219. Llewellyn now devastated much of Pembrokeshire, leaving Marshal on the verge of financial ruin. According to one source the damage was estimated at a cost greater than Richard I's ransom to Leopold of Austria.[45]

Despite Llewellyn's success there was growing resentment among the Welshmen of the south that the Prince of Gwynedd was becoming too powerful, and this led to conflict between Llewellyn and his son. When trouble arose in the middle March in 1220 Pandulf had been quick to defuse the situation with a truce. Nevertheless Marshal's continued feud saw him successfully drive the prince from Cardigan and Carmarthen in 1222. Once the truce became unstable Pandulf placed Wales under an interdict while the Archbishop of York and his suffragens were also instructed to publish an excommunication notice against Llewellyn in early October 1223.[46] The lack of assistance from Henry to Marshal to subdue Llewellyn caused resentment, however. In response, the council proposed a marriage between William and Henry's sister, Eleanor, which seems to have been acceptable to all parties.[47]

In many ways the continued threat from Wales was the first

genuine military challenge the sixteen-year-old king had to face in his own right. He held a great council in Worcester before meeting his army in Gloucester. In September 1223 he and Hubert moved from Hereford to relieve the castle at Builth, located in modern-day Brecon, before moving on to Montgomery on the 19th. Over the next few years the town and castle were heavily fortified, replacing the earlier wooden motte and bailey. Peace with the Welsh was reached on 8 October 1223, thanks in part to the mediation of the Earl of Chester.[48]

Henry received a visit in September 1223 from John of Brienne, King of Jerusalem, about a new crusade. Henry was courteous in his dealings with the visitor, but any pledge of money for a crusade probably never materialized.[49] Instead, Henry's focus remained on the ongoing issue of the surrender of royal castles. He still faced opposition, particularly from his closest allies. The loyalty of the Earl of Chester, Falkes de Breauté, des Roches and Aumale was threatened, as they had the most to lose. Several letters were written between September and December relating to the surrender of royal castles, including one from Honorius to Henry in November 1223 confirming that it was up to the king whether or not they were acted on.[50]

Many of the issues regarding the castles were blamed on the Justiciar. In November 1223 the discontented barons hatched a plan to overthrow Hubert. On hearing of the plot, the king returned from Wales. Once it was clear that Henry was returning the barons halted their plan, retiring to Waltham on the 28th. Despite this, some of them approached Henry in person and demanded Hubert de Burgh be removed from office. A plan was devised by the Earl of Chester and others to seize the Tower of London, but this did not materialize. When the lords met the king at a conference arranged by Langton they argued for the dismissal of de Burgh on the grounds that he had been squandering finances. Heated words were also exchanged between de Burgh and des Roches, leading to the conference being dissolved without the key issues being resolved.[51]

On 8 December Henry reclaimed Colchester, entrusting it to the Bishop of London.[52] Henry wrote to Honorius on 19 December thanking him for his help, and he asked for the Pope's continued assistance in appeasing the hostile barons. Evidently, Henry was under the impression that some of the barons had written individually to the Pope at this point.[53] Divisions between the king and the rebels soured the mood at the Christmas court. While Henry celebrated at Northampton with Langton and some of the other bishops, most of the rebels joined together at Leicester. As the situation escalated, Langton threatened the discontented barons with excommunication. After receiving assurances that the surrender of the castles was fair and unbiased, the Earl of Chester and his comrades agreed to the order, including the castles at Shrewsbury and Bridgnorth, on 29 December 1223. Legal tokens of surrender were presented to all on both sides and within the next three months the castles were back in the hands of the king.[54]

3

THE FIRST KING OF ENGLAND

Seven years had passed since Henry's first coronation, but the problems that blighted the reign of his father remained. Sustaining good relations with the barons was often difficult, particularly those who had been gifted estates by John. None the less Langton's triumph had at least secured the surrender of most of the royal castles. The archbishop's continuing power had now reinforced Henry's status as king and the future of himself and Hubert while Henry was still in minority.

This was too much for des Roches. In January 1224 the Bishop of Winchester secured a letter from the Pope to Henry, reminding him what John owed to the papacy and warning him against interfering with the bishop's see at Winchester. Exactly how Henry replied is not recorded, but it seems from the available evidence that on being sent to Rome the royal agents did not receive the Pope's full attention. As for des Roches, his specific complaints were concerned with safeguarding his own position following the castle surrender and his feud with the Justiciar, rather than personal problems with the king.[1]

The King of France died on 14 July 1223, shortly after a fiery-tailed comet had been seen in the skies above France. Philip's demise inaugurated the reign of his son, henceforth Louis VIII.

As the year drew to a close Honorius wrote to Louis, congratulating him on his accession but also demanding that he continue his father's peace with England.[2]

Philip's death brought an end to the good relations. On hearing of the event Henry instructed that ships be made ready on the south coast to ensure the swift restoration of Normandy. In Paris the former legate, Pandulf, attempted to convince the Pope to postpone the coronation of Louis until Normandy had been restored to England. Louis, perhaps sensing their intention, ensured that the coronation was performed quickly. Henry sent ambassadors to Louis demanding the return of Normandy and other possessions, to which Louis remained stubbornly opposed. He also maintained that his invasion of England was just and would happen again. On hearing that the Pope's intention was to reclaim the Holy Land rather than launch a crusade in the South of France against the heretical Cathar movement Louis abandoned his plans for a military expedition to the South and ordered an attack on Poitou.[3]

Poitou was proving particularly problematical for Henry. Six months after Pandulf's departure from England the Pope was called on to intercede in the dispute between Henry and his stepfather, Hugh de Lusignan. Previously the count had promised Pandulf to make peace with Henry and settle any outstanding issues relating to the restoration of the royal castles in their possession. The Dean of Bordeaux was brought in to ensure that everything had been carried out and at the appropriate time and to excommunicate Lusignan if it had not. By June 1222, however, nothing more had been done, leading to fresh criticism from Honorius. Within a week Honorius wrote another letter, at Henry's request, to the Archbishop of Poitou threatening Lusignan for his disloyalty, but by November the issues were still unresolved.[4]

Lusignan's eventual agreement in January 1224 to comply with the papal instructions was better news for Henry, but the intransigent behaviour of the new King of France was now pressing. Honorius's intention to launch a crusade in the east rather than the South of France against the Cathars inadvertently changed the situation for Henry. Louis's delay in replying to the English demands until 8 November 1223 had ensured that the truce remained in effect until April 1224, by which time Louis was prepared for war. Honorius wrote to Louis in February and April, exhorting him to make peace with Henry, but the new King of France was unresponsive. He waited until the truce of 1220 ended in May 1224 and then launched his invasion.[5]

The French invasion of Poitou threatened to reduce further what little remained of Henry's Angevin empire. John had lost Normandy, and with Poitou overrun English control was limited to Gascony, thanks largely to its trade links with Bordeaux. In June Henry held a council at Northampton to address the situation in Poitou. News from the French court was not encouraging. When Louis met with the English envoys at a great council in Paris he stated his view that his reclamation of John's land was just: the forfeiture by John had been absolute, thereby depriving the offspring of John of the right to rule as King of England or duke of his French possessions.

Henry's stance was equally firm. Like his forefathers he styled himself Duke of Normandy, Duke of Aquitaine, Count of Anjou and Count of Poitou. In light of their feud, including Louis's failure to abide by the terms of Lambeth, Henry refused to acknowledge Louis's rule, and for the first time since the Norman Conquest the King of England did indeed rule over parts of France without any feudal subjection to the King of France.[6]

Though the later years of Philip's reign nearly saw the fall of Poitou, at the time of Louis's invasion only Poitiers remained in

French hands. Every other major city and castle acknowledged Henry as both King of England and Count of Poitou. Nevertheless rule of Poitou was by no means an easy business. In practice the feudal lords were happy to give homage to Henry provided they suffered no great interference. During Henry's minority this must have appealed to both sides. Furthermore, it also allowed the Justiciar, a man always in favour of peace, the opportunity to concentrate on running the kingdom.

Since 1221 the Seneschal of Poitou had been one Savary de Mauleon, a mercenary of great intellect and strength. Mauleon was of the great house of Thouars. In the past he had fought for John, and he still maintained estates in England.

Even when Poitou seemed secure, however, there was always a threat from the powerful counts of La Marche, the leader of whom was Hugh de Lusignan. Isabella reasoned to Henry that the marriage between her and Hugh de Lusignan was of great benefit to the king in creating an alliance with the counts of La Marche. Up to this point, however, the marriage had gained Henry nothing, while Louis used the opportunity to profit from Lusignan's treachery. As Henry's advisers and the Pope negotiated a further truce, Louis made treaties with the barons and Hugh de Lusignan once again forsook Henry.[7]

Louis's forces met at Tours on 24 June 1224 and continued on foot through Thouars to the seaport of La Rochelle. Later immortalized for its legends associated with the Knights Templar, La Rochelle was the strongest of the Poitevin cities and, owing to its location and activities, the one that had the closest affinity with England.

Mauleon's position was in great peril. Despite his loyalty to Henry, Louis's numerical advantage forced Mauleon to relinquish Niort. By 3 August La Rochelle was in French hands and the Seneschal was fighting on the side of the French. With La

Rochelle taken, all of Aquitaine north of the Dordogne followed. As Poitou changed allegiance, Henry's stepfather was rewarded with a grant for the English-ruled Isle of Oleron – a small island off the Atlantic coast. Continuing his march, Louis set forth on a mission to conquer Gascony, taking all but the loyal city of Bordeaux.[8]

How did this happen? Had the King of England acted, Poitou and Gascony might well have been saved. But the possibility of a mission to Poitou was put on hold by one of the strangest events of his long reign.

Despite peace being restored at home by the end of the previous year, dissent still raged among certain individuals regarding 'novel disseisin' – unlawful appropriation of men's land. In early spring the king's justices travelled throughout the country to hear pleas, including thirty acts of 'novel disseisin' against Falkes de Breauté – at least sixteen of which he was guilty. When Breauté was brought before the king's justices at Dunstable, rather than have charges heard against him he conspired with his brother William to kidnap the justice of the bench, Henry de Braybrook, and shut him up, with two others, in Bedford Castle.[9] At the time Henry's forces had gathered in Northampton, awaiting the command to head to Poitou. Instead, these troops were sent to Bedford. After three days of failed requests Henry ordered the recapture of the castle by siege.

In many ways what followed was the greatest military challenge of Henry's reign. Bedford Castle was a great example of Norman ingenuity, and its fall proved incredibly difficult. King John had strengthened the castle for the precise purpose of withholding such a siege. Its strong towers and baileys were successful in keeping the king's forces out for two months. The kidnapping of Braybrook occurred on 16 June, and the resulting siege lasted from 20 June to 14 August. Of the eighty prisoners only three knights, who were accepted as Templars, were spared.[10]

Despite being excommunicated by Langton, Breauté had retained the support of the papacy. It seems reasonable to believe that the Pope was not fully aware of Breauté's actions prior to the siege.[11] For Henry the siege offered other complications. In addition to being unable to defend Poitou, the unexpected expedition required the issuing of a new scutage to meet the costs of the siege.[12] Breauté escaped to Wales before Bedford was captured, seeking help from Ranulph and Llewellyn. On this occasion Ranulph recognized the stupidity of Falkes's plan and instead joined up with the royalists. Falkes eventually handed himself over on the advice of the Bishop of Coventry while taking sanctuary in a local church.

Honorius wrote to Henry on behalf of Falkes on 17 August, requesting that he end the siege. In his letter Honorius advised Henry not to be overly hard on his loyal subjects. At around the same time Honorius wrote an even sterner letter to Langton. Shortly after the Pope's missive the king received another letter from a chaplain in Rome recommending that he reply firmly but well. Evidently, the king was unwavering in his view that Falkes's attack had ruined any endeavour in Poitou.[13]

In the eyes of some, Breauté's refusal to surrender had an even greater significance. The departure of Louis and removal of foreigners had accelerated a growing feeling of English national identity that would also contribute to the xenophobic attitude of several magnates in Henry's later reign. As a result the failure of a Poitou mission could be blamed on foreign troublemakers such as Falkes, who became victim of fresh hatred.[14] For Falkes the consequences were potentially disastrous. In a bid to appease the king Falkes surrendered the money he had with the Templars to Henry and ordered the gates of his castles in the West Country to be opened to the royals. Despite having his excommunication lifted, he was banished from the realm and for a time put in prison under Louis.[15]

The recovery of Bedford at least allowed Henry the opportunity to plan a defence of Poitou.[16] Honorius wrote to Louis again in August demanding no encroachment on English territories. He also wrote to Henry informing him of his communication with Louis and urging reconciliation between the two. A day earlier Honorius also wrote to the Bishops of Saintes and Limoges, in addition to the Dean of Bordeaux, ordering the excommunication of Hugh de Lusignan unless he restored to Joan, sister of the king, her dowry.[17]

Despite the struggles at Bedford and abroad, Henry was successful in winning back many castles. Hugh de Lacy gained power in Ireland, which also helped appease elements of discontent in Wales. The Welsh situation was also affected that year when Henry oversaw the marriage of his beloved sister, Eleanor, to the Earl Marshal.[18]

The Christmas court was held at Westminster, following which a council convened in January 1225. Once more the treasury was bereft of funds, owing partly to the cost of winning back Bedford, while Hubert painted a bleak picture of the situation abroad.[19] During the assembly the Justiciar attempted to rally the magnates to aid Henry with generous gifts of money, including a fifteenth of all movable property in England, not excluding ecclesiastical. In response Langton asked Henry to grant the liberties of the Church, resulting in a further issue of the Magna Carta and Forest Charter.[20]

Papal backing was still with the king. While Henry agreed to a third reissue of the charter Honorius wrote to Henry asking that he be just in every way, while also writing to the bishops of England asking them to assist Henry as appropriate.[21] In France the Legate of the Apostolic See, Romanus, attempted to use his influence to ensure Louis handed over Normandy, Anjou and Aquitaine to Henry.[22] Unsurprisingly Louis refused to comply with the terms discussed at Lambeth, leading to Henry sending his brother Richard as part of an expedition to Gascony in March.[23]

Richard was sixteen years of age at the time of the Gascony campaign. Despite his youth he was no stranger to conflict. He had already accompanied his brother on the Welsh expedition of 1223 and was also present in Poitou at the time of John's failed endeavour of 1214.[24]

Richard's campaign marked the beginning of a fine military career. At the time of John's death he had been offered refuge in Ireland, but Henry III decided against it. He was made Governor of Chilham Castle in Kent early in Henry's reign and spent most of his early years at Corfe Castle, under the supervision of the Poitevin, Peter de Mauley. But now Henry had bigger plans for his brother. Henry knighted Richard on 2 February and eleven days later granted him the lucrative Earldom of Cornwall. It is possible that Henry bestowed on Richard the county of Poitou as well. On 23 March he left England with a strong fleet and arrived in Bordeaux to a rapturous welcome.

The mission was successful. Richard captured St Macaire and Bazas swiftly and soon wrote to Henry claiming that Gascony was saved, with the exception of one town. The only major military objective that remained was the siege of La Réole, which took practically all summer and autumn. When the town finally fell on 13 November the Lord of Bergerac hailed Richard as lord.[25]

Though Gascony had been saved, the naval strength of the former seneschal around the Bay of Biscay hindered communication and trade between England and Bordeaux. For the second time in the young king's reign the Cinque Ports would prove of vital importance, leading to fierce fighting at sea.[26] Richard's role in the proceedings was praiseworthy. In addition to his military success, alliances were made with the counts of Auvergne and other enemies of the King of France, including an awkward union with Raymond of Toulouse, at the time in sympathy with the Cathars. The Duke of Brittany was also won over by an offer to inherit the Earldom of Richmond, which he had long coveted, and there was talk, and perhaps even a vague promise, that Henry would marry the duke's daughter.[27] Marriage discussions included the daughter of Leopold of Austria, while negotiations also took place over a union between Henry's younger sister Isabella and Henry, son of Frederick II, but this came to nothing following the murder of the Archbishop of Cologne, the project's most ardent proponent.[28]

In December Louis once again incurred the wrath of Honorius for the invasion of Henry's lands.[29] Around that time Honorius wrote to Henry informing him that England would receive a visit from a nuncio named Otho. As to Otho's exact purpose, speculation was rife. Roger of Wendover referred to 'important business of the Roman Church', whereas the historians William Hunt and Henry Richards Luard suggested the envoy was present to seek a pardon for Falkes de Breauté. According to Francis Gasquet Otho's aim was unclear, but interceding on behalf of Breauté was a possible consideration.

News of Otho's visit went down badly among some of the clergy. Prior to the nuncio's arrival Romanus had promised agents of Henry that he would attempt to hinder Otho on his journey to England. In June the legate had written to Henry to assure him that Louis would allow Breauté to travel freely in France, rather than suffer imprisonment, until he was reconciled with Henry.[30]

Eventually Otho arrived in England, probably in the autumn. As a nuncio he did not hold the powers of a legate, but he did argue for papal demands that a prebend be assigned to the Pope in every cathedral and a similar provision from every bishopric, abbacy and monastery. The king, eager to maintain good relations with the papacy, replied that the situation must be discussed, perhaps secretly knowing it would never get the approval of the magnates.[31]

The year 1225 had been an important one for the Church. Roger of Wendover recorded that in this year a decree was sent out from the Archbishop of Canterbury and his suffragens with new instructions for priests and concubines. In particular, it was announced that the concubines of any priest or clerk would no longer be given the right to be buried in consecrated ground without absolution, while the keepers of concubines were to be prohibited from receiving the kiss of peace or Holy Communion. The subject of illegitimate birth was also brought up, as was penance for any woman, married or not, who was found guilty of sex with a priest.[32]

Also around that time the Franciscan mission was making its way to England. Born in 1181 to the son of an Italian cloth merchant, Giovanni Bernadone, nicknamed Francesco on account of his flamboyance and love of French songs and romances, formed a new branch of Christianity when, at the age of twenty-five, he claimed to have been compelled to kiss a leper and to have had an epiphany. Following the command of a local priest, the 'little poor man' of Assisi set forth on a mission of preaching and living through beggary, travelling barefoot and refusing all ownership of property. His life of destitution found steady support among the clergy, particularly his continued adherence to the teachings of the papacy. Innocent III authorized his mission in 1210, and over the coming decade his following continued to grow. In 1224 a party of nine Franciscan 'friars' landed in Dover, leading to the establishment of friaries in Canterbury, London and Oxford within six months. Despite his death in October 1226, ravaged by sickness and age, and according to witnesses plagued by the symptoms of stigmata, Francesco's memory caught the imagination of many Christians in Europe and England throughout the reign of Henry III.

Christmas 1225 was celebrated at Winchester, following which the king moved on to his palace at Marlborough.[33] Henry summoned a council at Westminster on 13 January, despite his absence at Marlborough through illness. The reason for the council was to deal with the requests of Otho – according to the king, requests that concerned the whole nation – while the fate of Breauté was also discussed. Otho extracted some money from churches, two marks of silver under head of procuration (fees in support of papal officials in England), though the nuncio's demands were not met. Otho was recalled to Rome at the request of Langton and left England shortly after with little money.[34]

Honorius wrote to Lusignan on 8 January 1226 expressing anger that he had broken faith with Henry, and he threatened him once again with excommunication.[35] Recovery of the lost land in France remained a priority, though any chance of a military campaign in Poitou was ruled out when Honorius wrote to Henry in April demanding he refrain from interfering with Louis's crusade against the Cathars (the Albigensian Crusade). Honorius also requested that no pact be made between Henry and Raymond of Toulouse, a first cousin of the king, owing to his alliance with the Cathars. Honorius also made a similar demand to Louis regarding Henry's territories. On receiving the Pope's letter Henry agreed to postpone his expedition and passed on the news to Richard in Gascony.[36]

In May Henry was directed to expel a man named Robert Travers from a church in Ireland, coming around the same time that possessors of the royal castles in Ireland were required to surrender them. Back in England, a council met on 4 May at St Paul's to discuss the latest requests from the Pope. What was said was interesting. While Honorius acknowledged the past evils of the Roman Church, highlighting greed and scandal, he also pleaded that at the root of such things was poverty and that it was the duty of good Christians to see to the Church's needs. Once the papal letters had been read Langton made the point that recently similar demands had been made and rejected in France. Henry responded to the Pope that England's reply would be 'no more backward in obedience' than any other country; in other words, he would comply if other countries did.[37] Evidently, Henry had remained in favour in Rome. Also in May Henry and Cornwall were rewarded for their good relations by becoming exempt from excommunication unless done by specific order of the Apostolic See. The same direction was also sent to Romanus. In June Honorius offered Richard complete assurances that the papacy would provide for the welfare of himself and Henry.[38]

Henry's decision to abide by the Pope's wishes should have brought an end to any chance of a Poitou recovery, yet that changed following the sudden death of Louis in Auvergne on 8 November, apparently as predicted by an astrologer.[39] His successor was his son, Louis IX. As the new king was a minor, his reign, like Henry's, began with a regent, his mother Blanche of Castile.

Dissent against Blanche raged among the French. Hoping to take advantage, Henry made contact with nobles in Anjou, Normandy, Brittany and Poitou, looking to encourage support for an English invasion. The instability of the Angevin territories was clear for all to see. Just six weeks after the death of Louis VIII many of those who had conquered Poitou for the former king were now in league with Henry. The most notable to defect were Lusignan and Savary de Mauleon. Once again the key instigator was Cornwall, who, despite his young age, was proving a wise head on young shoulders and a key ally of Henry.[40]

Henry's appetite for kingship was evidently starting to grow. After spending Christmas at Reading he travelled to London and demanded 5,000 marks of silver from the city on the grounds that they had given the same amount to Louis on his departure in 1217. On 8 January 1227 a council met at Oxford, during which he declared himself of full age and sacked des Roches and several other governors.[41]

Effectively, Henry's full reign started here.[42] His first course of action was to question the charters of his minority, taking his lead from the clause back in 1218 that no charter made during his minority would be valid in his majority without confirmation. He threatened to quash the Charter of the Forest, insisting that a heavy tallage (feudal duty or land tax) be laid on the towns for its renewal, while the clergy were finally forced to hand over the fifteenth on movable property demanded in return for the reissue of the Great Charter in 1225.[43]

Des Roches's fall from favour was perhaps to be expected. Discontent with the Bishop of Winchester had been building for some time, particularly concerning his involvement with the rebels in 1223. With no bishop or legate to hinder him, Hubert de Burgh was at last able to enforce sole guidance over the king. In recognition for his faithful service he was made Earl of Kent. For des Roches the situation was bleak. Shortly after his dismissal he left England, intending to join the crusade in which he had so long vowed to participate.[44]

On 18 March 1227 Pope Honorius died. His last act in England was to ask for money to support another crusade. During his supremacy he had continued along the path of reform begun by his predecessor and added to the corpus of canon law and the reorganization of papal finances. He supported the evangelization of Spain and the Baltics and was instrumental in backing of Franciscan and Dominican orders.

Honorius's successor was the nephew of Innocent III, Ugolino da Segni, from now on Gregory IX. Shortly after his election

Gregory wrote to Henry on the subject of supporting a crusade. Papal backing was again to be of great importance to Henry. In April 1227, with Hubert's backing, Gregory IX renewed the bull of 1223, decreeing that the nineteen-year-old was able to rule by himself.[45]

While France still occupied Henry's attention, he entered marriage negotiations with several princesses. Among those mentioned were Iolenta, daughter of Peter of Dreux, the Duke of Brittany; Margaret, daughter of Leopold VI, Duke of Austria; and one of the daughters of Premysl, King of Bohemia. The king sent ambassadors to each, and he also sent warm wishes to Frederick II, Lewis, Duke of Bavaria, and princes of the empire to help ensure he had allies should the situation in France develop any further.[46] Meanwhile, the ambassadors who had travelled to France returned with the bad news that the lords, including Lusignan, had made peace with Blanche, leading to the Treaty of Vendôme. The catalyst this time was the presence of the French army south of the Loire, leaving the Poitou region susceptible to easy conquest. With Peter of Brittany also coming to terms with Blanche, the marriage between Iolande and Henry was shelved. Henry was now particularly vulnerable. Thanks to the quick thinking of Richard, Henry made peace with France in July for another year before Richard returned to England with Poitou still technically under English rule.[47]

Despite Richard's good work, Henry and Richard quarrelled over the latter's rights to a manor that had previously been part of the Earldom of Cornwall. Richard fled Henry's court on 9 July and joined with William Marshal, the son of the former regent, the Earl of Chester and several others. The earls made their demands to the king, particularly further complaints against Hubert and the condition of the Forest Charter. A meeting was arranged for 2 August in Northampton where Henry granted some demands to Richard.

At the same meeting the barons agreed to support Henry with £1,200 in addition to the tax of one-fifteenth that had already been granted.[48] The threat of rebellion was quietened, and all were at peace when Henry celebrated Christmas 1227 at York.[49]

In France, papal relations continued to complicate the situation. Like his predecessor, Louis was advised to restore all lands due to Henry, while Romanus was forbidden from excommunicating Cornwall or Henry without papal approval. Though Henry's position was secure, he was still forbidden from extending his hand towards his lost dominions on account of his truce with Louis, who was at war with the Albigensians. Evidently the Holy Land was still on Gregory's mind. In December he sent a letter once more stating the importance of a new crusade.[50]

Problems with France had reached a temporary stalemate. No sooner had that happened than Henry received news, in August 1228, that Llewellyn had attacked the recently fortified castle at Montgomery.[51] Hubert, the castellan of the castle, went in person to defend it, levying the charges on the kingdom. The king accompanied him in marching his army there and witnessed a Welsh retreat. Following the siege, the king continued west to Kerry in Powys and razed the monastery to the ground, depriving the Welsh of the chance to use it as a place of arms. In its stead building began on a castle.

Unknown to Hubert and the young king, many of the lords remained in league with the prince of Gwynedd, resulting in the English being caught off guard. In the resulting chaos the Welsh captured William de Braose, one of the strongest marcher lords. After failing to defeat the Welsh or meet the costs for the new castles, Henry made peace with Llewellyn. In October he returned to England without securing the return of William.[52]

4

UNWANTED VISITORS

The Treaty of Vendôme in 1227 had proved a major disappointment for Henry. The legal terms of the truce between Richard of Cornwall and Blanche already confirmed that Henry's French possessions had reduced dramatically since John's peace with Philip following Bouvines in 1214, while the agreement at Vendôme had also strengthened France's hold on Poitou through the agreement of future marriages between the Lusignans and French royals.

From a domestic perspective the treaty was not all bad. Favourable terms for Isabella effectively put aside disputes between Henry and his mother over Isabella's dower from John, with Hugh now surrendering any rights to Bordeaux as promised to him by Louis VIII.[1] The result was a brief respite following several months of grumbling from some of the barons over Henry's regular demands for money. So great was the threat that Gregory wrote to Henry directing that certain tournaments should be stopped as some of the barons and nobles were using them as opportunities to make compacts to resist the king's policy.[2]

It was recorded in the annals of Dunstable that a serious disagreement occurred between Langton and Henry about the privileges of the See of Canterbury. Though Henry eventually agreed to comply with the rights of an ancient royal charter, Langton became seriously ill soon after. The archbishop died in July 1228, losing both Henry and Hubert a key ally. Around the time of Langton's death Henry attempted to calm relations between the Holy Roman Emperor, Frederick, and the Pope. In April Henry had been informed that Frederick had been excommunicated. Tensions between Gregory and the Emperor had been running high for some time, and the Pope was less than impressed when Frederick delayed undertaking a crusade through illness. Henry also wrote to Gregory in July requesting permission to have his father's body moved to Beaulieu, the originally intended location for his burial, and about joining the sees of Waterford and Lismore in Ireland.[3]

In Plantagenet England the election of a new Archbishop of Canterbury was rarely a straightforward affair. On hearing news that the monks of Christ Church had elected their fellow brother, Walter of Eynsham, Henry looked to quash the election. While he undoubtedly coveted the see for one of his allies, on this occasion he might have had other reasons. In certain circles Walter's credentials were not altogether respected. Walter was getting on in years, and there was a question-mark as to his intelligence. When Henry sent agents requesting that the Pope dissolve the election, he gave them permission to offer the latter a tenth of all property in the kingdom to aid his war with Frederick. On hearing the news Richard Grant was appointed, not elected, to the See of Canterbury.[4]

A similar problem occurred that year regarding the election for the See at Salisbury after the transfer of Bishop Poore to Durham. While Henry was still dealing with the Canterbury election, the monks' choice of Robert de Bingham was put to Gregory. Two canons of Salisbury were then chosen to go to Rome, seeking papal confirmation of Bingham's appointment. Though the outcome of the election received a favourable response from the cardinals in Rome, the canons were received especially well by Otho. By mid-December the see was filled, followed soon after by Grant at Canterbury.[5]

It was also in this year that Richard de Burgh, Hubert's nephew, was made Justiciar of Ireland. His possessions in Ireland had been steadily rising, having inherited Hubert's brother's castles at Tipperary and Limerick, while a year earlier Henry III had also recognized his ancient claim to Connaught, further developing the influence of Hubert's close family.[6]

Another papal visitor came to England in 1229, this time a papal chaplain and messenger called Stephen, charged with the task of collecting tithes.[7] Henry called a council at Westminster on 29 April, during which Stephen read papal letters relating to the previously promised tithe of a tenth on all property. At the time of his visit news had reached England that Frederick II had triumphed in the sixth crusade of 1228, though the recapture of the Holy City did little to win over Gregory.[8] Among the letters, the Pope highlighted Frederick's misdemeanours, including entering the Church of the Holy Sepulchre on the feast of the Annunciation, being crowned in the church despite being excommunicated and ordering Christian girls to entertain Saracen men at his palace. There was also an accusation that Frederick respected the Sultan, with whom he had treated concerning the return of Jerusalem, more than the Pope. Concerning the tithe, Henry had already agreed to the chaplain's demands, the price of Grant's appointment, though he had not discussed the matter with his council. The result was chaotic. Money was collected, but the manner in which it was done was appalling. According to the chroniclers, many of the papal collectors were joined by usurers, forcing the clergy to borrow money at high interest in order to meet the tithes, leaving many clergymen impoverished.[9]

War with France was mooted at the Christmas court in Oxford as recent good relations between the Bretons, the Poitevins and the regent of Louis IX had begun to deteriorate. Gregory was against Henry warring with France and once again wrote to both kings looking for a peaceful solution. In April 1229 he identified the Abbot of Cîteaux to act as mediator between Louis and Henry.[10]

News of dissent in France was appealing to Henry, though any future military campaign had to wait after Hubert arranged another truce with France until July. April had seen a further turn of events when the regent, Blanche, triumphed over Raymond of Toulouse in the Albigensian Crusade, leading to the Treaty of Meaux, guaranteeing Raymond's dominions for the King of France through the marriage of her second son, Alphonse, to Raymond's daughter.[11]

Nevertheless in the north of France the barons were growing restless. While Henry was celebrating Christmas 1228 at Oxford he received letters from Normandy and Poitou inviting invasion. On Hubert's advice he waited till autumn, and on 9 October Peter of Brittany arrived in Portsmouth and greeted Henry as King of France.[12] Peter finally inherited the Earldom of Richmond and was recognized by Henry as Duke of Brittany, a title the kings of France had failed to formally acknowledge. The expedition was set for launch on 15 October, but this was postponed when the king realized he had too few ships, leading to dissension between Henry and Hubert. On the advice of Peter, Henry postponed the planned military expedition until the following spring.[13]

Christmas 1229 was spent at York, alongside Alexander II of Scotland, during which time Henry concentrated on preparations for his invasion of Poitou.[14] Having learnt from the failures of the previous year, he assembled a large fleet, consisting of about

230 ships, each capable of carrying sixteen or more horses, and a total of about 4,000 men. The expedition left Portsmouth on 30 April 1230, marking the first military campaign on foreign soil by a king of England since King John in 1213. In his absence the king entrusted the running of the government to the Chancellor, Ralph Neville, and Stephen Seagrave, a judge of some talent.[15]

Henry's forces stayed in Guernsey on the night of 2 May before landing at Saint-Malo the following day. The Duke of Brittany was present to welcome him, paying homage to Henry. On 8 May they proceeded to Dinant, the designated meeting place for the army, and following some discussion they continued to Nantes. Henry's intention had been to meet his mother and her husband, but not for the first time his mother let him down.

In principle the timing of the attack was perfect. Many of the French magnates were at war with the poet-count of Champagne, Theobald, leaving the French resistance under strength.[16] Nevertheless Louis was aware of Henry's arrival. Stirred by the English forces, Louis assembled a large army at Angers to ensure Henry stayed out of Poitou and subsequently moved to Oudon, a castle about four leagues away.[17]

Talk among the Norman allies was for Henry to go to war in Normandy, though this was dismissed as outrageous. Both the Bretons and the lords of Poitou generally paid Henry homage, though some fortified their castles against him, fearing a siege. By June, Henry had received the allegiance of all the lords in Poitou except for Lusignan and the Viscount of Thouars.

As summer progressed, Henry demonstrated his inexperience. Though his forces had set out with the intention of conquering lost lands, in reality there was no real sense of purpose on either side. Henry's forces marched largely unopposed through Anjou and from there into Poitou. He crossed the Loire on 1 July and back again in September. The only siege of note was taking back the castle of Mirebeau, located in the Upper Saintonge. The castle was the only place *en route* that withstood English pressure, and the siege occurred between 21 and 30 July. A decisive factor had been the arrival of the knights of Gascony, who brought with them a siege train from Bordeaux.[18]

With Mirebeau conquered, Henry continued to Bordeaux where he stayed for about a week before returning effectively along the same route by which he had arrived. On 15 September the campaign ended at Nantes with very little progress on either side. In the same month Henry wrote to Geoffrey de Lusignan, son of Hugh de Lusignan, confirming his intention to return to England. He also mentioned that many of his men, including both himself and his brother, had been plagued by illness.[19]

The expedition was over at the end of October, when they left from Saint-Pol de Léon and arrived back in Portsmouth. On Henry's orders the Earls of Chester, Pembroke and Aumale and the Duke of Brittany stayed behind, along with some 500 knights and 1,000 men at arms, ensuring Poitou was defendable. On his return Henry wrote to Louis IX about enforcing his surrender of the territories lost by John.[20]

In England the lack of progress in Poitou was severely criticized by the magnates, particularly on the grounds of cost. So bad was the situation that some of the poorer knights had been forced to sell their horses or arms for food. There was better news for Henry, however, when peace was agreed between Frederick and Gregory. After the Holy Roman Emperor had clashed with the papal forces on his return to Italy, a truce was agreed in August. The Emperor received complete absolution from the Pope at the pontifical palace and stayed there for three days, thus ending the hostilities of the past two years.[21]

In Wales Llewellyn was once more on the warpath. William de Braose was still in captivity following the failure of the 1228

expedition and only succeeded in winning his freedom on agreeing to wed his daughter to Llewellyn's son, thus conceding
Builth to the Welsh. Llewellyn was true to his word until the
prince discovered that during his captivity William had seduced
his wife Joan, half-sister of Henry III. The Welshman's retribution was swift. After seizing William from Builth at Easter he
hanged him from a tree in front of an estimated 900 witnesses.

Llewellyn's rage led to widespread carnage. Over the coming weeks he laid waste to much of the south of Wales, predominantly the lands of Pembrokeshire and Gwent that were under
the control of Marshal.[22] The truce of 1228 was at breaking
point, but for Henry the timing could not have been worse.

It would be the start of yet another gruelling challenge.

5

THE RULE OF THE 'POITEVIN'

Henry was at Lambeth for Christmas 1230, less than two months
after his return from overseas. The outcome of this French
expedition drew strong criticism from among the barons, leading to further tension between Henry and the Justiciar.

Henry's lack of progress in Gascony was a problem not only
in military terms but financial ones. On 26 January a council
met at Westminster to deal with the fall-out. Since about this
time, though perhaps as early as 1223, Henry had a small private
seal of his own, used for chancery and exchequer business, though
larger expenditures still needed the approval of the magnates.[1]
The discussion was of Henry's request for three marks from all
fiefs, laity and clergy to compensate him for his losses the previous year.[2] The new Archbishop of Canterbury, Richard Grant,
opposed it, but the difficulty was overcome when Henry issued
letters further guaranteeing the liberties of the clergy set out in
the Magna Carta. Henry received another excommunication
exemption notice from the papacy in January 1231, followed by a
similar exemption that prohibited the royal chapels being placed
under interdict except by specific order of the Apostolic See.[3]

In April Gregory wrote again to Henry, asking him to make
a lasting peace with Louis.[4] Though this did not happen, another

expedition to the land of his forefathers was no longer a priority for Henry. Of greater concern was news of an escalating feud between the Archbishop of Canterbury and Hubert de Burgh over the possessions of the young Earl of Clare, including Tonbridge Castle in Kent. As a minor, Clare was unable to obtain these possessions in his own right, leading to accusations from Grant that by taking control the Justiciar was intruding in the archbishop's jurisdiction. When Grant took the case to Rome he complained vehemently about the extent of Hubert's power in England. He also raised other issues, including Hubert's marrying a wife to whom his first wife was closely related and failing to respect the rights of the See of Canterbury.[5]

In April 1231 Llewellyn's resurgence in Wales boiled over following the surprise death of William Marshal, a fortnight after the marriage of his sister to the Earl of Cornwall. Henry was upset by the news. On hearing of Marshal's death Henry is reported to have cried out, 'Woe, woe is me! Is not the blood of the blessed martyr Thomas fully avenged yet?'[6] He swiftly marched against the Welsh, leading them to retreat. Yet almost as soon as he had departed Llewellyn invaded the marches, where Hubert de Burgh had several estates. Much of the damage occurred around Montgomery Castle. As the violence of Llewellyn's soldiers escalated, the English who were defending Montgomery Castle cut off their escape route and captured and killed many of them. This was a success for the Justiciar. On his orders all the prisoners were beheaded and their heads presented to the king.[7]

Llewellyn retaliated violently. The Prince of Gwynedd assembled a large army with great haste and inflicted a great deal of damage on the Welsh border. His crimes included the burning of churches full of women, nobles as well as peasants, and physical attacks on clergy.

Henry was furious. By 13 July he had assembled a sizeable force at Oxford. In his presence were all of England's nobles, priests and bishops. His forces proceeded to Hereford with great urgency, while Llewellyn had gathered his in a meadow not far from Montgomery Castle. The area was wet and marshy, far from ideal for traditional warfare. Instead, Llewellyn planned to survey the action from a distance and, should the opportunity allow, ambush the English soldiers as they left the castle.

What followed is a rather strange story recorded by Roger of Wendover. In a bid to trick the English soldiers Llewellyn sent a Cistercian monk from the nearby Cwmhir Abbey to Montgomery Castle to offer news of the Welsh progress. When asked what news there was of the enemy, the monk replied that he had seen the prince in a meadow close by, awaiting reinforcements. News of Llewellyn's presence aroused the attention of the soldiers. When asked if it would be safe for their horses to cross the river, the monk replied that Llewellyn had destroyed the bridge, fearing an attack; however, the river was safe for crossing, and Llewellyn's numbers were few.

Satisfied by the monk's words, the Constable of Montgomery, Walter de Godardville, ordered his men to assemble and mount their horses. They spotted the Welsh, who pretended to flee to the nearest woods. Too late did the English realize the trap. As they pursued the Welsh those at the front sank in the marshy riverbank. The Welsh seized the advantage, broke from cover and mercilessly slaughtered all who failed to escape, both human and beast.[8]

Though he was of a generally peaceful nature, Henry's response on hearing the news more than matched his ancestors' ferocity. The tithe barn of the abbey was looted and razed to the ground, and the same fate would have befallen the abbey itself had the abbot not offered to pay £200 to save its fine buildings.

Henry, also renowned for his piety and gentle nature, eventually calmed down and ordered that the abbey remain untouched.

The English made little progress against the Welsh. The only activity of note was the rebuilding in stone of Maud's Castle, sometimes known as Painscastle or Colwyn Castle, the previous building having been destroyed by the Welsh. While Henry was there the Duke of Brittany and Earl of Chester visited him, bringing news of a three-year truce with the French. Since Henry's departure in 1230 attempts by the Earls of Chester and Richard Marshal to conquer Anjou and Normandy had been unsuccessful, while the culmination of the French expedition against the Count of Champagne saw the forces return, leaving the lost territories of the former Angevin Empire too well defended for the English to risk further war. The earls negotiated for a truce with Louis that was concluded on 4 July 1231. Henry's former tutor, Peter des Roches, was particularly influential in the negotiations, appearing in France as he was returning from his crusade.[9]

A dispute followed with Richard Marshal about his inheriting his brother's rights, but this was later settled.[10] In October Henry returned to England, where he was talked out of marrying the sister of Alexander II by Chester on the grounds that Hubert had married the elder sister and it would not be seemly for a king to marry the younger. He spent Christmas at Winchester in the company of his former mentor, the recently returned Peter des Roches.[11]

Three other events of note took place that year. In keeping with his usual values, Henry is recorded as having intervened to ensure that scholars at Oxford and Cambridge were not overcharged for their accommodation.[12] Back in Canterbury the see was once more vacant after Richard Grant had died abroad, still angry about the feud with Hubert that had led to his journey to Rome. Though he succeeded in obtaining an audience with the

Pope, the archbishop died in August while in Italy.[13] Finally in that year the young Simon de Montfort received the prestigious Earldom of Leicester.[14]

The truce with Louis should have allowed Henry the opportunity to concentrate on Wales. Throughout 1232 Llewellyn's forces again inflicted much misery on the lands of the barons, leaving a trail of wreckage in their wake. When des Roches and many other royal counsellors brought the matter before the king, he argued that there was nothing he could do without funds. When the issue was discussed at a council at Westminster on 7 March 1232, the barons refused aid for a war with Wales, leaving Henry with just one option: to attempt to raise funds through demanding payment of revenues, including from various sheriffdoms. In this he achieved only limited success, and had to leave Llewellyn unchecked.[15]

Further problems awaited. On 7 June 1232 Gregory wrote again to Henry, this time complaining that one of his messengers had been killed and another left for dead. The catalyst was a series of events that occurred at Eastertide 1232. As the collection of tithes by papal emissaries continued to be scorned by large elements of the country, a knight named Robert de Twenge took it upon himself to relieve the Romans of their gains to give them to the poor.[16] On hearing the news Gregory was furious with Henry. On 9 June he wrote to Hubert asking him to ensure that the rights of the Roman Church remained unharmed. On being challenged over the matter Twenge went to Rome with letters from Henry, requesting the Pope hear his case personally.[17]

Henry's popularity was suffering, most notably among his subjects. Something was about to give, and on 29 July Henry made a big decision. Just one month after being appointed Justiciar of Ireland for life Hubert was sacked as Justiciar of England. His dismissal was undoubtedly a combination of the problems with Grant the previous year, failure abroad and with Wales and meddling on the part of des Roches. In his place Henry appointed Stephen Seagrave as Justiciar, in addition to allocating important roles for the Poitevins Peter des Riveaux and Robert Passelew.[18]

Despite Seagrave's lowly status as the son of a Leicestershire landowner, the humble lawyer had already gained experience of the Justiciar's post during Henry's absence in Poitou in 1230. Riveaux was a Poitevin clerk of questionable experience and referred to as the nephew of des Roches though word had it he was actually his son. Passelew was experienced at the papal court as the agent of Chester and Falkes de Breauté and was evidently well known to des Roches.[19]

Des Roches wasted little time in making changes, including bestowing nineteen of the thirty-five sheriffdoms on Riveaux by August and effectively stealing the Earldom of Gloucester from Hubert. Hubert, meanwhile, fled to Surrey, following which the king attempted to rally the citizens of London into tracking him down. After initially taking sanctuary with the canons of Merton he was later captured at a chapel near Brentwood in Essex.

The fall of Hubert is one of the more peculiar occurrences of Henry's reign. For so long this man had been the central figure in Henry's life, yet now he was accused of all sorts of ridiculous charges ranging from murder and treason to magic and witchcraft. One of the most interesting was an accusation that Hubert had stolen a precious stone, now in the hands of Llewellyn, believed to be something of a talisman in battle. After his removal as Justiciar Henry ordered an immediate investigation into the state of royal treasure that had been paid into the exchequer during his tenure, including in John's reign, and the debts still owed to the king. A similar report was also demanded on all his demesnes (land belonging to a manor) in England

and elsewhere, in addition to the situation regarding scutage, carucage and many other issues for which he had been made responsible.[20] Henry's behaviour here seems to confirm two things: how important the Justiciar of England was at the time and how lax he had been in keeping his affairs in order.

Henry held a council at Lambeth in September 1232, at which point he succeeded in obtaining a grant of a fortieth of all movables from the laity on payments to the Duke of Brittany, thereby bringing the costs of the recent Poitou and Gascony expedition slightly more under control.[21] The following month the barons lost their leader following the death of Ranulph de Blondevilles at the age of sixty. Described as 'almost the last relic of the great feudal aristocracy of the conquest', Ranulph had made a fine name for himself under Henry and, previously, John. According to the poet William Langland, the Earl of Chester enjoyed fame similar to that of Robin Hood, though no rymes of this man's exploits have survived.[22] On Ranulph's death Richard Marshal ascended to the head of the baronage and immediately warned the king that the presence of Poitevins would cause the English to withdraw from court. Evidently Henry feared this possibility, leading to argument between Marshal and des Roches.[23]

Meanwhile Hubert was brought before the king on 10 November. Owing to his past good work he was allowed to keep his lands and was received with sureties by Richard of Cornwall, Warenne, the Earl of Surrey, Marshal, the Earl of Pembroke and de Ferrers, the Earl of Derby, and from then on allowed to remain under the watch of four of their knights at Devizes Castle which was still Hubert's property. On the orders of the king he was to be held in captivity until he either agreed to become a Templar or was released with the consent of his keepers and the magnates.[24]

Fifteen days of terrible thunder from 12 November proved the prelude for troubles to come.[25] With Hubert imprisoned, it did not take long for des Roches to extend his influence. While celebrating Christmas with the king at Worcester he replaced all the English officials with Poitevins – many of whom had only recently reached England – causing dissent in both England and Rome.[26]

In the absence of Hubert, Henry was at least learning the art of kingship for himself. He was enriched by Hubert's treasures, handed over with permission of the master of the Temple and was also taking a more hands-on interest in running the kingdom.[27] On 10 January 1233 Gregory wrote to Henry declaring null and void any oaths sworn under duress at his coronation not to recall the grants made in prejudice of the rights of the Crown through concern that such oaths could compromise his ability to rule.[28] Arguably this was the clearest sign that Henry was ready to rule alone.

Returning to the conflict with Wales, Henry once again feared trouble around Whitsuntide 1233. He had been at Gloucester on 23 May for Pentecost and from there continued on a tour through the Vale of Evesham. On 1 June he was at his manor at Feckenham, famed for its magnificent fishponds.[29]

A council was summoned for 24 June to take place in Oxford. When the magnates refused to attend, Henry received word through envoys that discontent was rife owing to the large influx of Poitevins since the removal of de Burgh.[30] A Dominican, Robert Bacon, complained personally to the king about des Roches, warning him that trouble might follow. The news deeply alarmed Henry – particularly the threat that should things not improve he would be driven from his kingdom together with the interlopers.

To ensure no uprising would occur Henry demanded hostages as security. This was potentially dangerous territory. While he watched developments nervously the Bishop of Winchester continued to press him to confer more honours on the Poitevins as they would protect the kingdom.[31]

Gregory wrote again to Henry, imploring him to make long-term peace with France. In May Gregory was also forced to intercede between Henry and Hubert, confirming that English nobles were not to be tried abroad.[32] Des Roches was also keeping a close eye on Hubert de Burgh.[33] He had already succeeded in turning the tables on the man responsible for his downfall in 1227, but now Hubert's life was in danger. Without drawing too much attention to the significance of the imprisoned former Justiciar, des Roches asked for custody of Devizes Castle.[34]

Before any progress was made Hubert got wind of this plan and sent word to two of his sergeants.[35] On 29 September 1233 these men capitalized on the fact that the castle guards were sleeping and freed the prisoner, though with great difficulty; as he was shackled it was necessary for him to be carried. On escaping the castle the sergeant proceeded safely across the moat. It was noted in the chronicles that the devout servant put the former Justiciar down only when they reached the high altar of the nearby parish church.

News of Hubert's escape did not take long to spread. The castellans, fearing the wrath of the bishop and the king, turned out in dramatic fashion and frantically searched the nearby area. When news reached them that the former Justiciar had taken sanctuary in the church they descended on him in numbers. Hubert was found praying in front of the altar. Though he was in sanctuary he was taken by force back to the castle and severely beaten by the guards.

The castellans had made another mistake. When Robert, Bishop of Salisbury, heard of this he demanded Hubert be returned to sanctuary. He excommunicated the guards who refused to obey and took the case before the king. Henry heard the news on 1 October at Oxford. Several bishops also attended, keen to lecture the king on the right of sanctuary. Two and a half weeks passed before the issue was resolved. On 18 October Hubert was sent back to the church from which he had been taken, though Henry was not in a forgiving mood. He agreed that sanctuary could never be violated but wasted little time before writing to the county sheriff ordering him to besiege the church.

The king did not anticipate what happened next. Hubert was indeed returned to the church at Devizes, but from there he was rescued by a small group of armed men who dressed him up as a knight. He made it as far as Wales, thanks to the assistance of the rebel barons Gilbert Basset and Richard Siward.[36]

Little did the king know that things were about to take a nasty turn.

6

THE FORGOTTEN WAR

During the summer and autumn of 1233 England was experiencing civil war. Certain barons, unhappy at the rising influence of the Bishop of Winchester and the influx of inexperienced officials from Poitou, were starting to cause trouble for the king.[1]

As indicated, the king had ordered a council to be held at Oxford on 24 June 1233, but this was later dissolved as most of the magnates failed to attend. Another was announced to take place at Westminster on 5 July, but the same thing happened. Des Roches then suggested a third date of 1 August, for which failure to attend would result in being labelled a traitor. Attendance for the August council was at least great enough to ensure that the event went ahead. Rumour in some quarters suggested many of the nobles agreed to appear only after being bribed, but for now there was at least general support for the king, even if they did not approve of his advisers.

Among those planning to attend was Richard Marshal, son of the former regent and, after the death of his brother, inheritor of the Pembroke estates. Like most of the barons Marshal had refused to attend the first two councils, but he, too, had been won over for the August council either by threats or monetary gain. While making his way to Westminster, however, Richard received word from his sister, Isabella, that the treacherous Bishop of Winchester had set a trap for him. Without waiting to see if she was right Marshal changed direction and fled to Wales.[2]

The scene was set for rebellion. All tournaments were cancelled owing to fears of an uprising, while des Roches ordered the seaports to be put under constant surveillance for messengers of the Earl of Pembroke.[3] After the council on 1 August the king sent for a number of foreign troops – this time from Flanders and once again on the advice of des Roches. Henry's forces gathered at Gloucester on 17 August, and the new mercenaries caught up with them at Hereford. Officially Marshal had been declared a traitor, and the king ordered that his lands be confiscated.[4]

By early September the king's forces had taken Marshal's castle at Usk. Faced with out-and-out conflict, Marshal agreed to the castle's surrender on the basis that it would be returned within fifteen days – once the king had corrected 'whatever needed to be corrected in the kingdom, with the counsel of the bishops'.[5] By 8 September Henry was satisfied with the earl's fidelity, but further problems arose when Marshal went missing while at Woodstock, travelling to a council at Westminster. Despite the agreement Usk Castle was not yet returned.[6]

Outraged by Marshal's disappearance, Henry seized his lands and dismantled his castle at Inkberrow, Worcestershire, and several of his manors, including Crendon and Hamsted Marshal.[7] The Westminster council was held on 9 October, at which point the king was urged to make peace with Marshal. In response to the earl's being labelled a traitor, it was argued with some accuracy that it was only right that Marshal be tried by his peers. In reply des Roches responded, rather condescendingly, that 'there were no peers in England as there were in France'.[8]

A renewed outcry now raged against des Roches, leading to threats from the bishops to excommunicate the king's Poitevin counsellors.⁹ This was the spark for all-out conflict. Two barons, Gilbert Basset and Richard Siward, who had recently been deprived of land by des Roches, began a rebellion, while Marshal retrieved Usk and, incredibly, now took up arms against Henry in alliance with his arch-enemy Llewellyn.

While Hubert was being freed from Devizes, war raged in the south of Wales. Between them Marshal and Llewellyn wreaked havoc in Glamorgan, which at the time formed part of des Roches' Gloucester inheritance. Several castles fell in a short period, including Cardiff and Abergavenny, while another branch of their army made some progress in Carmarthen.

Henry gathered his forces at Gloucester on 2 November before leading them towards Chepstow, the centre of Marshal's land in Gwent. Since Richard had devastated the land so severely the king's forces were in danger of starving. From there Henry moved up the Wye Valley in the direction of de Burgh's castles of Skenfrith, White and Grosmont.

Henry spent several days resting at Grosmont until the night of 11 November when the opposition forces surprised his sleeping soldiers. On this occasion no soldiers were slain or captured, but many lost horses or possessions. Following the setback and the flight of some of his men Henry returned to Gloucester.¹⁰

While the king was retreating to England another fierce clash took place in the shadow of Monmouth Castle on 25 November. As Richard attempted to pass with a small band of men at arms the group was suddenly attacked. Incredibly the Marshal held his own against twelve men, until the castle warden finally captured him. In the following mêlée the warden was shot by a crossbow arrow, and in the confusion his men scattered. By the time Marshal had resumed control the rest of his men had regrouped, allowing him to overrun the opposition. Against all odds Richard took possession of Monmouth Castle.¹¹

On hearing the news Henry was furious. Richard's success at Monmouth allowed him free passage to join with Llewellyn and mount an attack on Shrewsbury. On 22 December the king offered terms, but Marshal refused. Several days later, with Henry still at Gloucester, another group of royalist troops was beaten.

War was proving a disaster for the people of England. Roger of Wendover provided a shocking account of the state of Gloucestershire. 'It was a wretched sight for travellers in that region to see on the highways innumerable dead bodies lying naked and unburied, to be devoured by birds of prey, and so polluting the air that they infected healthy men with mortal sickness.'

War with Marshal continued until January 1234, culminating in the capture and burning of Shrewsbury.[12] For a time Henry had vowed never to make peace with Marshal, but with Siward still active and laying waste to the lands of both Richard of Cornwall and the Bishop of Winchester he declared his intention to leave Gloucester and return to the heart of his kingdom.[13] After enduring a joyless Christmas with des Roches at Gloucester, a council was held at Westminster on 2 or 4 February attended by most of the bishops, including the Bishop Elect of Canterbury, Edmund Rich. Once again the prelates warned Henry about des Roches and his evil counsellors and argued for their expulsion. Henry considered his next move while he undertook a pilgrimage to Bromholm Priory in Norfolk, two years after attending one with Hubert de Burgh. On his travels he visited Bury St Edmunds, Walsingham, Castle Acre, Ramsey and Peterborough, while Marshal returned from a brief trip to Ireland to subdue any threats to his lands in Leinster, followed by an attempt to recover some of his possessions.

Henry's temper had been calmed by the end of February, and negotiations for peace with Llewellyn and Marshal were now at last ready to begin.[14] He now asked the Bishops of Coventry and

Rochester to negotiate with Marshal; a truce was agreed on 6 March and confirmed at a council on 9 April.[15]

Evidently Henry's patience with des Roches was also exhausted. In the council on 9 April the new Archbishop of Canterbury came to Westminster and threatened Henry with excommunication. Henry relented and dismissed des Roches to his diocese and removed Riveaux from the treasurership. With the Poitevins gone Henry became reconciled with the lords he had previously alienated, including Hubert de Burgh. Yet even for Hubert there was no real return to power. Throughout his time on the throne Henry had never ruled without a regent, a legate or a justiciar. Des Roches's dismissal was the break from his past that Henry needed. From this point on the king filled his government with low-ranking officials and became his own chief minister.[16]

Returning to the situation with Marshal, unbeknown to the king things had taken a turn for the worse. Prior to the truce the king, along with des Roches, had attempted to take the war to Ireland. Ireland was of great significance for Marshal, since he had inherited estates owned by his father as Earl of Pembroke. Early in 1234 the Bishop of Winchester and the Justiciar both wrote to the Justiciar of Ireland, Maurice Fitzgerald, and other enemies of Marshal seeking their help in capturing or killing the earl. Many of his enemies agreed, and they did great damage to his lands. On hearing that some of the family estates in Ireland were under attack Marshal returned to Ireland and was met on his arrival by the former justiciar, Geoffrey Marsh, a long-time enemy of his and, unknown to the earl, also part of the conspiracy.

Limerick was back in the earl's hands after a short siege, following which his enemies requested a truce. The earl demanded a meeting with his enemies on 1 April on the Curragh of Kildare, leading to initial discussions through Templar intermediaries. However, these came to nothing following a deceitful piece of advice from Marsh to reject any offer.[17] Undoubtedly Marshal must have seen what was coming. Marsh left, claiming he could not fight for Marshal as this would involve conflict against his brother-in-law, leaving Richard with just fifteen knights to defend him. Outnumbered nine to one, he was captured. He was taken to Kilkenny, previously his own castle until it had been seized by the Justiciar. On being presented with a royal warrant that justified his opponents' recent actions, Marshal was requested to authorize entry into his castles. He had survived almost certain death during his capture, and though his condition initially improved he became much worse after receiving medical treatment from a surgeon, and on 16 April he died from a fever and was buried at the Franciscan church.[18] Whether his death was the work of the surgeon or the consequence of his earlier wounds is uncertain.

Marshal had died while the king was seeking peace. Despite making mistakes, Henry was never accused of having been involved in the conspiracy. He learnt of Marshal's death in the second week of May. At the time he was at Woodstock, one of his favourite palaces. He was greatly saddened by the news. The annals of Dunstable say of his reaction that he 'mourned for his friend as David had lamented Saul and Jonathan'.

This was the Poitevins' final mistake.

7

THE HOHENSTAUFEN
ENDEAVOUR

The priority Henry gave to waging war against Richard Marshal
had caused many problems for England. Since the start of the
rebellion he had been unable to halt isolated outbreaks of violence, notably on the part of Siward and Basset in the south-west,
while his government struggled to cope with the rising costs.
As Justiciar Seagrave lacked the capability of his predecessor
and was largely swayed by the influence of des Roches, and in
consequence the administration of the kingdom had suffered
since 1232.

The long-vacant See of Canterbury was also proving particularly problematical for the king. The longer Canterbury
remained without an archbishop, the longer the Church remained
inactive. Had Grant's successor had been elected sooner, the
kingdom would have had a senior cleric to help moderate the
rising influence of the Bishop of Winchester and the papacy.
Relations between Henry and Gregory had also slipped slightly.
The Pope had remonstrated profusely with the king over his
treatment of Hubert de Burgh and was vocal about his attitude
towards both Agnellus of Pisa, the first English provincial of the
Franciscans, and Richard Marshal, whose father was still fondly
remembered.

When asked about Grant's successor at Canterbury Gregory rejected Ralph Neville as Henry's first choice and was also dismissive of his second choice, the Prior of Christ Church, through concerns about his age and an alleged lack of knowledge for the position. When the third choice, John Blunt, was also vetoed on the advice of the reinstated Simon Langton, brother of Stephen and now Archdeacon of Canterbury,[1] the Pope succeeded in persuading the monks of Canterbury to accept Edmund Rich or, as he was later known, St Edmund of Abingdon, a man whose greatness would earn him fond memories.[2]

Before his appointment Edmund had been treasurer at Salisbury. He came with a reputation as a fine scholar, having taught theology and arts at both Paris and Oxford, and despite lacking experience for his new role he possessed great strength of conviction. He was present along with the suffragens on 2 February in supporting the integrity of Marshal and was unequivocal in his warnings to the king over his past favouritism for the Poitevin faction.

His consecration as archbishop was confirmed on 2 April 1234. Merely a week later he threatened to excommunicate the king unless Henry put an end to the ongoing dispute that plagued the kingdom. This was the push that finally led to the removal of the Poitevins. After talks with the king Edmund went to Wales at Henry's request to attempt to make peace with Llewellyn and Marshal (whom Henry still believed to be alive).[3]

The king set out for Gloucester on 23 May to meet the archbishop on his return. At the council that followed on 28 May the Poitevin counsellors were dismissed and a truce with Llewellyn was discussed in detail. Siward was forgiven for his rebellion, and Gilbert Marshal inherited the offices and titles of his childless brother. As a show of forgiveness Henry himself dubbed Gilbert a knight. Also present was the former Justiciar, Hubert de Burgh, now pardoned for any past offences. As a token of good faith Hubert formally resigned any claim to resume the position of Justiciar, but he was reinstated as a counsellor and granted ownership for the second time of the three castles of Gwent: Grosmont, Skenfrith and White.[4] Henry also imposed fines and ransoms on those who fought for Marshal in Ireland and thanked Richard de Burgh for his support, allowing him to take over the government of Ireland.[5]

While the king was at Gloucester Edmund and the other bishops returned from their discussions with Llewellyn. Terms had been agreed, involving formal reconciliation between the king and the noblemen he had alienated. A two-year truce with Llewellyn was confirmed on 21 June 1234, conducted at a location between Shrewsbury and Ellesmere. This brought to an end the difficulties between Henry and Llewellyn ap Iorwerth. Peace continued until his death in 1240, with the truce being renewed from time to time.[6]

Of the previous administration, only Neville remained in his job. After ousting Seagrave as Justiciar Henry left the role unfilled, arguing that there should be no senior magnate, either church or lay. This was his chance to exercise to the full his powers as king. Past criticism of his officials had undoubtedly influenced his decision, as perhaps had murmurings of their lack of affinity with some of his subjects. Various clerks filled the role of treasurer, each time temporarily, but Henry appointed no official replacement. In essence, England was again ruled in a manner similar to that of his grandfather, Henry II: the subjects of the king became faithful but capable followers once more, rather than undermining his authority.[7]

News of recent developments was welcomed by Gregory, who wrote to Henry in April to congratulate him. Two months earlier the Pope had written to Louis asking for peace with

Henry. Before his dismissal des Roches had been sent to discuss long-term peace with France.[8] Though Henry sent some aid to the Duke of Brittany in May, he refused to support further military action abroad. Louis's increasing strength and Henry's poor financial situation brought both kings close to peace, but any chance of a permanent solution was hindered by Lusignan's demand for the Isle of Oleron, as promised to him by John. On hearing of Henry's stance the Duke of Brittany had little choice but to withdraw his homage to Henry and make peace with Louis.[9]

In many ways 1234 had been the most challenging year of Henry's reign so far. In addition to the threat of war in France and Wales, this was the third successive year of sickness and famine in England. Though this was not directly the fault of the king, it imposed a significant burden on the lives of the common people, and their affinity with their king and protector was becoming further isolated after the recent uprising.[10]

Despite Henry's problems, his pilgrimages and religious tours had left him invigorated.[11] In September the English prelates were once again implored by the Pope to aid the Holy Land, following which the clergy fell prey to a further wave of abuses by papal collectors, many of whom were accused of keeping tithes for themselves.[12] Gregory was intent on bringing an end to hostilities in the Holy Land, and he once again attempted to make peace between Henry and Louis, writing to both in November.[13] Lusignan's refusal to cooperate still hindered the truce, leading to further letters between Henry, Lusignan and the Pope, while Henry asked for the Pope's assistance in dealing with the Duke of Brittany.[14] Also that year the Pope had written to the Bishops of York and Carlisle in January, directing them to caution Alexander II of Scotland to respect the treaty with England and observe the fealty due to Henry, and he also wrote to Alexander personally.[15]

In December Henry received another letter from the Pope, paving the way for what would prove to be the main event of 1235. In February 1235 two members of the Knights Templar came to visit Henry on behalf of Frederick II. Also in the party were several knights and messengers who brought with them letters sealed with gold, delivered personally from the Emperor. The reason for the visit was Frederick's desire to marry Henry's younger sister, Isabella.[16]

Henry evidently found the idea interesting and discussed it with the bishops and nobles for three days. The match already had the approval of the papacy, and by 27 February there was unanimous agreement. Isabella was brought from the Tower of London and appeared before the envoys. She was in her twenty-first year, immaculate in behaviour and appearance and dressed as befitted a princess. On seeing her for the first time the envoys were particularly captivated by her well-educated manner and her fine voice. They presented her with a ring as a sign of her betrothal, followed by unanimous shouts of 'Long live the Empress!'

Frederick was overjoyed on hearing the news. In response to the agreement he sent the Archbishop of Cologne and the Duke of Louvain to England with a large party to escort the empress-in-waiting to her new home. On Henry's part, no expense was spared. Among his gifts to his sister was a gold crown, decorated with sculptures of the four martyred kings of England, festal robes made of silk and wool, a fine bed of silk, muslin draperies and several horses of docile nature. The agreement also cost Henry a dowry of some £20,000, leading to the issue of a hidage of two marks on every hide.[17]

When the arrangements had been made a solemn celebration took place at Westminster Abbey on 6 May, attended by the Archbishop of Cologne and various messengers. The following day the king, Isabella and their entourage began their journey to the coast. After passing Rochester and Faversham Abbey they stopped at Canterbury to pray before the shrine of St Thomas, before continuing on to Sandwich, close to the spot where Hubert de Burgh had achieved his important victory over Eustace the Monk some eighteen years before.

Isabella's party left England on 11 May. According to Roger of Wendover, over 3,000 knights gathered at the spot. As Henry watched the ships sail away into the distance it was noted that he did not hide his tears. Although such a sign of affection was not out of the ordinary in the thirteenth century it perhaps suggests that Henry's tendency towards lavish spending was a sign of love for his favourites as much as recklessness.[18]

At the time Frederick was at war with his son, preventing Isabella from seeing him. After remaining for a time in Cologne, Isabella finally received word that she was to join Frederick at Worms. On 30 July they married.[19] In gratitude to Henry Frederick sent three leopards and other gifts to England.[20] The marriage between Frederick and Isabella brought the approval of the papacy and a key ally for Henry. The event also passed without interference from France, as Louis was happy to agree to honour Gregory's request that there be no disturbance to the marriage.[21]

By 1235 relations between the kings of England and France were much less hostile, but official peace continued to be obstructed by Lusignan. In March the Pope wrote to the Archbishop of Bordeaux and Bishop of Bazas requesting their compliance in compelling Lusignan to restore certain vassals to Henry, and three weeks later Gregory also wrote to Simon Langton on the matter.[22] A grant of an annuity from Henry to Lusignan resolved the issue in July.[23]

Gregory wrote to Henry on 1 July, absolving him from an

oath previously taken to alienate certain rights of the Crown, as it appeared contrary to the oath taken at his coronation to preserve them. He also informed Henry that he had received his most recent messengers and had written to Louis on the situation in Poitou.[24]

The remainder of 1235 was quiet. That summer Henry spent much of his time travelling around his kingdom; he met the abbots and priors of various religious houses including Wood-stock, Gloucester, Bath, Marlborough, Reading, London, Northampton and Nottingham. He gained pledges of financial support from many of them, but of more importance was his ability to build a rapport with his subjects.[25]

On a related note, it was in 1235 that the Benedictine monk of St Albans, Matthew Paris, began his acclaimed work *Chronica Majora*. Over the next twenty-four years the 35-year-old would go on to write several historical works, many of which detailed the events of Henry's reign. Though his bias, often fervently anti-papist in manner, has led to some issues regarding the validity of his work, what separated Paris from other chroniclers was his tendency to illustrate his work, largely through watercolour washes. He enlisted a wide range of sources, including letters and first-hand documents, but was also known to have met many key people, including Henry III himself and the Earl of Cornwall.[26]

Henry's mind was alive with activity during that summer of travel. Fresh from witnessing the marriage of his sister, his thoughts now turned to finding himself a suitable partner. He was twenty-eight and finally secure on the throne of England, enthusiastically getting to grips with the running of his kingdom and famously devoted to his Church. On account of his religious faith he deprived himself of mistresses, unlike many of his Plantagenet ancestors, and was regarded as being in a state of spiritual purity.

Until now talk of marriage had been influenced by the changing political situation. Better relations with Louis, Llewellyn, Frederick and his own barons had given Henry the chance to govern in peacetime, diminishing the urgency of needing to marry solely for an alliance. He had reigned for twenty years, but if he was going to lay the foundations of a dynasty like his grandfather's he would need the support of a family.

The pious king was now ready for a queen.

8

THE RULE OF THE SAVOYARDS

Throughout 1235 negotiations took place for Henry to marry. The woman concerned was Joan, daughter of the Count of Ponthieu. At some point before 8 April 1235 both parties had gone so far as to pledge themselves to one another, *verba de praesenti*, a binding constitution that could only be broken through the consent of the papacy. Henry also wrote to the count requesting that Joan should come to England at Pentecost so that they could be married and Joan crowned on the feast.

The match had its advantages. Successful union would have gained Henry a strong presence in the north-east of France, in addition to an alliance with a powerful family. This possibility was unwelcome to the French. A combination of the diplomacy of Blanche and Louis himself was needed to convince the count and the Pope not to allow the union, and by 16 July Henry was writing to his envoys at Rome telling them not to proceed with their attempts to confirm the agreement.[1]

While negotiations were still ongoing with Joan, Henry wrote to Raymond Berenger, Count of Provence, and his brothers Amadeus, Count of Savoy, and William, Bishop Elect of Valence, on 22 June proposing marriage to Berenger's daughter, Eleanor. Raymond was a man of fine pedigree and valour, more at home on a battlefield than anywhere else. He had ruled the county of Provence since 1219 as a vassal of Frederick II and was the Count of Forcalquier to the north.[2] In his younger days he had married a strikingly beautiful woman, the daughter of the Count of Savoy. The marriage had not only benefited Raymond as a political arrangement but produced four attractive and elegant daughters, the eldest of whom, Margaret, had already married the King of France.[3]

The possibility of a marriage between the King of England and the second daughter of the Count of Provence had many advantages. Though Henry would gain no dowry, an alliance with Eleanor's father as well as a family connection to the King of France was highly tempting to the magnates. The marriage of Louis and Margaret, having taken place on 27 May 1234, had not only cemented relations between Provence and the monarchy of France but brought with it arbitration over unresolved issues between Raymond Berenger and his rival, Raymond of Toulouse, Henry's kinsman and natural ally in the south. For Henry any alliance with the families who dominated the Alpine passages potentially allowed a presence in the south and east of France.[4]

Henry celebrated Christmas in Winchester, the city of his birth, anxiously preparing for the return of his envoys.[5] In Provence Raymond had welcomed Henry's envoys in early October. News of the King of England's desire to marry his daughter went down well. The proposal was accepted, involving a dower to Eleanor that was not dissimilar to that enjoyed by previous queens of England – approximately one-third of the king's possessions. It was also necessary for Raymond to allocate Eleanor a marriage portion, established for the benefit of future children. Henry clearly had spent much time contemplating the matter and sent six sets of letters, his demands ranging from 3,000 marks to 20,000. When the count made his will in 1238 the amount allocated for Margaret and Eleanor was 10,000 marks.[6]

At the castle of Tarascon on 23 November 1235 Eleanor entered *verba de praesenti* with Henry. She was then entrusted into the guardianship of her uncle, William, the Bishop Elect of Valence. By 15 December she had reached the city of Vienne, at which point William, as dean of the cathedral, confirmed the marriage agreement. From Vienne they continued towards England, together with her retinue and Henry's ambassadors. For five days they travelled through the land of Theobald, Count of Champagne and King of Navarre, during which time he bore their expenses with great optimism. These were undoubtedly large given that 300 horsemen were accompanied by an even greater number travelling on foot. When they reached the border of France Louis received word of their request for safe passage. On hearing the news that the sister of his wife was to marry the King of England, Louis received them with great honour and according to at least one source may have personally accompanied them to Wissant.[7]

The party reached Dover by 10 January, and within a few days they arrived at Canterbury. There Henry met his new bride for the first time. He was immediately captivated, and they married at Canterbury on 14 January 1236 in a ceremony conducted by Archbishop Edmund.[8] Though she was praised for her elegance and beauty, no description of Eleanor's appearance has survived. Based on later evidence, the new queen seems to have inherited the same physical traits of her mother and sisters and was charming and well educated. Strangely, equally little is known of Henry's appearance. According to the only description that survives, included in the chronicle of Nicholas Trevet, he had smooth skin but a slight drooping of the right eyelid, perhaps hiding part of the pupil. If his later tomb at Westminster is any indication of his physique, he was about 5 feet 6 inches (1.68 metres) in height, about the same as his father, and was of strong stature.

Five days after the wedding the king and queen arrived at Westminster in preparation for the crowning of the queen the following day.[9] The chronicler Matthew Paris described in enormous detail how the city of London was alive with wonder. A plethora of fine decorations filled the streets, arousing the delight and enthusiasm of the commoners. It was an ancient right accorded to Londoners that on such a day they should perform the role of butler to the king. While the party travelled to Westminster the people of London walked in procession, set out in columns according to rank, carrying in their hands 360 cups made of silver and gold.[10] The crowds waved, people cheered and royal trumpeters played. As recorded by Paris, 'All the pleasure and glory the world could pour forth was on display there.'

The prelates of the kingdom performed various roles, as did the lay magnates. The Lord Marshal, Gilbert Marshal, Earl of Pembroke, carried a rod before the king; the Earl of Chester carried the sword of St Edward; the wardens of the Cinque Ports held a canopy for the king. Behind the king, dressed in full regalia, his new bride followed, also walking beneath a canopy and alongside two bishops chosen to accompany her to the abbey.

On reaching the door all stopped for the Archbishop of Canterbury to recite the first prayer before continuing inside. As in the coronation of kings Eleanor's head was anointed with holy oil. The archbishop blessed the rings and the crown of lilies, before placing the crown on her head. It is possible that Eleanor held a virge and sceptre, as indicated by a seal used until 1259. After the ceremony came the great feast. There was a place at this point for a young Simon de Montfort, 6th Earl of Leicester, to provide the king with bowls of water before he dined.[11]

Eleanor of Provence was only twelve or thirteen at the time of the wedding. Despite the age gap she got on well with her new husband and went on to enjoy a happy marriage. She was compliant in nature and in her early years probably slightly naïve, though well trained for her future environment by her diligent parents. It has been suggested that she grew to be taller than Henry, evidence supported by the height of their future sons. She shared her husband's piety and took an interest in the life of St Edward the Confessor, to whom Henry was famously devoted. She developed a fine manner and intellect, an interest in literature and a fascination, instilled also in their first son, for the legend of King Arthur. Henry and Eleanor are recorded as visiting Glastonbury in the summer of that year, perhaps inspired by the Arthurian legend.[12]

Most importantly, unlike Henry's predecessors, no hint of scandal ever harmed them. At a time when marriages were often arranged for political reasons, this pair was among the few who enjoyed a loving marriage.[13]

After the wedding festivities were over Henry attended a great council at Merton in Surrey on 23 January. With the exception of the earlier reissue of the two charters, the meeting at Merton was arguably the most important legislative event of his reign so far. The various revisions of the charters had already had a significant impact on the laws of the country, particularly the stipulation that no man would be deprived of lands and chattels unless actually convicted of an offence, but other issues were not altogether resolved. Of greater concern at Merton was the legal situation regarding the rights of widows to inherit their late husband's dower at the time of his death. It was henceforth decided that any widow who had been forced to enter legal proceedings to inherit their late husband's dower should receive everything due, beginning on the day of the husband's death.

A further issue was the practice that people who had brought a case of novel disseisin were often disappropriated again by the same person despite winning their case. This was rectified with a threat of prison against their challenger, while the charging of interest to a minor on his father's debts was also denounced. Finally of interest, the council also assured that the right of access by tenants to common pastures was reserved to them in the event that a lord of the manor was to enclose common land.[14]

Another matter discussed at that time, though separate from the 'statute of Merton', was the legal position regarding the status of children born out of wedlock. At the time the position in common law in England differed from civil and canon law, leading to debate between various parties over the law's amendment, most notably the status of children born out of wedlock to parents who later married.[15] Among the chief proponents of the change in status of children born out of wedlock was the new Bishop of Lincoln, Robert Grosseteste, a man of fine learning from his time at the universities of Oxford and Paris.[16]

Though the status of first-borns was not resolved at Merton, the events of 1236 had a marked effect on the running of the kingdom. Despite persistently agreeing to abide by the Great Charter, Henry's actions were coming more regularly into question. His ability over the past two years to run his government with the aid of his clerks had tightened his grip on the country, assisted by the loyalty of his close advisers. As the year progressed a rumour developed that Henry had established a twelve-man secret council. In April word of this caused quite a stir among the magnates, who strongly opposed the empowering of foreigners, most notably William of Valence. Fearing for his safety, Henry sought refuge in the Tower of London before moving on to Westminster to meet the council on 28 April – the magnates having refused to attend the Tower. Henry agreed to the appointment of new sheriffs with the aim of easing past corruption, and he made changes to the household, including recalls for former justiciar Seagrave and Passelew as justices. Somewhat surprising was the appointment of Riveaux as keeper of the wardrobe.[17]

An abnormally wet winter followed by a prolonged drought played havoc in England in 1236, damaging the corn crop. The year closed with another Christmas at Winchester, followed by a council to consider the financial situation of the country in January 1237. Aid was requested on the king's behalf by his clerk, William of Raleigh, who proposed that any money should be entrusted to a committee of magnates who would be empowered to authorize expenditure on the upkeep of the kingdom. The reaction was negative, for the usual reasons. Henry's poor financial situation, particularly in the light of his recent marriage and a debt owed to the Emperor as part of Isabella's dowry, induced him to offer concessions. He promised greater freedom for the barons should he receive a thirtieth of all movables. Other reforms were mooted, including the election of three barons as advisers to the king and the excommunication of anyone who refused to abide by the Great Charter. On 28 January Henry received formal absolution from Edmund for past violations of the charters at a ceremony at St Catherine's Chapel at Westminster attended by the bishops.[18]

From a financial perspective the council was useful. Aid was given to Henry, but the presence of Valence saw much of the money squandered, usually on enriching his favourites. Henry's decisions led to further criticism on the part of the magnates. At the end of May he sent two envoys to Rome, requesting a papal legate. No legate had been present in England since Pandulf. Henry had apparently asked for one before the Poitou campaign, but he withdrew the request in 1230 after criticism from the magnates that he had acted without consultation.[19] Henry's request was answered in February 1237, in a typically mixed response. Richard of Cornwall was as displeased as any at his brother's subservience to the Pope. Also under scrutiny was his tendency once again to favour foreigners, including the up-and-coming Simon de Montfort.[20]

The new legate was Otho, a man already familiar with England. Edmund met him on his arrival at the end of June, acknowledging the legate with his usual reverence, though the latter's visit was not well received by the clergy. There is reason to believe the magnates suspected Henry had an ulterior motive for the legate's arrival. As a papal legate Otho had the Pope's permission to absolve Henry from any oaths that might prejudice the rights of the Crown. Intriguingly, the Pope had written to Henry in June 1236 explaining that his coronation oath refused him the power to give up rights of the Crown.[21]

Peace with Scotland was again a priority. In June 1236 Henry had been present in York to meet Alexander II, looking to settle the Scottish claim to Northumbria.[22] Further friction arose between the king and Hubert de Burgh after the new Earl of Gloucester, a minor, married Hubert's daughter without the king's permission, though this was eventually resolved.[23] In September 1237 the king returned to York, and he held a council with Alexander II on the 14th, at which point the latter's claims were settled. The talks with Alexander also involved Otho, appointed by Gregory as legate of Scotland as well as England. Alexander II formally agreed to give up his claim to the northern districts of England in return for receiving several manors in ancient Northumberland and Cumberland to the value of £200 a year, the most notable being Penrith. These lands were to be held on Henry's behalf by Alexander in return for delivering a goshawk each year at Carlisle Castle. The event was known as the Treaty of York, confirmation of which occurred in 1242.[24]

In England trouble continued to brew. A tournament at Blyth at the beginning of the year had threatened to develop into an orgy of violence. As the year continued, Otho was able to appease the dissident barons, and his attention then turned to bringing reform to the clergy. He met them at a synod at St Paul's on 18 November, at which point his appointment as legate was published and talks took place on matters of ecclesiastical discipline. The 'Constitution of Cardinal Otho' that followed would prove to be an important event, as it formed the framework of ecclesiastical law for centuries to come.[25]

At around the time of the synod the archbishops of England, acting on behalf of the clergy, presented a long list of grievances to the king. There followed a threat of excommunication by the prelates against all who had violated the Great Charter.[26] The king had again succeeded in bringing calm – but at a price.

9

THE DEVIL AND HIS HORSEMEN

The year 1238 started with an event that would cause Henry much future aggravation. One week into the New Year Henry presided over the second marriage of his sister Eleanor, widow of the Earl of Pembroke, to her new husband, the young Earl of Leicester, Simon de Montfort.[1]

Simon was around thirty years old at the time of the marriage. Since coming to England seven years earlier he had become firmly established as a favourite at court. As a de Montfort he came from a prestigious family. His father, Simon de Montfort III, held his seat at Montfort l'Amaury, some forty kilometres from Paris, and was famed for having brutally slaughtered his fair share of 'heretics' in the Albigensian Crusade. Simon III's brother, Guy, had joined Philip Augustus in the third crusade of 1191, while Simon III himself fought with distinction in the fourth crusade before becoming involved in the new crusade to the south. As a general in the war he excelled, building up a large territorial empire. Yet with success came claims of excessive brutality. His death in 1218 left the de Montfort name infamous in that part of the world.

The rise of the crusader's son Simon de Montfort IV, who would later inherit the Earldom of Leicester, was more due to influence from his mother's side of the family. Simon's grand-mother, Amicia, inherited the right to that title after her brother, Robert de Beaumont, 4th Earl of Leicester, died childless. As the eldest son of Amicia, Simon III was acknowledged to be the possessor of that title when he visited England around 1206. When his son arrived in England some twenty-five years later he took the title from Ranulph, Earl of Chester, in acknowledge-ment of his right of succession.[2]

The wedding aroused discontent. Henry was himself one of only a few attendees at the ceremony, which took place in his small chapel at Westminster.[3] Richard of Cornwall, in particu-lar, was vocal in his criticism of the union and reproached Henry for allowing the service to go ahead without discussion among the magnates. He was also scathing that Henry had allowed his ward, Richard of Clare, to marry the daughter of the Earl of Lincoln without prior consultation.[4]

Richard took to arms and amassed an impressive gathering at Kingston. The uprising surprised the king, who once more sought refuge in the Tower.[5] Otho and des Roches both approached Henry, emphasizing the severity of Richard's actions, following which the nobles took up the matter. Henry was under pressure but not just from the magnates. His decision to reinforce the Tower's inadequate defences drew criticism from the people of London, who saw it as a symbol of oppression. In an attempt to defuse the situation Henry held a conference on 2 February at which he agreed to submit to plans for reform, supported by the nobles and the legate. Before progress could be consolidated Richard abandoned the cause of reform and made peace with both Henry and Simon.[6]

Evidently the Earl of Cornwall was not the only magnate angered by the Earl of Leicester's marriage. The Archbishop of Canterbury was equally astounded when he heard the news and declared the marriage void, as Eleanor had ignored her vow of chastity. In response Simon was forced to take the case to Rome to prove that nothing improper had taken place.[7]

Otho's position had become quite secure in England since the synod, despite objections from the Archbishop of Canterbury who had taken his complaints to Rome. The legate's recall to Rome was deferred after he successfully obtained a letter of support with the seal of the king, Cornwall and the bishops asking him to stay. Almost immediately further trouble followed. While the king was at Abingdon on 12 March he received a surprise visit from the legate, who complained of his servants' treatment by students of Oxford University.[8] At the time Otho had been staying with the canons of Oseney, during which time his visit had caused much interest among the nearby students. When one party arrived at the abbey, hoping to pay their respects to the legate, their request was rejected by an Italian porter, prompting them to return with several clerks who entered the abbey by force. An impoverished chaplain from Ireland then found his way into the kitchen. His pleas for food were rejected by the cook who poured a pot of scolding broth on him. In the chaos that followed, the cook was killed by a crossbow arrow while Otho sought sanctuary in the tower. Though the legate managed to escape, his servants were forced to seek refuge until the king's forces relieved him. In retribution, the legate placed the university under an interdict, and in consequence Henry suspended all lectures at the university.[9]

In April Henry was on hand to welcome another foreigner, Baldwin II, Emperor of the Latin Empire of Constantinople. The pair met at Woodstock, where they discussed issues in the east, including Frederick's second excommunication by the papacy in the space of eight years.[10] Henry bestowed on Baldwin a gift of 500–700 marks and promised him troops to assist

Frederick in his war with Italy. He also agreed to write to the Pope on Baldwin's behalf, which brought English business in the Roman Curia to a temporary halt.[11]

Around the time of Eleanor's wedding to Simon the King of France received a distressing message from envoys of the Saracens. Unrelated to troubles in the Holy Land, a previously unknown race of people had emerged from beyond the Near East. The leader of these people was Genghis Khan, Emperor of the Mongols. News of his barbarity spread like wildfire, fuelled by tales of his warriors having heads too large for their bodies or dining on the raw flesh of animals and humans. Though these fearsome warriors remained far from England they caused much mischief for the English. In Great Yarmouth fish dealers faced bankruptcy as their customers from Russia or the Baltic failed to make their usual orders. Throughout Europe rumours that the forces of Tartarus had been unleashed caused havoc. It seemed there was nothing that could be done to thwart the progress of the so-called Devil's Horsemen.

By 1238 Khan had brought over half the known world under his rule. While John had been attempting to avoid the Charter of Liberties, Khan's forces had taken Peking. China had been invaded and the Mongols' march continued into Persia and Russia. Their horsemen were feared for their ability to ride at great speed, changing from horse to horse at full gallop, and for their ruthless abilities in battle. Khan was famed for his tactical and military strength; though illiterate he chose steady and learned advisers with great success; and, despite his ruthless streak, he showed a unique respect for religion and a willingness to learn from the ways of others that also aided his advance.

After visiting Louis the Saracen envoys sent another envoy to England. Henry took the issue seriously and talked the matter over with his former adviser, Peter des Roches, himself a veteran of the crusades. However, on the subject of assisting the Saracens des Roches advised that Henry should 'let these dogs devour one another' and complete a conquest of the Holy Land once this was done.[12]

Des Roches died on 9 June that year. Since his dismissal four years earlier he had redeemed himself by fighting for the cause of the Pope but returned to England in 1236 a weary man. He was reconciled with the king he had once tutored as a boy, and he spent his last two years in quiet retirement.[13]

With des Roches dead, the Winchester See needed to be filled for the first time in Henry III's reign. Henry's preference was his new uncle, William the Bishop Elect of Valence. This decision met with resistance as William was already in line for the prince-bishopric of Liège, though Gregory granted him permission to take both Winchester and Liège. Nevertheless, the monks of St Swithun's resisted, preferring the chancellor, Ralph Neville, also Bishop of Chichester, and after two quashed elections the see remained vacant.[14] Henry was noticeably angry – so much so that on 28 August he deprived Neville of the great seal, the chancellor's chief responsibility, placing it in the hands of two keepers. He changed his mind the following April, but on that occasion Neville refused to take it.[15]

In September Henry was the intended victim of an assassination attempt. While he was staying at his palace at Woodstock one of his clerks, who claimed he was rightful king of England, attempted to kill him. On being apprehended by the guards the man admitted to being sent by various persons, including the outlawed William de Marisco, who was living a life of piracy on Lundy Island.

What saved Henry was actually his marriage. Rather than being alone in his chambers, the king was sleeping with Eleanor.[16] His initial relaxed attitude to the intruder changed dramatically when he became aware of the real purpose of the attack. Matthew Paris described in vivid detail the man's punishment. 'In the first place, he was dragged asunder, then beheaded, and his body divided, into three parts; and each was then dragged through one of the principal cities of England, and was afterwards hung on a gibbet used for robbers.'[17] Though it was not until 1351 that the punishment of hanging, drawing and quartering became common in England, this may have been the first recorded incident.

Henry spent Christmas 1238 in Winchester, to the irritation of the monks of St Swithun's. The occasion was tense. During the festivities the king insulted Gilbert Marshal, allegedly arising from suspicion concerning the Woodstock treason, and the earl left the court early in a fit of rage.[18]

With the troubles of 1238 behind him, for Henry 1239 proved to be largely a year of celebration. On 17 June he became a father. His son was named Edward after St Edward the Confessor. The prince would later be remembered as Longshanks, the hammer of the Scots, and King Edward I, a great king of England. The legate baptized Edward on 28 June after he had been initiated by the Bishop of Carlisle. Also present were the prince's godparents, Richard of Cornwall and Simon de Montfort.[19] On news of Edward's birth all in the kingdom offered their congratulations, including the city of London, where the prince had been born. On receiving many gifts from its citizens Henry inquired what had been brought and by whom and in certain cases demanded they be returned for better offerings. News of his dissatisfaction was greeted with further scorn; on hearing the news a man called Norman remarked, 'God gave us this child, but the king sells him to us.'[20]

The appearance of a comet preceded an outburst that would potentially ruin the kingdom. At the queen's churching (a tradition of blessings to a mother after recovery from childbirth) the king had a violent quarrel with de Montfort. Accusations, whether true or not, were rife that the new favourite had seduced his new wife before their marriage. Worse still, he was accused of obtaining money, with which he bribed the Roman court to procure a dispensation for his marriage, using the king's name as security. In the resulting uproar Simon and Eleanor fled to France, ending the first of many disputes between the king and Simon over the next quarter of a century.[21]

In the autumn the inevitable requests for aid came in for the Pope's war against Frederick. Under the direction of the legate all foreigners holding benefices in England were to be deprived of a fifth of their annual revenues in addition to the collection of a general subsidy.[22] A rumour also abounded that Gregory intended to grant Roman citizens who helped against Frederick benefices in England.[23]

Christmas 1239 was once again spent at Winchester. During the festivities Henry bestowed the Earldom of the Isle of Wight on the young knight, Baldwin de Rivers.[24]

Early in 1240 a meeting took place between the legate and the bishops to resolve fresh complaints against the king and his advisers. Among the key issues were consistent abuse of the rights of the clergy and the prolonged vacancy of various sees. Grosseteste wrote to Edmund around this time, voicing his concern over the future of the Church should matters not improve. Before the council ended the king had received messengers from Frederick, upset that his excommunication notice had been published in England. Henry's reply noted his obvious conflict of interests, particularly his own ties to the papacy. He also wrote to Gregory on behalf of Frederick, though this had little effect on the stubborn Pope.[25]

Another council was held in London on 18 February. While initial discussion took place regarding general observance of the stricter regulations imposed on the clergy since the synod, Otho also announced news of his recall to Rome owing to concerns over criticisms aimed at the Roman clerics. Grosseteste was particularly vocal in his criticism of the legate, leading to complaints to Edmund and demands that Otho be removed from England.

Further disagreement arose between Henry and Edmund, this time regarding Edmund's desire to fill sees that had been vacant for more than six months with his own appointees. Though Edmund received the backing of the papacy, on this occasion it was Henry who demurred, successfully persuading Gregory to change his mind.[26] All this was too much for Edmund. After remonstrating with the king over recent events, particularly Gregory's demand that 300 English benefices should be allocated for distribution among relatives of any Roman who aided the war against the Emperor, he fled the kingdom in despair and died abroad on 16 November. Thus passed away one of the greatest clerics and theologians in English history.[27]

Henry's request that the legate remain saw Otho's position in England once again secure by July 1240, though opposition north of the border the previous year significantly weakened his position as legate of Scotland.[28] A fresh meeting of the bishops was called in July at Northampton during which time Otho's call to take a fifth of the bishops' goods was rejected by the prelates.[29]

By October Gregory had decided to recall Otho. A final meeting between Henry, the legate and the prelates was recorded as having taken place on All Saints' Day, at which Henry supported Otho in his mission to extract money from the clergy. Otho remained in England for Christmas at Westminster. At the banquet he was reported to have been invited to sit at the head of the table, the seat designated for the person who ruled the realm.[30]

Much was changing in England. Henry had made the decision to withdraw protection from all foreign merchants who remained in England after a certain date, yet he continued to oversee the rise to prominence of outsiders.[31] In July 1239 he had received another of his wife's uncles, Thomas of Savoy, enriching him with a gift of 500 marks and granting him a tax on English wool that passed through his jurisdiction as Count of Flanders. William of Savoy's clerk, Peter of Aigueblanche, gained the See of Hereford, but the biggest beneficiary was William's brother, Peter of Savoy, who became the second foreigner in fifteen years to be invested with the prestigious Earldom of Richmond.[32] This was another decision that enraged the magnates.

10

PRELATES, POITOU AND THE BIRTH OF PARLIAMENT

Otho departed on 7 January 1241, leaving England without a legate or an Archbishop of Canterbury. His time in England had provoked large-scale resentment among the prelates, while taxes for the purpose of war, levied by the legate, had caused unrest both at home and abroad. For Henry the situation was particularly troubling. His sister was still enjoying a satisfying marriage with Frederick, and Henry was reluctant to fund the papacy's military campaign against his brother-in-law.[1]

Valence was poisoned in November 1239, an event that saddened Henry and Eleanor, though his death was largely unmourned by the monks of Winchester. Earlier in 1239 Henry had replaced the prior of St Swithun's with a foreigner named Andrew, tasked with the responsibility of persuading a majority of the monks to support Valence as Bishop of Winchester. Early in 1240 Gregory had quashed the election and asked Otho to enquire into the legitimacy of the proceedings. He also wrote personally to the king regarding his continual interference. In response to the legate and the king, Gregory asked that Otho ensure freedom was given to the monks to elect their preferred candidate but also to ensure that the candidate would not be a nuisance to Henry.[2]

Eleanor gave birth to a baby girl named Margaret on 2 October 1240, an event widely welcomed by all at court and none more than the doting father.[3] The departure of the Earl of Cornwall on crusade (severely grieving the recent death of his wife, Isabella) gave Henry more freedom in his dealings, particularly as he was eager to empower relatives of the queen. With Valence dead, Henry attempted to obtain the See of Winchester for Boniface of Savoy, another of his wife's uncles, and unsurprisingly he faced similar problems. The monks succeeded in electing William of Raleigh, though, somewhat unexpectedly, Henry was unhappy with the election of his loyal clerk.

Other ecclesiastical issues also dominated the early part of 1241. There was considerable disagreement between the monks of Durham and the king over the successor to Poore as Bishop of Durham, but this was resolved after the withdrawal of the prior, who had previously been seen as the leading candidate in the local community. In Rome Gregory IX died on 22 August, aged about ninety-three. During his time on the throne of St Peter he had continued in the spirit of his predecessors to establish papal supremacy throughout Europe, leading to persistent trouble with the Holy Roman Emperor. He died with his enemy at the gates of Rome and the future of the papacy under severe threat. On hearing news of Gregory's death Frederick wasted no time in ordering the seizure of papal collectors.[4]

Henry abandoned his attempts to obtain Winchester for Boniface and moved on to convincing the monks of Christ Church to elect Boniface to the See of Canterbury. Little was known about Boniface other than that he had been Bishop Elect of Belley, a dependency of Savoy, since 1232, yet he was still only a subdeacon. Nevertheless, the monks realized that the election of the wrong man could cause problems. Before his departure Edmund had placed Christ Church under an interdict, requiring that the monk receive absolution from the Pope. Understanding that the assistance of the king and papacy was paramount to lasting peace, Boniface was elected to Langton's throne.[5]

Meanwhile the situation in France had taken another turn. The King of France's brother, Alphonse, had been knighted on 24 June 1241 at Poitiers and invested with the county of Poitou. While Hugh de Lusignan reluctantly paid Alphonse homage, Isabella was furious at an apparent insult she had received at Poitiers from Blanche and Louis. After seeing his wife sulk for several weeks back in her home county of Angoulême, Hugh entered into an alliance with the Gascons at Pons and planned an uprising against the King of France and his regent mother.[6]

News of the discontent evidently made its mark on the King of England, but for now any hope of obtaining aid for a campaign in France was dependent on relations with Wales. The lengthy truce between England and the Prince of Gwynedd had allowed Henry to concentrate on other things, but the situation threatened to deteriorate after Llewellyn's death in 1240. Llewellyn's son, Dafydd, or David, now became Prince of Snowdon. His personality was both impatient and hostile. To combat the threat, Henry sent his army to Gloucester and from there on to Shrewsbury on 2 August 1241. The threat was too much for the young prince, who submitted without the need for conflict.[7] Peace lasted less than a year, however. On the recommencement of hostilities, Henry made terms with the wife of David's half-brother Griffith, and later that year he led a force from Chester into north Wales. Griffith was David's prisoner but was released following David's submission to Henry.

Heated exchanges occurred that year between Henry and the Bishop of Lincoln over Henry's desire to provide his clerk, John Mansel, with the prebend of Thame – located within Lincoln Cathedral. Despite the backing of the papacy, Grosseteste was once again infuriated at the laxity of Rome in enriching a favourite of the king with such a wealthy and undeserved award – particularly as it was stipulated in the General Council of the Lateran in 1215 that no clerk could hold more than one benefice. On this occasion trouble was avoided when Mansel resigned any claim to the prebend.[8]

Across the Channel, the pious Louis IX paid £25,000 to the Saracens of Damietta to take possession of the relic of the True Cross. Relic-hunting was something of an obsession for Louis, who had two years earlier succeeded in purchasing the Crown of Thorns from the bankrupt King of Jerusalem; he was also said to own a cloak once worn by Christ, the alleged head of the spear used by Longinus and the sponge that had been dipped in vinegar.

In recognition of this momentous event, work started on the magnificent Sainte-Chapelle, built to house the treasures. The chapel was built in the Rayonnant style, so named for its rose windows, and celebrated for its incredible architecture and decoration.[9] Coincidentally, in the same year Henry commissioned a shrine of pure gold to be made to house the relics of St Edward the Confessor. The shrine was created by skilled goldsmiths using precious stones, the cost being met by the king alone.[10]

Returning to matters of state, 1242 became another epic test of Henry's kingship. At Christmas of 1241 he received word from his stepfather that the time was ripe for a military attack on Poitou. Though Lusignan spelled out the need for military assistance, he also offered seemingly secure guarantees of support from the Gascons, the Poitevins, the Count of Toulouse and the King of Navarre.[11]

What happened next was a landmark moment in the history of the nation. Henry summoned a council on 29 January, referred to by Matthew Paris as 'the first authorized account of a parliamentary debate'. All of the magnates appeared, as did the recently returned Earl of Cornwall. Henry asked for aid for war with France. On this occasion the barons insisted on examining the status of the truce and refused to approve aid while it remained valid.[12] It was also suggested that the king probably already had enough money without the need for further allowances.

Justifying the war was a problem. Henry's marriage to the sister of the Queen of France, both nations' good relations with the papacy and the fact that the countries were still officially under truce until 1243 made it difficult to justify an invasion. Gregory's death the previous year had lost Henry the support and guidance of the Pope but also led to a fall in papal demands for money. After failing to get the lords' approval in public, the king turned to private negotiation. He met with several of the lords the following day and succeeded in winning some provision for war, though not as much as he had been asking of the Parliament.[13]

It was enough to launch an invasion. He began his preparations for war with a series of pilgrimages, including visits to Waltham, Bury St Edmunds, St Albans and Bromholm.[14] By early May his forces were ready to depart. They left Portsmouth around 15 May with some 300 knights, seven earls and thirty casks of money. In his absence the king delegated the safekeeping of the kingdom to the Archbishop of York, while Queen Eleanor and Richard of Cornwall accompanied him to France.[15]

On 18 May their forces reached Finisterre, and about a day later they landed at Royan at the mouth of the Gironde.[16] After staying for several days in Royan they advanced to Pons in Saintonge, where Hugh joined them. There they engaged in their first conference, culminating in sending messages to the King of France. Exactly what they expected to achieve is still unclear. At the time Louis was laying siege to one of Lusignan's castles, at which point Henry's messengers caught up with him. Intriguingly, when the messengers met Louis they were well received and Louis responded that he had not broken any truce and would happily extend it and return the land due to Henry according to the agreement at Lambeth in 1217, though he questioned Henry's involvement with Lusignan.[17] Within days the English forces had reached Saintes, where the king penned a declaration of war against Louis, dated 8 June.[18] Henry's forces continued to Tonnay and Taillebourg and then to the south of the Charente. Around that time he sent letters back home to the bishops asking for prayers for their success and safe return. He also penned a letter to the Archbishop of York asking for further knights, soldiers and money to aid the endeavour and insisted that the 500 people to whom he gave alms on a daily basis must continue to be well fed.

While Henry was touring the lower regions Louis's army was also on the move. The French took many castles in Poitou, including Fontenay, giving Louis a position of dominance north of the Charente. He took Taillebourg without opposition, making a mockery of any guarantee that Henry had from its lord that Taillebourg was to be given up to him.[19] In mid-July events took a turn for the worse when Henry's forces, a combination of Englishmen and Gascons, advanced from Saintes up the river. For the first time the foes came face to face, separated only by the River Charente. On seeing the large number of tents on the opposite side, the English retreated. Had it not been for a one-day truce negotiated by Richard of Cornwall on 20 July Henry would have been in personal danger.[20]

Once the truce had ended Louis pursued the English. The French advanced uncontested to the capital of Saintonge, where the numerically inferior English did little to combat him. Most of the action took place in vineyards and narrow lanes to the west of the city rather than on an actual battlefield. Both sides fought valiantly, but eventually the numerical superiority of the French resulted in another English retreat. A skirmish between Lusignan's forces and a party of French was followed by an encounter near Saintes, leaving Henry little choice but to head in the opposite direction. He retreated to Pons and from there to Barbezieux. While still in retreat Henry was advised that Lusignan had deserted to the French, yet another act of betrayal by his stepfather.

Henry was now fleeing for his life. As Louis's forces closed in, the English escaped only by a thirty-hour march to Blaye. The ordeal not only lost the king any hope of victory but a large amount of his baggage. After going for over forty-eight hours without food, his forces regrouped at Blaye and continued to Bordeaux.

Bordeaux remained safe in no small part owing to an out-break of sickness among the French. Laid low himself, Louis offered a five-year truce in September, to which Henry readily agreed. A letter, written by Henry to Frederick, narrated the fail-ings of the campaign, notably his receiving the 'kiss of Judas' from Lusignan and Reginald of Pons and their return to Gas-cony. Henry's force left Bordeaux in September 1243, during which time he became a father for the third time, landing in Portsmouth on 25 September before returning to London.[21]

The truce with France was concluded in April 1243, allowing Henry to concentrate on problems in his kingdom. The failure of the second Poitou and Gascony venture resulted only in the arrival of more Poitevin relations in England, most significantly a visit from the king's mother-in-law, Beatrice, the Countess of Provence. Henry received her well and spared no expense. She was already an important ally for Henry, holding his castles in Provence at a cost to the king of some 4,000 marks a year.

Joining Beatrice in England was her daughter, Sanchia, another woman of great beauty. While the expedition in Poitou had been going on, the new Bishop of Hereford had travelled to Provence to negotiate a marriage between the Earl of Cornwall and Henry's sister-in-law. At the time Henry undoubtedly welcomed the idea, viewing the marriage as a further opportunity to cement the allegiance of Raymond – or at least to avoid the need for war with Louis. Richard married the sister of Eleanor in November 1243.[22]

In May 1243 the former justiciar, Hubert de Burgh, died at his manor at Banstead. Henry had now lost the final link with his minority. Hubert was buried at the Dominican convent in London, to which he had given generously throughout his life. His lands went to his son, John, except for those he had held with his wife, Margaret. With his death also died the Earldom of Kent.[23]

The brief tenure of Celestine IV as Pope was succeeded by the election of Innocent IV in June 1243, nineteen months after Celestine's death. It seems evident from Innocent's early letters that the long interregnum had allowed some of the English benefices to keep much of the funds allocated to the Romans who possessed them. During his first few months as Pope Innocent was particularly vocal in his contempt for the treatment of agents seeking revenues, as well as critical of papal collectors who charged fees.[24]

While the pontifical see remained vacant a serious argument had arisen between Grosseteste and the convent of Christ Church over jurisdiction. After Grosseteste had issued an excommunication notice against an abbot of Bardney for failing to appear before the court of the archdeacon, followed by an interdict on Bardney Abbey, Grosseteste was himself excommunicated by the convent, in the absence of Boniface, though this had no impact on him, and the issue was resolved on the eventual election of Innocent IV.[25]

Meanwhile, despite the election of Boniface at Canterbury, the new archbishop was still to be confirmed. Furthermore, the situation regarding the See of Winchester was also to be resolved. On his return from Gascony the king continued to persecute William of Raleigh, resulting in further conflict with the bishops. So volatile was the situation that Raleigh fled to the continent to pass on his concerns to Innocent IV in person. The Pope agreed the transfer of Raleigh from Norwich to Winchester in September 1243, the same day that he confirmed Boniface as Archbishop of Canterbury, two years after his initial election. Following the ratification of Raleigh's election, the Pope wrote to Henry asking him to continue to ensure the protection of the Church and not to interfere with the ecclesiastical affairs of the bishops. Still Henry refused to acknowledge the new bishop. Instead, he ordered the shutting of the gates of the city against Raleigh, forcing the new Bishop of Winchester to place it under an interdict and return to France.

On hearing the news Grosseteste took up the case of the new bishop and wrote to Boniface about enforcing the Pope's view. Henry wrote to Rome and Oxford, arguing that Raleigh had secured the post by unworthy means, so Grosseteste came to Reading to see him, only to find that he had moved on. Henry sent his messengers to Rome, requesting Raleigh's removal, but on this occasion one of Henry's papal agents foresaw the inevitable repercussions of such an approach and returned to England. When Grosseteste and the other bishops who had travelled to Reading finally caught up with Henry at Westminster they criticized him for his tyrannical behaviour and threatened to place his chapels under interdict. For now, Henry pleaded merely to hear the Pope's response. Between 20 and 25 February he received a severe warning from the papacy urging him to accept the Pontiff's decision. The issue was finally resolved, and Raleigh entered his cathedral on 29 August 1244.[26]

Further problems arose for the king early in 1244 when another papal messenger arrived in England looking to replen- ish the papal coffers, which were severely depleted as a result of the war with Frederick. The man sent was Martin, a clerk rather than a nuncio or legate, to whom Innocent seems to have granted more extensive power than was normal, such as the right to excommunicate. Martin's visit was the least popular yet among the clerics. His actions included forbidding unhelpful prelates from giving less than thirty marks to the papacy and proposing the assignment of a prebend to the Pope's nine-year-old nephew.

The behaviour of the papacy seriously affected the welfare of the Church, leading to further calls for Henry to intervene. A document was drawn up by the clergy arguing that since the reign of Ethelbert religious houses had been endowed to support religion and protect the poor, but due to the recent heavy finan- cial demands from the papacy this mission was under threat. On this occasion Martin's actions seemed too much even for Henry, prompting him to write to Innocent protesting at the severity of the papal provisions.[27]

Some time in 1244, possibly October, the king summoned the barons and prelates to the refectory at Westminster and asked for a subsidy. Among the attendees was the recently returned Boni- face; the chancellor, Neville, had died on 1 February.[28] Among Henry's arguments for aid was a renewal of the threat from Wales and potential problems with Scotland. He also argued that the failure in Poitou and Gascony was partly the fault of the barons, as it was they who had backed the campaign. He was met with the usual criticisms of his past wastefulness and a demand that he uphold the provisions of the Charter more closely, but on this occasion there was some willingness to help him as long as

he agreed to further reform. For now Henry attempted to pro-
long the discussions, perhaps with the aim of wearing down the
opposition. The Pope's reply to Henry's letter about Martin's
demands, dated July 1244, insisted that the clergy must help the
'beloved son' as he needs.[29]

After six days the council was adjourned, with a decision
on the king's debts to be delivered at a later date.[30] Prior to the
council's dismissal Martin had appeared, once again asking for
funds. Suspicion was rife about his intentions: intriguingly he
produced several new papal documents, leading to talk among
the prelates that he left Rome with forms sealed before they had
been filled in. Among his requests was one for 10,000 marks to
the papal exchequer.

The Pope's demands encountered strong opposition, not
only from the magnates but the Emperor. In England there were
murmurs that the papal demand for money was to aid a war
against the man whom the Pope had asked the sister of the King
of England to marry. Despite protests from the papal visitor,
Henry gave permission for letters delivered by Frederick's messengers to be read aloud at the same council, imploring Henry
not to fund the Pope's war on him. Among other things, the
Emperor highlighted Gregory's attack on towns and villages that
were not rightfully his and his desire for peace with both England
and the papacy.[31]

Henry moved north in the summer of that year, looking to
renew peace with Alexander II. The idea of Alexander's son
marrying Henry's daughter had been mooted, but Alexander's
own marriage to Mary, the daughter of Enguerrand de Coucy,
less than a year after the death of Henry's sister, Joan, had led to
tension between the two kings. Henry turned to the queen's uncle,
the Count of Flanders, for help and ordered his forces north to
Newcastle in August 1244. Fortunately, the issues were resolved

without military action, and confirmation of the truce was granted by Innocent. In April of that year papal confirmation had also been given to Henry to loan 4,000 marks to his father-in-law, taking five castles as security.[32]

The council reconvened, probably after the king's return from the north, to announce a decision on the king's subsidy. Unlike the Pope's requests, there was a willingness to grant aid to Henry, but only on the condition that he was to seek the council's advice on how it should be spent. Among the issues highlighted was Henry's continued tendency to rule without a justiciar or chancellor. A new scheme of reform was drawn up, prompted by recurrent claims that the Great Charter was frequently broken. From now on a new charter was to be put into effect, including its provisions together with the appointment of four magnates as the king's advisers on the council, creating the office of 'guardians of liberties'. Finally the king was to allow a chancellor and justiciar to be chosen by the council and judges to be elected. Henry agreed in person to abide by the Charter, as decreed by the terms of his coronation oath. By the end of February 1245 the council formally agreed aid to provide for the marriage of the king's daughter, but they refused to do anything more.[33]

The granting of aid to the king was less welcome in the eyes of the papal collector, who saw his own attempts to collect money potentially suffer. After receiving no support from the prelates at either of two councils he instead focused on making demands upon individual prelates and monasteries, taking most of the money he received to offset his own expenses.[34]

In Rome the constant threat from Frederick's imperial guards forced Innocent to take flight. On his way to France envoys of David of Wales met the Pope in Genoa and offered to surrender Wales to the papacy on the condition that Henry would no longer wage war upon Wales. The Pope gave the proposal considerable thought, and he later wrote to the Abbots of Aberconwy and Cwmhir inquiring whether the original oaths made by the princes of Gwynedd to the king of England were made under duress or free will. The abbots summoned Henry to appear before them, which he refused. As a result the idea came to nothing. During the course of that year Griffith broke his neck attempting to escape from the Tower of London.[35]

Innocent arrived in Lyon around 2 December 1244. On 22 December he celebrated Mass in the cathedral and announced the thirteenth ecumenical council of the Church for 24 June 1245, aimed primarily at resolving the situation regarding Frederick II. In England there was talk at the time that the Pope should be invited to England, though the idea was dismissed owing to concerns that many among the Pope's entourage would be looking to profit from England.[36]

The council of Lyon sat for three sessions in June and July. During that time discussion centred on several issues, including the long-term safety of Jerusalem, the Latin Empire of Constantinople, the Mongol threat, clerical abuses and, most notably, the war with the Emperor. In addition to his excommunication Frederick was officially deposed by Innocent, the first dethronement in two centuries.[37]

Attendance among the English prelates was low. In their absence the king sent his clerk, Laurence de St Martin, to be his proctor and representative. On 20 May he had arrived in Lyon, following which the Pope wrote to Henry saying he was satisfied by the excuses for non-attendance. He also granted Henry right of patronage to churches of royal dignity, such as the royal chapels, thus allowing him greater freedom regarding bestowing benefices, in addition to clarifying the papal stance on Wales.[38]

Prior to the council, Henry also directed that inquiries be made into the revenues received by the Romans and Italians who held

benefices in England. The result was astounding. Initial inspection suggested that they amounted to as much as 60,000 marks,
which at the time exceeded the annual income of the Crown. On
hearing this, Henry wrote to the Pope protesting the tribute of
1,000 marks originally agreed by John in May 1213 and the abuses
of papal collectors. Evidently this was not surprising to Innocent,
who had heard whisperings of dissent since arriving in France.
On reading the letter, Innocent responded to Henry's concerns
with a reminder of what the papacy had done for him and his
father and asked for greater effort in providing for the Holy See.

Among those who did make their way to Lyon was the Bishop
of Lincoln. Grosseteste left England in November 1244 and was
later joined by Boniface and the Bishops of Hereford and Worcester. Also from England were the Earl of Norfolk, Roger Bigod,
and one William de Powick, Henry's spokesman. Evidently
Henry had concerns about the event. Speaking beforehand to
those who planned to attend he issued a warning, especially to
the prelates, of the need to safeguard the interests of the kingdom during the council.

From an English perspective the Council of Lyon had more
important issues to deal with than the situation with Frederick.
One of the first items on the agenda was the canonization of the
recently deceased Edmund Rich, which had the backing of eight
archbishops and over twenty bishops. Other English concerns
were voiced in July by the proctors, most notably de Powick. These
included the 1,000-mark tribute of King John, recent monetary
demands, the bestowal of English benefices on foreigners and
criticisms of Martin for acting with more powers than a legate.

Despite a vague promise from the Pope to deal with these
problems they were largely ignored. The English agents in Lyon
threatened that no further payment of the 1,000-mark tithe would
be made during the king's lifetime. On hearing this, Innocent

rounded on the English bishops individually and forced their agreement to the 1213 charter of King John, infuriating Henry. On his return to England Grosseteste spoke to Henry, using his best endeavours to calm the king before writing to the Pope, once again confirming Henry's love for the papacy, while asking for his understanding in ensuring the long-term survival of the Church in England.[39]

Meanwhile back in England Martin came to Henry around 30 June complaining that the lords wanted him to leave as a result of arguments with the prelates. When he asked for 'safe conduct' Henry is said to have replied, 'May the devil grant you safe conduct to hell and all through it.' Martin left England in mid-July, heading straight for the Pope in Lyon.[40]

In reality, the decisions reached in Lyon did little to improve the welfare of England or its Church. Demands by Innocent IV on the clergy were particularly large in 1246, drawing fresh criticism. So bad had things become that on this occasion the king forbade the prelates from collecting, resulting in another frank discussion with Grosseteste. Henry assembled a Parliament in London on 18 March 1246 to discuss the ongoing problems, particularly the news from the Council of Lyon. Henry and his barons wrote separately to Innocent, though the barons went into more detail. Messengers from England carrying these letters set out for Lyon on 9 April 1246. Among them was William de Powick. Before they left, a new papal letter requiring a subsidy of 6,000 marks was being circulated by the Bishop of Winchester.[41]

An answer to the king's letter came at a council at Winchester on 7 July. Innocent was unwilling to compromise, and the messengers returned home with nothing new to report. For a time Henry was still reluctant to give in to the Pope, though his stance changed on the advice of the Earl of Cornwall, effectively saving his country from interdict.[42]

Owing to Henry's continued financial problems he issued a tallage on the city of London, leading to further discontent among the Londoners. Throughout his reign Henry had struggled to develop an affinity with the city. Now, in certain quarters, criticism of him was growing louder. He was described as the 'lynx with eyes that pierced all things' in the prophecy of Merlin.[43]

11

HENRY THE BUILDER

Away from the turbulence of war and politics, a quieter revolution was under way – one that would provide an enduring physical legacy of Henry III's reign. This was a sweeping architectural movement that was spreading throughout much of Europe.

Three centuries would pass before the term 'Gothic' was originated, but the style is easily identified. No structure in England exemplifies the Gothic style better than Westminster Abbey. At the time of Henry's second coronation Westminster Abbey was a far cry from the building that had replaced it by the end of his reign. Almost exactly two centuries earlier Edward the Confessor had ordered the rebuilding of a small Benedictine monastery, located close to his royal quarters – the name Westminster being used to distinguish it from its sister structure St Paul's, at East Minster. Sadly Edward was gravely ill at the time of its consecration and did not live to see it.

By 1245 Henry had decided to rebuild Westminster Abbey, and over the next twenty-two years he oversaw a programme of building work that led to its becoming the new centrepiece of England's spiritual community.

Evidently the idea of remodelling the abbey existed long before Henry III's grand design was conceived. In 1220 he had appeared at the abbey the day before his coronation to lay the foundation stone of the Lady Chapel.[1]

His vision for the eventual design was sketched out early. Though he had never visited the cathedrals of France he was inspired by stories of their elegance and hoped to create something that equalled the greatest buildings of his time. The Rayonnant structure of Sainte-Chapelle was in development as a fitting home for Louis's religious relics, while the great modern edifices at Rheims, Chartres, Bourges and Amiens, constructed in the Gothic style, had enhanced the reputations of those cities considerably.[2]

Henry took on full financial responsibility for the construction of the new Westminster Abbey and showed a keen interest in its progress. He commissioned an expert in Cosmati work (a type of mosaic, originally from Rome) from Italy to work on the base of the shrine of Edward the Confessor and also the choir pavement, which was very rare in England if not unique. Inspired by the stories of the cathedral at Rheims, Henry sent his masons to France to visit the building first hand and learn the techniques needed to carry out the work. His chosen architect was Henry de Reynes, probably a man of French birth. The high vaults, flying buttresses and numerous chapels also bore a marked resemblance to the French style, as opposed to the square choirs or retrochoirs of England.[3]

Henry and cathedrals were destined to have a special relationship. During his reign they became not just religious houses but also status symbols and, potentially, business ventures. They attracted pilgrims from all over Europe and from England, and many of the windows paid tribute to their creators or donors. For Henry there is reason to believe they held more significance than most. Not only were they viewed by Christians of the age as the closest thing to God on earth but they made a strong connection for Henry between his past and his vision for the future.

One of the most important cathedrals in England was at Worcester. The tomb of King John, located in between those of St Oswald and St Wulfstan, became a regular haunt for Henry when he visited the city. He was present at Worcester in June 1218 for the cathedral's reconsecration after it had been damaged by fire in 1202. Construction of the Lady Chapel was under way in 1224, though this was in the Early English style rather than the new Gothic, while work on the choir and retrochoir continued between 1224 and 1269.[4]

Not far from Worcester, Henry's coronation at Gloucester marked the beginning of his reign, and it also gave the abbey (now a cathedral) a special place in his affections. A large number of very fine windows decorate the modern-day cathedral, their ages ranging from the fourteenth to the twentieth centuries. One of them is the coronation window, dating from 1860, depicting the coronation of Henry under the watchful eyes of the nervous barons and prelates. Henry evidently enjoyed a strong affinity with the cathedral and donated 110 oaks from the Forest of Dean to benefit it in 1232. The central tower was completed in 1222. In 1242 the nave was completed by the monks, three years following the rededication. Around the same time construction began on a tower to the south-west side.[5]

In London the first cathedral at St Paul's had been destroyed by fire as early as 1087, and a second fire in 1136 was a further setback. While Westminster Abbey was used for the crowning of monarchs, St Paul's had occupied a strong place in the hearts of the people of England and was often chosen as the site of national celebrations. The central tower of the third cathedral was completed by 1221, and further changes were made before the end of Henry III's reign.[6]

The first cathedral in Lincoln was started in 1072 after the victor of Hastings, William the Conqueror, ordered Bishop Remigius to establish a cathedral there. The fortress-like Norman cathedral was added to by Hugh, Bishop of Lincoln, between 1186 and 1200; a new polygonal apse and five new chapels were added to the east end. The additions were the first sign of the new Gothic architecture, illustrated by pointed arches, flying buttresses and ribbed vaults. By the time Henry gained the throne larger stained-glass windows had been added, developing the cathedral into a glorious structure. The nave was completed by the middle of Henry's reign, and the west end was extended in the Gothic style together with further work on the great transept and the chapter house. The central tower collapsed, necessitating further work that reached its pinnacle in 1256 when Henry granted a licence to extend beyond the walls.[7]

Becket's shrine was installed at Christ Church in 1220, leading to an influx of pilgrims who would in later years influence the work of Geoffrey Chaucer. Work on the cloisters at Canterbury occupied the years 1236–8, during which time developments had also taken place at Rochester.[8] The cathedral at Rochester is one of the smallest in England but also one of the finest. It dates back to the early seventh century, and the nave is believed to be the oldest in England. Though much of its construction took place before Henry's reign, a number of notable features were added during his lifetime. These included the eastern and northern transepts, built between 1200–27 and 1240–55 respectively, adding to the western transept which had been completed in the period 1170–1200.[9]

The octagonal chapter house at Lichfield Cathedral is unique in England. The structure dates back to the 1240s and comprises two storeys: one for meetings of the clergy, the other a library. The cathedral is famous for its literature, including the famous

Lichfield Gospels, while other elements of the Gothic structure include the nave which dates from the 1260s and the transepts from at least twenty years earlier. The west front includes several statues of the kings of England in the Gothic style. The original was begun in 1265, though much of what can be seen today is a later addition.[10]

In the North of England the twin west towers of Durham Cathedral were completed in 1220 and the original central tower in 1262, adding to the superb Romanesque structure that already existed. In 1242 work also began on the Chapel of the Nine Altars located to the east side of the cathedral. Around the same time building work took place on the fine cathedral at Carlisle, including the choir and aisles, which was completed around 1292.[11]

While most of the examples mentioned were a hybrid of the new Gothic and the older style, during the reign of Henry III several great structures were rebuilt entirely in the Gothic style. Among the highlights were the reconstruction of York Minster, Salisbury Cathedral and Beverley Minster, all of which began in the 1220s. When the decision was made to move the cathedral at Salisbury to a new site, some two miles away, plans were put in place for its rebuilding in the newer Gothic form. Work on Salisbury officially commenced with the laying of the first stone by the legate, Pandulf, in 1220, and work on the Lady Chapel also commenced that year. Seventeen years later the choir was completed and the bodies of past bishops were moved from the previous site. The building was finished in a relatively short period of time, and consecrated in 1258. In 1263 work began on adding the cloisters, and this continued into the reign of Edward I.[12]

York Minster can officially be dated back all the way to the seventh century, but much of the early structure had been destroyed by fire during the reign of King Stephen. Construction of the new cathedral began in 1171 and had progressed sufficiently by 1221 for it to be chosen as the location for the marriage of Alexander II of Scotland and Joan, the sister of Henry III. Four years later work had begun on the north transept, and by 1242 the south was completed. In 1251 York Minster was again selected for the wedding of a Scottish king to a daughter of a king of England, this time Alexander III and Henry's daughter, Margaret.[13]

No cathedral in England epitomizes the flourishing Gothic style more than the cathedral at Wells. The west front, in particular, completed in 1260, is arguably the finest of its type. Work began during the reign of Henry's grandfather, Henry II, but developed during Henry III's minority and continued throughout his reign. So great was the effect that in 1239 Wells was already dedicated, and in 1244 it was put forward for cathedral status.[14]

In the South of England building of the abbey at Beaulieu was under way in 1203–4, when John founded it for the Cistercians. It was completed by 1246 and officially dedicated by Henry III in the presence of his wife and seven-year-old son, Edward.[15] St Albans had to wait until 1877 before becoming a cathedral city, but the building itself dates back to 1077. Much of the abbey can be dated to 1214–35. Repairs were undertaken on the foundations in 1257 following damage by an earthquake in 1250 and took sixty years owing to lack of funding.[16] Henry's beloved Winchester Cathedral was also developed in the 1200s, leading to the formation of the retrochoir and a lady chapel by 1235.[17]

The Cistercian abbey at Rievaulx in the North of England was one of many to be given a Gothic facelift. During Henry's reign many other abbeys were built, including Lacock in Wiltshire by the widow of William Longspee, an illegitimate son of Henry II, the Cistercian abbey of Grace Dieu in Monmouthshire in 1226 and the nearby Tintern Abbey shortly before the king's death.

Like the king, Richard, Earl of Cornwall, was particularly dedicated to his faith and founded a number of religious houses, the most spectacular being Hayles Abbey in Gloucestershire, inspired by his return from Poitou during a heavy storm. The foundations were laid in 1245–6, and the dedication ceremony followed in 1251, attended by Henry and Eleanor.[18]

Shrines were also favourites of Henry III's. Further to the translations of the relics of St Edward the Confessor and St Thomas Becket, Henry was at Ely Cathedral in 1251 to witness a shrine to St Ethelreda being placed in the retrochoir. A number of lady chapels were also begun during his reign, including at Oxford in 1220, Hereford in 1226, Bath in 1248, Chester in 1265 and Peterborough in 1270. In Ireland, the cathedral at Down, generally held to be the burial place of St Patrick, can be dated to the 1220s according to a petition put forward to Henry by the monks, which informed him that construction was under way.

It was not just religious buildings that were developing in thirteenth-century England. Castles, too, constructed in a wide variety of styles and sizes, had for some time prior to Henry III's reign become progressively more significant features of the landscape. By the end of the reign of Henry II the Saxon-style motte and bailey had largely made way for the imposing stone Norman façades that often consisted of a strong, square keep and additional defences.

Castle construction was of great interest to Henry, as was the fortification of existing structures. The most famous example of Henry's role in fortification was the Tower of London. At the beginning of his reign the Tower consisted of one stone keep, the famous White Tower, and a surrounding wall. The square structure, built on the orders of William the Conqueror, had developed a reputation as the main command point of the city of London and was seen by the citizens as a sign of oppression. Before Henry's reign it had never been used as more than a place of refuge and lacked royal favour on account of its uncomfortable living accommodation.

Development of the Tower took place on two occasions during Henry's reign. During the 1220s a water gate was established on the southern wall, running alongside the river, next to the new Wakefield Tower. A second tower, the Lanthorn, was also constructed, probably intended to be used by the queen. In 1238 further work was commissioned, this time on a new curtain wall to the north, incorporating eight new towers, including the Bloody Tower, a western gateway and a moat.

The reasons for the new work need little explanation. London's defences had been easily breached by Louis in the barons' war and were viewed by the regency as weak. In 1238, when Henry shut himself up in the tower in fear of his brother's uprising, he undoubtedly saw the unmoated out-of-date structure as susceptible to attack. It was also here that the greatest prisoners of the day were kept, including Hubert de Burgh in 1232 and the Welsh prince, Griffith.

Upgrading of the defences was not the only change. Henry ordered the refurbishment of the living quarters, including the queen's chamber, and decorations and new stained-glass windows for the chapel of St John the Evangelist in the White Tower and St Peter ad Vincula in the bailey.[19] While work was taking place in 1241 a peculiar story arose that construction of the Beauchamp Tower was plagued by 'divine intervention'. When a new wall fell suddenly a priest who witnessed the event spoke of a horrifying vision that the 'turbulent priest' Thomas Becket had emerged and struck the wall down with his staff; as a Londoner he insisted that the walls were 'not for the defence of the kingdom but only to oppress'.[20]

Though Henry III can be credited as having the greatest effect on the structure of the Tower of London, and responsibility for making it appear as it does to visitors in the twenty-first century, perhaps the most imaginative of the additions was a new house added in 1237 to accommodate the leopards sent by Frederick. Menageries were much favoured by the Plantagenet kings. Henry's grandfather, Henry II, had been the first of the kings of England to establish one in his park at Woodstock, where he kept a number of beasts, including lions, leopards, lynxes and even camels and a porcupine. His successor was also recorded as having an interest in animals. While on crusade Richard I captured a crocodile that later escaped into the Thames. Henry III's menagerie at the Tower of London, however, outdid them both. Historians are not entirely sure of its exact location, but part of it seems to have been housed within the appropriately named 'Lion' Tower, which no longer survives. Among the animals housed at the Tower were the leopards from Frederick and two bears, one a present from the mayor of Northampton, the other a polar bear sent from Norway.

Like the great cathedrals castles were an essential part of medieval England, and each served its own purpose. When William the Conqueror came to England in 1066 he established a network of castles to secure and demonstrate his dominion over the realm. As the king extended his conquest from the south to the central areas of England he built many castles, including the mighty fortresses at Warwick, Nottingham, Lincoln, Cambridge, York and Huntingdon. The castle was a status symbol but also a protection against attack. Unlike the Saxon castles, many of the Norman castles were constructed of stone from the outset, including the White Tower, Pevensey, Colchester and Exeter, in order to be able to withstand siege.

Nevertheless, by the time of Henry III's reign many of the castles established by his forebears were incapable of withstanding prolonged attack. Aside from the Tower, Henry took his builder's instincts to other parts of his kingdom. In York the later-dubbed Clifford's Tower was still a ruin at the time of Henry's visit in 1244 after being partially destroyed by a gale sixteen years earlier. On seeing the remains Henry commissioned two craftsmen to rebuild it at a cost of some £2,600.[21] His father had spent £1,400 on Corfe Castle, his favourite royal residence, and Henry himself spent a further £1,000 on adding new walls and towers.[22]

On the coast, control of the Cinque Ports was of vital strategic importance during the latter years of the reign of King John and the early years of Henry. From the Iron Age through to the early years of the Second World War a fortification at Dover was the most important structure in England used to combat invaders. After his victory at Hastings William's forces headed straight for Dover and spent eight days enhancing its defences. Henry II ordered its complete reconstruction, carried out between 1168 and 1188, at a cost of some £6,000. Its fortifications were reinforced by both Richard and John, resulting in it being the only Cinque Port Prince Louis was unable to conquer, despite gaining control of the barbican and the east tower. This event encouraged Henry III to spend a further £7,500 on extending the castle, including the establishment of the great hall in the 1240s. By 1256 the castle was at its peak, its structure largely as it has remained to this day.[23]

On John's death at Newark the castle there fell into the hands of rebel barons. Having won the war in 1217 Henry was present before the walls of Newark the following year and took the castle after an eight-day siege. By the end of the century the original Norman castle had been rebuilt and the work undertaken at Henry III's direction restored the castle to the status of a royal favourite. So impressive were the improvements that the castle successfully withstood at least three sieges by the Parliamentarians in the English Civil War.

Rochester Castle was retaken by the king's forces at the end of the first barons' war and was badly in need of repair. Restoration took place between 1217 and 1237, costing in excess of £600, most of which was spent on the keep. The outer curtain wall was also strengthened, a ditch placed outside the town and a new chapel built in the castle. In addition to the defences, Henry also gave a facelift to the residential areas, and an almonry and stables were added in the 1240s. Shortly after, work was undertaken on the gatehouse, followed by further repairs to the keep in the 1250s.[24]

Work on Hadleigh Castle began some time early in the reign of Henry III after Hubert de Burgh had been granted permission by John to build a new castle. By 1235 a park had formed around the castle, including woodland, a fishpond, stables and a park lodge. There were also terraced gardens along the south side. Hubert's fall saw the castle confiscated by Henry in 1239, including its 140-acre estate. In 1249 a large watermill, used in the making of bread, had been constructed in the grounds, but by the 1250s it was already falling into disrepair.

Like most castles in Surrey Guildford was built shortly after the arrival of William the Conqueror and continuously developed over the next two centuries. The additions of Henry III were of considerable note and led it to be described thereafter as a palace. Eleanor took a keen interest in the improvements: there was a new window in her rooms, flanked by two Purbeck marble columns, and windows with coloured glass in the great hall – an expensive luxury in the thirteenth century – and the walls were painted to depict the story of Dives and Lazarus. A screen near Henry's chambers illustrated the legend of St John and Edward the Confessor, while his chambers were painted green with gold and silver stars. Other additions were made for his son, and in later years Edward's wife, while in 1245 Henry also bought land to extend the inner bailey. A similar painting of Dives and Lazarus was added to the great hall of the castle at Ludgershall, which Henry visited on a regular basis after he had turned it into a hunting lodge.

The famous castle at Nottingham, for so long one of the strongholds of England, had been significantly strengthened by King John, who used it as an arsenal, prison and treasury. On taking the throne Henry added his artistic vision to repair and improve the royal apartments and ordered several other additions. He also asked the sheriff to build 'a good stone gateway with two towers', the only part of the original castle that remains.

In Wales, the 1245 campaign of Henry III saw an effort to rebuild the castle at Deganwy after it had been destroyed by the Welsh. The walls and towers that survive can be dated from that period. Henry was also responsible for the castle at Dyserth which was strengthened in 1246 with a watchtower, a well and a large catapult used to combat the Welsh. Henry's birthday while in Wales in 1223 marked the commencement of the rebuilding of Montgomery Castle in stone, while the trio of castles at Grosmont, Whitecastle and Skenfrith were all improved under the guidance of their castellan, Hubert de Burgh.

Among the possessions of the great Marshal family was the mighty Pembroke Castle in south Wales. William's most notable gift to the castle was the great round tower and much of the inner ward. When the Marshal family line ended in 1245, Henry III presented the castle to his half-brother, William de Valence, who added to its defences. In 1226 both Cardigan and Carmarthen once again became royal castles and benefited from the attentions of the builder king. On the border, the Norman castle at Chester fell into royal hands in 1237, following which it was used primarily as the headquarters for Henry's military action against the Welsh. Being located in such a strategic position its defence was of key significance, and Henry ordered extensive work on the outer bailey. Work on Beeston Castle also began under the rule of Ranulph in 1225, and when that, too, fell into royal hands it was judged by Henry too important not to be a royal castle.

The famous castle at Hever was another on which construction began during the reign of Henry III, while Tattershal, Tickhill, Stogursey, Pickering, Pontefract, the Black Gate of Newcastle Castle and Sheffield were all developed during Henry's reign. At the southern tip of England, the castle at Pevensey, so resolute in withstanding the siege in the aftermath of the Battle of Lewes, passed to Peter of Savoy in 1245 and remained in royal hands from that point on. In 1249 the king, worried by the threat of a French invasion, ordered Peter to construct a castle at Rye to protect the town, and this was completed soon afterwards.[25]

But of all the castles in England his greatest achievement was the one he undoubtedly most regretted. A relatively unimportant manor at Kenilworth was developed into a well-fortified Norman castle during the reign of Henry II, at which point the king purchased the castle for the Crown. Like his father, Henry III spent considerable funds developing its outer defences, including an impressive moat system, making it one of the most formidable castles in England. Unfortunately for Henry, his tendency to enrich his favourites saw him give Kenilworth to his sister, Eleanor, and consequently Kenilworth became the home of Simon de Montfort. The castle was superbly designed and constructed and, as events later demonstrated, extremely difficult to besiege and capture.[26]

Of important note in the history of the Middle Ages, prior to Edward's period of dominance over Wales, the first concentric castle was built in 1268 at Caerphilly. Henry had ordered the castle's construction under the supervision of Gilbert de Clare in order to withstand the threat from the Welsh. In 1270 it was already under attack, forcing building work to be delayed, though the castle was finished within eighteen months. The completed building was unlike anything seen in England or Wales before that time, and it changed the nature of warfare. The new design was a huge problem for traditional warfare as the gap between the outer wall and the centre was far greater than anything else in existence. The rectangular inner ward and surrounding towers were equally difficult to penetrate, and each entrance was guarded by two impressive towers. At its zenith, Caerphilly was possibly the greatest concentric castle ever created.[27]

Like Henry, Richard, Earl of Cornwall, had a profound interest in castles. In 1225 he inherited Berkhamsted, another castle that had featured prominently during the war with Louis, and he made many improvements over the next twenty years, including a three-storey tower. Perhaps most fascinating was his construction of Tintagel, inspired by the Arthur legend. Unlike most castles of Henry III's reign, Richard set out to build it in an older style, incorporating a series of long halls rather than a strong keep.

Henry had a profound impact on the palace at Westminster. During his reign Westminster's importance as a location of central governance developed enormously. New exchequer buildings were assembled north of the great wall in about 1270, while the Chancery, the courts of the king's bench and the Court of Common Pleas came to be assembled in the great hall. According to at least one source the throne was in place against the south wall no later than 1245.

Henry's greatest influence was the creation of three apartments: the Queen's Chamber, the Queen's Chapel and what came to be known as the Painted Chamber. The last was built as the king's private apartment, allegedly on the site where Edward the Confessor had died. In later years it was used to mark the state opening of Parliament, while certain paupers were also fed

Kings Henry II, Richard I and John, as they appear on the west front of Lichfield Cathedral, Staffordshire

Above: King John's putative murder in 1203 of his twelve-year-old nephew Arthur, Duke of Britanny

Left: The tomb of Eleanor of Aquitaine at Fontevraud. She died in 1204.

:

Ruins of the Templar Church near Dover, Kent, where, according to tradition, King John submitted England to the papacy in 1213

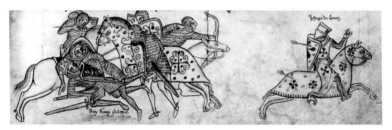

John's defeat at Bouvines in 1214; after an original thirteenth-century drawing by Matthew Paris

Dover Castle; Henry III spent over £7,000 on the fortifications. Dover was the one Cinque Port Prince Louis never captured.

Left: King John signing the Magna Carta

Top and above: A thirteenth-century depiction by Matthew Paris of Prince Louis's arrival in England and King John's tomb at Worcester Cathedral

Worcester Cathedral; Henry attended its rededication ceremony in June 1218

The Great Hall of Winchester Castle, Hampshire, added by Henry III between 1222 and 1235

Winchester Cathedral, where Henry III was baptized in 1207

Goodrich Castle, Herefordshire, which was under the command of Henry's regent William Marshal

Matthew Paris's thirteenth-century depiction of the Battle of Lincoln, 1217

Statue of Stephen Langton, Archbishop of Canterbury, from the west front of Christchurch, Canterbury, Kent

William Marshal's effigy on his tomb at Temple Church, London

Christ Church Cathedral, Canterbury, where Henry III and Eleanor of Provence were married in 1236

Far left and left: Henry III and a nineteenth-century engraving of a portrait of Eleanor of Provence

The Tower of London; much of its present appearance is due to Henry's redevelopment and building programme

Ludgershall Castle in Wiltshire; this was a fine hunting lodge during the reign of Henry III

White Castle in Gwent, one of three castles in the area to have been owned by Hubert de Burgh, Justiciar and 1st Earl of Kent

The Gothic spire of Salisbury Cathedral, Wiltshire

The Gothic west front of Lichfield Cathedral, Staffordshire

The quintessential Gothic façade of Wells Cathedral, Somerset

Above and above right: Henry III and Edward I

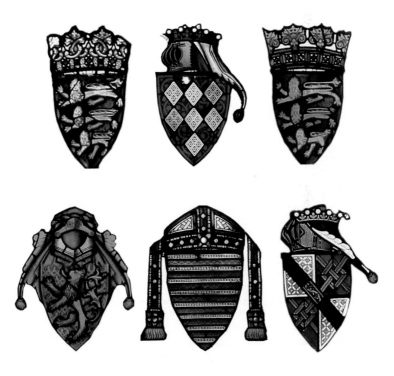

From top left: Arms of Henry III; Arms of Hubert de Burgh; Arms of Edward I; Arms of Savary de Mauleon; Arms of Aymer de Lusignan and Arms of Hugh le Despenser

The original site of Beaudesert Castle, Warwickshire, once home of Peter de Montfort, an ally, not a relative, of Simon de Montfort

The outside wall of Wolvesey Castle in Winchester, former palace of the bishops. Its complicated defences helped the royalists withstand a siege shortly after the Provisions of Oxford, 1258.

The ruins of the Priory of St Pancras, Lewes, Sussex, where Henry III spent the night before the Battle of Lewes in 1264

View of Lewes Castle from the priory

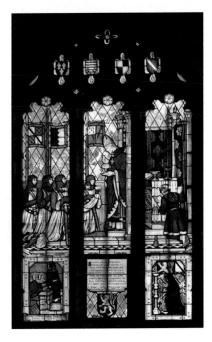

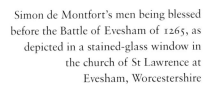

Simon de Montfort's men being blessed before the Battle of Evesham of 1265, as depicted in a stained-glass window in the church of St Lawrence at Evesham, Worcestershire

The Battle Symbol by Enzo Plazzotta, located near the priory. The monument was presented to the town of Lewes in 1964 to mark the 700-year anniversary of Montfort's victory

Edward saves his father from certain death at the 1265 Battle of Evesham

View across the battlefield of Evesham

Kenilworth Castle, Warwickshire, where the disinherited de Montfort rebels sought refuge following their defeat in 1266

Pevensey Castle, Sussex, where many of the Royalists successfully withstood siege from the rebels

Westminster Abbey from the south-east, as illustrated by Warwick Goble, in Gasquet (1908)

Top and above: Westminster Abbey the nave and choir from the west, as illustrated by Warwick Goble. Above right: Henry III's tomb at Westminster Abbey

Corfe Castle, Dorset, a favourite residence of both King John and his son Henry III

The mighty Caerphilly Castle, Glamorgan, on the border of Monmouthshire, a fine early example of a purpose-built concentric castle built during Henry's reign

The original grave of Henry's brother-in-law, Simon de Montfort at Evesham Abbey. He was killed in 1265.

John, Henry III and Edward I, as they appear on the west front of Lichfield Cathedral

there as well as in the Queen's Chamber and the Great Hall. The room was famed for its elegance, but what set it apart was its magnificent paintings, including one of St Edward the Confessor on the ceiling above the king's bed. Craftsmen began work in 1226 and continued for sixty years. Following the fire of 1263 some areas needed repair, and further damage was caused by mob violence in 1267.

But of all the castles that were to develop during the busy reign of Henry III perhaps the most famous, but also most forgotten among the people of today, was his impact on the long-time home of the royal family. When Henry married Eleanor of Provence Windsor Castle became one of their favoured residences, and it was their home for much of the year. Windsor was already one of the oldest castles in England, having been built either shortly before or after the Norman conquest. Little is known of its early history. Henry I held court there in 1110, and there is also mention of a chapel located somewhere in the castle. By the end of the twelfth century, however, it had developed significantly. Sieges in 1193 and 1216 did much damage, leaving the castle in a poor state at the beginning of Henry's reign. Thanks to its location, on a steep chalk cliff rising to a height of some 100 feet overlooking the Thames, it was not destroyed. An attempt to repair the damage finally began during the year of Henry III's second coronation and continued into the next year. More ambitious refurbishment took place during 1222–3, including work on the great hall in the outer bailey, the king's houses, the houses on the moat and the great tower. At around this time new towers were constructed to replace those at the south-west end of the middle and upper baileys, and a wall was built to connect them on the mount. The lower bailey was reinforced with walls and towers on the north and south side, after which three new towers were added between 1227 and 1230.

But Windsor's real glory days did not begin until Henry's marriage. Beginning in 1236 he made several improvements, including a new wing of royal apartments and a chapel dedicated to his favourite saint. The new accommodation comprised a building on the western side and continued south from one of the Norman corners at the north end. In 1241 the area was raised to two storeys, along with two Norman towers located east of the new building. The birth of Edward and their daughter, Margaret, led to the construction of new chambers and nurseries, probably west of the queen's lodgings. A new tower was built in the mid-1240s to the north, and in 1253 this was raised by an extra storey. While much of this new building apparently belonged to the queen, rooms for the king were built in the lower bailey in the 1240s, including additional accommodation for the queen and a chapel. Further work on the queen's apartments were undertaken in 1257, and the following year the royal chapel was also reconstructed.[28] These new additions had a major effect on the prestige of the castle, developing it into one of the finest homes in Europe.

During Henry's reign work was carried out at the royal castles and palaces at great personal expense to the king. Perhaps his greatest legacy was the consistent addition of a barbican – a fortified gatehouse – to the castles' outer defences, making the royal castles of England among the best defended of their day.

12

THE PRETENDER KINGS

War with Wales again threatened to break out in September 1245. Henry made an expedition against the Welsh at Snowdon. On this occasion no fighting took place. The under-strength Welsh avoided out-and-out conflict with the English, who were themselves capable of remaining camped only for so long. The main problem was finance. So bad was Henry's situation after Parliament's refusal to grant aid that funding came from the Earl of Cornwall, who took possession of the crown jewels as security, leading to a scutage of three marks being issued in 1246 to cover the cost.

The English suffered from the cold but also from lack of food. To ease the crisis the king called on support from Ireland, and their troops ravaged Anglesey, severely depleting the countryside. The major loss for the Welsh was not men but corn. When Henry's army returned to England he forbade trade with the Welsh, which led to many Welsh people dying from starvation. Combat stalled over the winter, but when Dafydd died the following year without an heir the future of that country became unclear once again.[1]

In 1246 Henry wrote to the Pope to request his assistance in protecting his rights in Provence after the death of Raymond

Berenger, father of the queen. Order on the continent was threatened when Charles, brother of the King of France, married Beatrice, the youngest daughter of Raymond, in January 1246 and claimed the right to Raymond's possessions in Provence.[2] The continued triumphs of Louis IX also brought about the ruin of Isabella and her treacherous husband. She left her husband and continued to Fontevraud, where she subsequently died.[3]

Relations between Henry and the Bishop of Lincoln were becoming increasingly strained in the year after the council of Lyon as Grosseteste's views on the limitations of Henry's power over the clergy became more obvious. Henry again failed in an attempt to gain a clerical position for one of his favourites, owing to the candidate's alleged ethical shortcomings, resulting in a difference of opinion with the Archbishop of Canterbury.

Despite his election and confirmation, the new archbishop was still to be consecrated.[4] Boniface's absence, coupled with the ineffective behaviour of the king, had seen the see fall further into debt. Boniface asked that the debt be repaid through aid from the whole province of Canterbury, though this was refused by the bishops. They also refused Innocent's decree that Boniface, as Archbishop, be allowed to take first pickings from all the benefices in the province. Nevertheless the situation changed in April when Innocent wrote to the Bishop of Hereford informing him of the need to assist Canterbury with aid from all vacant benefices for a period of seven years in addition to revenue from the archbishopric until 10,000 marks had been collected.

Henry was angered by the demands from Boniface and the Roman Curia for money and wrote to the bishops ordering them to refuse bulls of provision in their dioceses. The bishops' refusal to comply with the Pope's demands was followed by the usual threat of excommunication, which encouraged widespread compliance. In 1247 the creditors of the Canterbury See were again demanding repayment, and in response Innocent gave permission to ignore claims for which there was no clear proof that the money had been borrowed and used by the see. As the creditors' demands became heavier, Boniface also received permission to take up to 12,000 marks rather than 10,000.[6]

No sooner had Henry given in to the Pope's monetary demands in 1246 than Innocent ordered a new subsidy of 11,000 marks. The pressure on the English treasury was intense. The 1246 subsidy of 6,000 marks was due at the Temple in the Strand on 15 August, while in October the Pope commissioned a Franciscan, John the Englishman, to collect the second.[7] He was actively seeking support for a new crusade at the end of 1246, at which time he sent several new preachers to England to enforce past crusader vows or exchange them for money to assist Constantinople.[8] When Parliament met on 2 February 1247 even the king was vocal in his complaints against the Pope. On this occasion the bishops agreed not to attend, giving greater freedom for their representatives to present their grievances. Henry listened with sympathy and agreed that a joint appeal should be made to the Pope from the clergy and people of Canterbury. Back in Lyon, the Pope had already been informed of the situation before the messengers left England. Innocent dismissed Parliament's arguments and considered placing an interdict before being dissuaded by the counsel of an English Cistercian, John Tolet.[9] Opposition to his demands was in any case withdrawn by the Easter Parliament at Oxford, leaving the clergy little choice but to pay the 11,000 marks. Evidently, it was not just in England that the actions of the papacy were causing distress, as papal interference in France was similarly having a negative effect on the faithful.[10]

Another nuncio came to England late in 1247, dubbed 'another Martin' on account of his name, Marinus, and his task of collecting money. Parliament again met on 9 February 1248 to

consider the new demands. On this occasion most of the magnates attended, the still absent Archbishop Boniface being one
of the few who did not. Debates took place about Henry's own
monetary needs and the lack of evidence that his previous agreements to abide by the Charters had been kept. When the king
attempted to offer guarantees the magnates responded that his
behaviour should be monitored.[11]

Henry finally took up the cross as a crusader in 1247 and on
doing so wrote to the Pope requesting an entitlement to funds
for the crusade. Innocent was delighted when he heard the news
and wrote to Grosseteste and Walter Cantilupe, the Bishop of
Worcester, on the subject. At the time he was ordering fewer
benefices but still enough to arouse opposition.[12]

Peace with France had moved a step nearer following the
announcement of the crusade, while in Wales the death of Dafydd
without issue left the house of Gwynedd split between the sons
of Griffith ap Llewellyn, Llewellyn and Owen. As a mark of
diplomacy, the land of Llewellyn ap Iorwerth had effectively been
split into two, but while this might have successfully placated
the brothers the English Seneschal of Carmarthen used the
opportunity to capitalize on the weakness of the Welsh. As a
result of the English threat Owen and Llewellyn agreed to submit to Henry in exchange for being recognized as princes of
Gwynedd and Snowdon, culminating in the Treaty of Woodstock in April 1247.[13]

Since Henry's departure from Gascony the domain was
becoming increasingly fragmented. The irresponsibility of a
string of weak seneschals had failed to uphold English control,
and much of Gascony was plagued by internal strife. The feudal
lords were increasingly disconnected from their English over-
lords and saw homage as a formality rather than a serious act of
loyalty to the King of England.

Bordeaux in particular was disrupted by the rivalry of the Rosteins and the Colons, a feud not unlike the Montague–Capulet rift in Shakespeare's Verona. The valley of the Adour was the coveted prize of Theobald, both Count of Champagne and the King of Navarre, while Gaston de Bearn's annihilation of the town of Dax ensured that peace in Gascony would not be secured simply through casual surveillance from England. The lingering threat of invasion from Ferdinand of Castile and James I of Aragon must also have given Henry cause for concern.

Allowing Gascony to fall was unthinkable. Over the previous fifty years the King of England had already lost much of his ancestral lands, but Gascony had never formed part of France and hence had never been a fiefdom of the King of France.

Only a warrior could put down the unrest, and Henry found one in Simon de Montfort. The two men had largely been reconciled since the disagreement of 1239. Simon had briefly returned to England in 1240, seeking to raise money for his crusade, and later played a minor role in Henry's ill-fated Poitou expedition of 1242.[14] As the son of a fierce Albigensian crusader, Simon was well prepared. He was appointed Seneschal of Gascony on 1 May. Unlike his predecessors, he was entrusted with exceptionally wide-ranging powers and assigned to govern the duchy for seven years, with immunity from removal without his permission.[15]

Simon left for Gascony in the autumn, around the same time as the seventh crusade was beginning. Had Simon not been sent to Gascony he would almost certainly have followed Louis IX and many of his own compatriots to Egypt. After successfully negotiating extended truces with the King of France and an understanding with the King of Navarre, the new seneschal began his role with determination and vigour. Within the first three months he had stamped his authority on Gascony, and he subdued the Rostein faction in Bordeaux in 1249. He captured Gaston de

Bearn and sent the disgraced rebel to England to answer for his crimes. On the death of Raymond of Toulouse his heir, Alphonse of Poitiers, made an uneasy peace with Simon, building on the similar peace between de Montfort and Theobald.[16]

Despite the new seneschal's success, his harsh rule was not widely popular among the Gascons. Though he had succeeded in driving the troublemakers from Bordeaux, the threat of insurrection was always close at hand. Like his king, Simon's pressing concern was aid. But despite the occasional setback in Gascony, and complaints against his style of rule, when Simon returned to England in January 1249 he was warmly welcomed.[17]

Troublemakers from Gascony were not the only foreigners who had been making their way to England. After the death of Isabella Henry offered a home to three half-brothers and a sister from the marriage of his mother to Hugh de Lusignan, further infuriating the lords. Almost immediately his brother, also named William de Valence, married a wealthy heiress and was installed as Earl of Pembroke. His sister Alicia was married to the young John de Warenne, Earl of Surrey, while the king also gave in marriage two young Poitevin women to two of his wards, both of whom were apparently reluctant to go ahead with the arrangements.[18]

When Henry again pressed Parliament for aid on 9 February 1249, the response was emphatically negative. Questions of better security were raised, including his past recklessness and his continuing to govern without a chancellor, justiciar or treasurer. The financial situation was becoming critical.

The coinage was altered during 1247–8, having suffered deliberate sabotage, or clipping, apparently the work of criminals from Flanders; implementation of the change was time-consuming, but it did require cooperation between the king and his council. Henry had taken advice on the best way forward and decided on a change in form, as opposed to revaluing the coinage. He brought into the project his wealthy brother, the Earl of Cornwall, who lent him 10,000 marks, in addition to allowing Richard administration of the exchange and half of the future profits. The value of the new currency was set by 27 July, and the new money was due to be put into circulation by November.[19]

In July 1249[20] Henry was again in conflict with the lords, this time because he refused to allow the election of ministers as stipulated in the reform of 1245. Constant pressure for reform was becoming increasingly irritating to the king who claimed the lords were attempting to make a servant of him. When Parliament again deprived him of aid, he sold his jewels and plate to the city of London. Worse news was to come, however, when Innocent reminded Henry that 1,000 marks was due to be paid to the Templars, as Innocent had borrowed that sum from the order in anticipation of payment.[21] Also in that year Innocent issued a papal bull on 23 January giving Henry the right to reclaim royal estates that had been given away, notwithstanding any previous agreement, while the persistently absent Boniface was finally enthroned at Christ Church on All Saints' Day.[22]

Meanwhile, by the end of November, the fate of Gascony changed following Henry's decision to give it to his son, Edward, rather fulfilling his promise that it would be given to Richard. On 28 November Henry wrote to Simon informing him of the change and within three days wrote to him again declaring that his position as Seneschal was secure.[23]

Nevertheless, among the Gascons there was disappointment. The transfer of authority from the king to the prince was not particularly unpopular, but any hope they had of Edward replacing de Montfort was frustrated. The main problem Simon had to encounter was ruling an isolated area under threat from the expansionist French.[24] Irrespective of his methods, however, de Montfort had secured Gascony, and when he returned to England a second time in spring 1250 he still had the backing of the king.²⁵

Henry wrote again to the Pope early in 1250 about his lack of support from the ecclesiasticals in England. On 6 March he took up the cross and in a public ceremony asked the forgiveness of Londoners, who were still aggrieved at his money-raising attempts of recent years. He made an effort to curtail his spending, notably on shrines, though he did not eliminate his wastefulness altogether. Innocent replied on 13 April: in light of his taking up the cross Henry was given permission to take a tenth of all ecclesiastical revenues in the kingdom for three years, subject to the approval of the bishops. On 24 April there were also letters from Innocent to the bishops regarding crusade incentives for Englishmen.²⁶

The possibility of a crusade was increased following the death of Frederick II. Since 1229 Frederick had, off and on, been a thorn in the side of the papacy. To his allies and admirers he was known as 'Stupor Mundi', the wonder of the world. Born in 1194 near Ancona to Henry VI, the Holy Roman Emperor, and Constance, the last inheritor of the Norman dynasty of Sicily, he was parentless at the age of four and henceforth brought up by his new guardian, Innocent III. In 1215 he was crowned King of the Germans, sitting like those before him on the great marble throne of Charlemagne, and five years later Honorius crowned him emperor in Rome.

Critics of the emperor laid the shortcomings of his reign at the door of his lifestyle. Isolated as he was in Sicily's fine capital of Palermo, he ruled more like a Byzantine emperor than a European king. He kept countless concubines and was surrounded by splendour and wealth. Despite his upbringing he was sceptical of religion and referred to Christ, Moses and Mohammed as great deceivers. Though this had led to his excommunication, he was praised for his thinking and his writings, and for his military audacity. The last, however, also let him down. His feud with the popes left him short of allies in Europe, and a defeat in Vittoria in 1248 was compounded by another at Lucera in 1250. He died in the Italian city of Fiorentino, dressed in the habit of a Cistercian monk, and was later interred in Palermo alongside his father and grandfather. It was noted that his death coincided with an earthquake.

Meanwhile Louis's Egyptian expedition had proved disastrous. Two years on the road with insufficient provisions had brought the French forces to the brink of extinction, leading to a crushing defeat by the Saracens. It was written by the French chronicler Salimbene, a Franciscan friar of Italian birth, that over 2,000 knights and 15,000 soldiers were captured or slain by the enemy, and worse still Louis IX was also captured, though later freed on payment of a ransom. Equal misfortune befell Louis's brother, the Count of Artois. His losses also included at least 1,000 knights and over 7,000 soldiers. When news of these catastrophes reached the ears of Blanche of Castile the messengers were accused of lying and hanged. As the deaths became public knowledge the people of France were overcome with grief.[27]

In England, problems continued at Canterbury. When the synod met at Oxford in April to discuss the tax on all the benefices in Canterbury Henry attempted to protect his royal chapels and prohibited papal attempts to extract money to pay off debts.[28] Around this time Henry was also required to write to Innocent on behalf of Boniface regarding trouble with the Bishop of London and others after they had made accusations that Boniface was abusing his powers. Boniface used his influence to excommunicate the Bishop of London, eventually leading to a papal bull in November clearing him.[29]

By the end of September the See of Winchester was once again up for election following the death of William of Raleigh in Tours. Despite his eventual consecration Raleigh's time at Winchester continued to be plagued by differences with the king, and when he died he was estranged from the monarch. Henry now attempted once again to gain the see for one of his favourites. His new choice was his half-brother, Aymer de Valence, the youngest son of Isabella and her second husband. Henry met with the monks of St Swithun's, informing them of his choice and perhaps offering a vague threat of what could happen should his wishes not be taken seriously. A compromise was proposed that Valence be made bishop elect. Matthew Paris was particularly critical of this election. At the time Valence was still under thirty years of age, and his piety and intellect were questionable.

Christmas was spent at Winchester, a strategic move by Henry to demonstrate to the monks that he was not going to give in on this matter. He considered visiting Innocent later in 1251, but the Pope replied in April that the time was not right. Better news came when royal agents returned from Rome with the news that Aymer had been granted the See of Winchester, though his consecration was indefinitely postponed.[30]

Peace between England and France was extended for another five years in 1250, at a time when Henry's focus was once again on Gascony.[31] De Montfort came to Henry in January 1251 urging him to give further help. Henry promised Simon supplies and thanked him for his loyalty, though for the first time he questioned aspects of his government.[32] Reports had reached England regarding Simon's often over-zealous manner. Indeed, 1251 proved to be chaotic in Gascony. De Montfort was driven out by a revolt, and when he next came to England in November 1251 he was received coldly.[33]

Away from court a controversial movement was spreading across Europe. A sixty-year-old Hungarian monk was causing a stir with his teachings on the subject of Louis's capture in the Holy Land. The movement of the 'Pastoureaux' or the 'Crusade of the Shepherds' originated in northern France in 1251; thousands of Christians of the poorer classes became the monk's followers. As many as 100,000 mostly young peasants made their way to Paris where they were received by Blanche of Castile, who welcomed their vow to rescue the Holy Land.

Keeping a movement of that size in order was never going to be easy, but that was not the greatest problem. On his travels across France the monk preached against the church and the papacy, with the result that any clergyman who spoke against them was murdered, as were several Jews. The rampage continued until the 'crusaders' reached Bourges, by which point word of their behaviour had reached Blanche, and they were forcibly dispersed. Their leader was dispatched with a blow from a double axe by an angry bystander as he preached his message.[34]

Henry enjoyed a pleasant Christmas at York, giving his daughter, Margaret, in marriage to the newly crowned Alexander III, King of Scotland. Alexander also did him homage for Lothian, as required by the treaty of 1230. Events in Gascony once again dominated the early part of the following year, by which time the long-term future of the duchy had become increasingly unclear.[35]

Evidently Henry took the complaints against Simon seriously. His decision to send a commission of inquiry to Gascony early in 1251 had little effect, however, as it did not stop the accusations against the earl. Henry wrote to the complainants from York early in the New Year; he recalled de Montfort to England in May 1252 and put him on trial over the following month. The situation reached boiling point when Henry threatened to remove the earl from office, leading to Simon's reminder that the king had promised that his position was permanent. When Henry answered that he would have no compact with traitors, the disgusted earl replied, 'Were thou not my king it would be an ill hour for thou would thou dared to utter it.'

On de Montfort's return to Gascony he faced another revolt by Gaston de Bearn. His absence had allowed Bearn to make significant headway, but his return prevented the revolt from becoming too serious.[36]

As already indicated, Henry had already decided that Gascony would be passed to Edward rather than Cornwall. When the decision was renewed in April Henry ordered an assembly of all the Gascons who happened to be in London at the time, including the Archbishop of Bordeaux. According to the king, Richard had lost interest in Gascony and was happy for Edward to take it. In reality, Richard was so furious he stormed from court, cursing the king's fickle attitude.[37]

The Gascons, however, were delighted. All present swore fealty to the prince, and relations were promising at the feast that followed. Intriguingly, during the festivities several comments were made against Simon, including that he would either be banished or else cut up and fed to dogs. These sentiments were the prelude for what was to come. When the Gascons returned home Simon awaited their arrival with the support of a large force at La Réole. The scene was set for war. Still aggrieved with the seneschal, the Gascons tried to attract the attention of Simon's enemies, promising that a new lord, the prince, would soon get rid of him.

The rebels met Simon with a large gathering, but a lack of planning led to their being ambushed. As a skirmish began, the Gascons captured one of Simon's knights, coincidentally the very man Simon had placed in charge of the ambush. In a desperate bid to save his knight Simon got on his horse and charged at the enemy. He succeeded in freeing the knight, but his success was nearly short lived as he lost his steed. In the resulting mêlée the knight he had saved was said to have cried out that he must save

Simon as he had just been saved. Though both survived, a large battle ensued; the Gascon resistance was put down, ending the discontent against the earl.[38]

Away from Gascony, 1252 was dominated by talk of a further crusade. On the back of a letter from Innocent IV, Henry outlined his intention to go on crusade, and on 14 April he confirmed his date of departure as 24 June 1256. In June 1252 Innocent demanded that the 4,000 marks promised to Canterbury be raised through a collection by churches in the province.[39] At the time Henry was equally short of money. At a council in London on 13 October 1252 he laid before the prelates a papal mandate for crusade expenses, highlighting that the English clergy should pay one-tenth of its annual revenue to support his expedition, valued in the new currency rather than the old. Under the leadership of Bishop Grosseteste the bishops refused. In some quarters there was doubt as to whether Henry would actually go on crusade. Among the attendees was the new Bishop Elect of Winchester. Though Aymer supported Henry, his stance was swayed by the strength of the Bishop of Lincoln, which infuriated Henry.[40]

Henry enjoyed better luck when he limited his demands to a request for aid for the Holy Land. Criticism was labelled at the diocese of Canterbury for their business incompetence, and discussion also took place about both the reissue and replacement of the Great Charter. Henry allegedly swore horribly at hearing this suggestion. He attempted to talk the magnates round individually, starting with the Bishop of Ely, but on this occasion he was unsuccessful.[41]

Closely intertwined with the fate of the crusade was that of Henry's birthright on the continent. Though truces between Henry and Louis were easy enough to negotiate, in June 1252 Henry implored Louis to allow him the lands of his forefathers, as this would hasten his ability to go on crusade.[42] Henry and Louis had no desire for war, but formal peace was impossible without Henry ending his claims upon Normandy and Aquitaine.

Matthew Paris was particularly critical of Henry at this time. In addition to his criticism of Aymer, among his writings was a story, somewhat difficult to believe, regarding the benefice of the church of Preston. Following the death of William Haverhill, also the royal treasurer, the vacant benefice was bestowed on one of the chaplains of his half-brother, Geoffrey de Lusignan. Paris slated the capabilities of the man, but he is equally scathing of his treatment by Henry and others at court. One particular story is recounted, apparently witnessed by the chronicler, that when Henry and Richard were strolling in the orchard of St Albans one day this same chaplain was seen to throw sods of earth or pieces of fruit at them, or at other nobles, as if he was mentally insane.[43]

Henry's dubious practice of employing unworthy foreigners in positions of stately or clerical importance would appear to have been a deliberate strategy to arouse discontent rather than simply poor judgement. Nevertheless the effects were unsurprisingly negative. Discontent was rife in 1252 and nowhere more so than in London. When some of the king's servants violently inter-rupted a game of quintain – a type of jousting – he fined the Londoners who retaliated by attacking his servants.[44] Also around that time Henry attempted to win the favour of Richard de Clare, Earl of Gloucester, and promised that if his son would marry Henry's niece he would be rewarded with 5,000 marks. After failing to raise the money from several abbeys Henry eventually tried to force it out of the Templars and the Hospitallers.[45]

Innocent was now desperate for a contribution from England to the crusades. Throughout 1250 he had continuously written to Henry requesting he leave for the Holy Land. Since Henry took up the cross it was agreed he be granted three years of ecclesias-tical benefice money towards his expenses, for two years following the beginning of the expedition all money taken from those who took up the cross compounded for absolution from the crusading vow, plus other moneys such as the residue of all intestate estates. Henry also wrote to the Archbishop of Dublin to enforce this. The rumour was rife in Ireland and England that the king wished to extract more money from non-crusaders than crusaders. Henry also complained to the Pope that collectors had not sent him the money he was due. While Innocent wrote to his collectors he also promised Henry that the lands in France held by Louis would be returned to him.[46]

Boniface had returned to England in November 1252, at which point a serious argument arose between him and Aymer when one of Aymer's appointments was judged to have been within the jurisdiction of Canterbury. There was a small fracas when Aymer took a band of men to Maidstone and, after failing to find the person he was looking for, continued to Lambeth and captured one of the archbishop's officials. The case was finally resolved on 13 January 1253 under the guidance of the papacy, but the split was enough to create divisions between the Poitevin and Savoyard factions.[47]

Aymer had been with Henry for Christmas in Winchester, before the matter had been resolved. The event was remembered both for the generosity of the people of Winchester in bestowing a noble gift on the king for the Christmas ceremony, and the king's demeaning of the gift by extorting 200 marks from the city to replenish his depleted coffers.[48] Henry summoned the usual Parliament in London in April 1253, again looking for aid. After he had made a presentation of his needs and aims, a deputation of the magnates, led by Boniface, challenged him to grant the right of freedom of election in all ecclesiastical matters. This was effectively a criticism of Henry for promoting favourites rather than the most able candidates – ironic, bearing in mind that the four bishops in the deputation included Boniface and Aymer.

There was now progress on both sides. On hearing the magnates agree to his demands in exchange for a reissue of the Charter Henry was penitent. Cleverly he challenged the four bishops to resign what they had obtained through his patronage. In response the bishops asked that Henry's promise affect only the future, not the past.

The Parliament ended with the prelates finally giving in to Henry's monetary requests. They agreed to honour the papal decree that tithes amounting to a tenth of ecclesiastical revenue would be given to assist the king's crusade, to be paid when the crusade actually started, on condition that Henry agree to confirm the Charters.[49] Confirmation came on 13 May at a ceremony in Westminster at which the bishops announced that all who refused to abide by the Charters would be excommunicated.[50]

In Rome, it was now the Bishop of Lincoln who incurred Innocent's wrath. Like the majority of the clergy in his day who entered the Church for the right reasons Grosseteste was a highly intelligent man and a great theologian. Though of humble stock, he excelled at Oxford in the study of natural sciences, mathematics and theology, and in 1229 the then 59-year-old was elected its first chancellor. As Bishop of Lincoln he controlled the nation's largest see and therefore its wealthiest. As one of the three highest clerical magnates in England his relationship with the papacy was always of significance. On his first visit in 1245, while the Pope was at Lyon, he received a favourable response to his dispute regarding reforms in his own diocese, but the cordial atmosphere changed in 1250 when on a visit to the Roman Curia he criticized Innocent for using the revenues of the English Church to finance his war with Frederick.[51]

Grosseteste and Innocent clashed violently in 1253 when the former refused Innocent's demand to induct the Pope's own nephew, Frederick di Lavagna, into a wealthy canonry at Lincoln

Cathedral. On reading the bishop's letter of refusal Innocent was alleged to have said, 'By Peter and Paul, if I were not a kind man I would throw him into such utter ignominy.' The cardinals, however, were far more sensible in their counsel. The testimony of Giles, a cardinal from Spain, offered a fine appraisal of Grosseteste, confirming to the Pope that any sanction against him would be widely unpopular.

As the year progressed, Grosseteste's health began to deteriorate. By early August he was bedridden at his manor at Buckden, and on 9 October he died peacefully. It was recorded that at the time of the bishop's death the Bishop of London heard a strange sound in the air, rather like a bell from a church but not one he had heard before. On hearing the sound, and being close to Buckden at the time, he was instantly convinced that the bell was a sign. When he asked those with him if they could hear what he heard they replied that they could not. The party continued to Buckden with great haste, and on their arrival the bishop's beliefs were confirmed. The time of death was clarified to have occurred at the exact time the bishop heard the tolling of the bell. None of those present was left in any doubt that the strange event was indeed the work of the late Bishop of Lincoln, and the large number of witnesses, coupled with the fact that the place where the Bishop of London heard the sound was geographically removed from any known abbey, monastery, priory or church, makes the event all the more mysterious.[52]

Meanwhile, Simon de Montfort's four-year adventure in Gascony had come to an end by September 1252. The claim that he could not be removed by the king was resolved with a large pay-out, following which the earl retired to France.[53] Almost immediately the situation in Gascony deteriorated. Gaston de Bearn was again in revolt and had offered the duchy to Alphonso of Castile.[54]

Henry's reaction to the news was to begin negotiations for a marriage between Prince Edward and Alphonso's half-sister, Eleanor. There was also talk of Henry's daughter, Beatrice, marrying the eldest son of the King of Aragon.[55] Henry himself sailed with an army from Portsmouth on 6 August 1253 and landed in Bordeaux on the 15th, leaving the kingdom in the hands of his wife and brother. What followed was vaguely similar to his last outing. Initially Henry made some progress, taking Benauges, La Réole and several other castles in the Lower Garonne, but he made very little headway in the area as a whole. In some places the expedition was marred by the mindless violence of his troops who burned houses and vineyards.[56]

The biggest problem for the king was not necessarily the rebels but the possibility of attack by rival princes. He shored up his relations with the King of France by negotiating a continued truce, followed soon after by talks with other local lords. But undoubtedly the most important was his completion of a truce with the King of Castile. When Gaston de Bearn fled to seek help from the King of Castile he was shocked to hear that the marriage of Edward and Eleanor had already been agreed.

Henry remained in Bazas for Christmas actively preparing for the pacification of the realm. Thanks to Simon's return, the duchy was largely restored to order. Back in England a council met on 28 January 1254. The prelates refused to grant an aid from the clergy, but they did grant one from themselves in case the King of Castile invaded. The lords also announced their preparedness to travel to Gascony if called on, though Cornwall reminded them that no general aid could be made without the publishing of the Charters.[57]

Peace was settled between Henry and Alphonso in April, at which point there was also talk of Henry changing his crusade to join Alphonso in Morocco or Tripoli, for which he would receive half of any lands conquered in Africa.[58] In the king's absence a Parliament met at Westminster on 26 April. This was another landmark in English history and a clear sign of what was to come. For the first time since the reign of King John two knights from each shire were summoned, and also present were members of the diocesan clergy, the first attendance of its kind at a Parliament.[59] Perhaps the most significant feature at the Parliament was the role of the recently returned Earl of Leicester. When the topic of money came up Simon took a stout view, arguing that the lords should not be deceived by the king's 'mousetraps'.

Once terms with Alphonso were settled Henry sent for his wife and sons. In May 1254 Queen Eleanor arrived in Bordeaux, followed by Edward and Edmund on 12 June. Also in attendance were the queen's uncle, the Archbishop of Canterbury and several of the magnates.[60]

Edward was welcomed at Alphonso's court at Burgos on his arrival in August and was knighted by Alphonso. Two months later he married Eleanor in the Cistercian monastery of Las Huelgas, and on 1 November Alphonso confirmed a charter renouncing his claim to Gascony.[61]

For Henry, the marriage of his son to Eleanor of Castile gave him the opportunity to concentrate more single-mindedly on domestic policy. On 14 February 1254 Henry created Edward the Duke of Aquitaine and formally assigned to him Ireland except Dublin and Limerick, the county of Chester, various royal castles and acquisitions in Wales, the castles of Peak, Stamford, Grantham and Bristol, the Channel Islands, Gascony and the Isle of Oleron.[62] Though Henry remained in control, from this point on writs were being made in Edward's name, and he could also now profit from the revenues made under his jurisdiction. Despite criticism by the chronicler of St Albans of Henry's decision to grant so much power to Edward, it is interesting to note with hindsight that the decision to allow Edward the opportunity to experience kingship first hand would have a profound effect on his later reign.[63]

Henry and Eleanor spent the summer in Bordeaux before leaving the city in good hands. On the way back, and following a short illness, Henry visited his mother's tomb at Fontevraud and had her body moved into the church and a mausoleum established over it. During the trip Henry and Eleanor also made a pilgrimage to the shrine of the recently canonized Edmund of Abingdon at Pontigny.

However, his main desire was to visit Louis. Henry sent his envoys to Paris, informing Louis of his wish to see him. It was also his wish to visit the great cities of which he had heard tales but never seen. Evidently, Louis was also keen on improved relations with his brother-in-law. Writing from Jaffa on his way home on 1 May 1254 he highlighted the importance of peace with England. At the time of Henry's request he had only recently returned to France following his captivity while in Egypt. On hearing the news his response was of great joy.

Once Henry had received assurances of a safe passage he assembled his household and headed for Orléans. His journey was well received, and on the orders of the King of France the people of the cities were to prepare for his arrival with great energy. Henry arrived in Chartres in December, where he met Louis for the first time. Both men came quickly towards one another, offered each other the kiss of peace, and conversation was friendly and enthusiastic. On 9 December they went on to Paris.[64]

As news of Henry's visit became known, the crowds of onlookers grew significantly. Alongside Henry and Eleanor in Paris were her three sisters, Margaret, wife of Louis, Beatrice, the Countess of Anjou, and Sanchia, wife of Richard of Cornwall. Joining the sisters was the proud mother, Beatrice of Savoy, who watched with delight as all of her four children joined together in the only occasion of its type. Louis's only regret was that the barons of France were not there.[65]

Understandably, the prestige of the occasion captured the imagination of the students of Paris. Rather than continue to study, lectures were missed, and the students expended their limited resources on candles and high-quality delicacies or 'quaintises' instead of their usual food and board. The students, particularly the English, joined the new crowds, singing and dancing and carrying in their hands leafy branches of flowers.

After seeing some of the sights Henry decided he would stay at the Old Temple, choosing the location due to its size and religious importance. In keeping with his usual wishes he ordered that the poor of the area be treated to a meal, and the following day a large number enjoyed the king's meat, fish, bread and wine. Early the following morning, both kings visited Sainte-Chapelle, one of the key reasons for Henry's journey. After taking his time to pray, he deposited gifts in honour of the relics, as was typical of pilgrims, and over the coming days he performed similar acts in other churches throughout the city.

Henry's fame spread, and the people clambered to meet him. His visit was noted for its great reverence and notably his generosity to the French people. Also singled out for praise was his retinue, whose fine clothes and friendly behaviour won the hearts of the people.[66]

When he parted from Louis he did so not only as a king from a king but very much a brother-in-law from a brother-in-law. On leaving Paris his retinue travelled to Boulogne, where they waited for a fair wind. Henry took advantage of the delay to visit the church of St Mary famed for its relics.[67] The trip, despite its cost of over £1,000, had made a favourable impression upon the French.

If only the same could be said of his own people.

13

THE PHONEY KING OF SICILY

On hearing of the king's return, the people of London took to the streets to welcome his arrival. Though Henry had often endured bitter relations with the city, gone were the days when the Londoners backed the invasion of rival lords. Not since 1238 had the city been the centre of an uprising, while the king's wedding to the daughter of the Count of Provence was still very much in people's memory.

In the king's absence alms had been distributed and prayers said daily for his safe return. When he did return he was warmly welcomed and presented with a gift of £100. Unfortunately Henry was less ostentatious in his gratitude than he was in his willingness to spend. Perhaps because similar gifts had often been given to him in the past, he gave the impression of dismissing the gesture as nothing out of the ordinary. The Londoners viewed his lack of gratitude as ungracious, and it reminded them of his behaviour at the time of Prince Edward's birth. None the less they decided to bestow another gift, this time a cup of some £200 in value, which Henry accepted more graciously.[1]

Around the time of Henry's return a strange event is said to have taken place in Rome. Despite the death of the Bishop of Lincoln the Pope had not forgotten Grosseteste's refusal to bestow the benefice at Lincoln on his nephew. On one occasion his anger boiled over, and in his rage he demanded that the bones of the bishop be exhumed as a mark of disgrace. Though his wish won little support among the cardinals, he ordered that a letter be sent to the King of England to that effect. The following night, the chronicler writes, the late bishop appeared to the Pope in a dream. Dressed finely in his robes of office, he stabbed him in the side with his pastoral staff and said to him, 'Sinibaldo, you wretch of a Pope, so you are going to cast my bones out of my church, to bring shame upon me and the church of Lincoln? How did you think of such a blind piece of folly? You, raised to a position of honour by God, ought rather to show respect to His faithful, even when they are dead. The Lord will no longer suffer you to have any power against me.'

What happened next astounded the papal attendants. Though Innocent was now awake he was plagued by a severe pain in his side, and he did not eat or drink that next day. As it turned out 1254 would be Innocent's final year, and when he died, on 7 December, he did so fearing that the wrath of God was imminent.[2]

During his time on the throne of St Peter the man formerly known as Sinibaldo Fieschi faced some of the severest challenges faced by a Pope. The issues presented at the Council of Lyon continued to plague the papacy throughout his tenure, and even after the death of Frederick political stability remained a challenge.[3]

Perhaps his most significant legacy was an event that had taken place some two years earlier in the Languedoc region. By delivery of papal bull *Ad extirpanda* Innocent IV developed his predecessor's decree into the Inquisition by allowing the inquisitors to use torture. The Albigensian Crusade had been nothing short of a bloodbath. Rather than a genuine attempt to deal with heresy, the declaration by Innocent III that the lands of the

Cathars were fair game for any nobleman who conquered them led to forty-five years of butchery at the hands of greedy lords from the north, leaving a trail of destruction in their wake and many dead Catholics.

At the heart of the inquisition was a group of friars, the order of St Dominic, famously dubbed the Watchdogs of God. Little is known of Dominic's early life. That he was born in Castile in 1172 is generally accepted. He was a devout Christian from an early age, and he spent his later life preaching. Among his journeys was a visit in 1206 to the Languedoc region of southern France where the Cathar sect dominated. Languedoc had always been a tough area for missionaries and was viewed by Innocent as suitable for the harder line of the Dominicans as opposed to the more passive approach of the Franciscans and the Cistercians. The order's interrogation techniques were often brutal and led to the execution of several Cathars or Cathar sympathizers, while those who confessed were often spared with life in prison. It is perhaps fortunate that the Inquisition never took root in England, where the 'Black Friars' concentrated on preaching, winning the respect of the nobles and even being employed by the King of England as confessors.[4]

Back in England, Alphonso of Castile wrote to Henry early in 1255 urging him to build on his visit to France with another truce with Louis.[5] Things were certainly going well between the kings of England and France. In further acknowledgement of his recent visit Louis arranged for an elephant to be sent to Henry as a gift. Though Henry already possessed a large number of animals – as already mentioned he had established an impressive menagerie in 1237 to house the leopards sent by the Holy Roman Emperor – this was the first elephant ever seen in England and quite possibly the first seen north of the Alps. The local people flocked to see the strange beast. The elephant was taken by water from Dover to the Tower, where it survived for four years. Its remains were then interred at the Tower bailey before being entrusted to the sacrist of Westminster Abbey on the king's orders. At the time of the elephant's arrival in England the Queen of France also sent her brother-in-law an impressive hand-basin in the shape of a peacock and constructed of many fine materials.[6]

Henry's poor behaviour in London was exacerbated by a protest. At Merton in January the king's council decided that in order to meet his costs in Gascony he should tallage his demesnes. Among those present were the Mayor of London and several other dignitaries from the city. The council asked for 3,000 marks from the city, but the Londoners refused and offered just 2,000 as a voluntary aid. This was rejected, and the Londoners were later forced into submission.[7]

The significant cost of Henry's Gascony campaign and visit to France led to further efforts to raise money. In April 1255 he asked Parliament for another sum of money and received the usual response regarding appointments – on this occasion Parliament insisted upon having elected ministers who could only be dismissed by the common council, as set out two years earlier. He was also refused on the grounds that past money had been wasted, and in response he decided to enforce payment of the tenth due from the clergy.[8]

During his expedition to Gascony, Henry became involved in an initiative that would go on to shape much of his reign. Innocent wrote to Henry on 21 May 1252 regarding papal conflict with Conrad, King of Sicily, and offered the Crown to Henry for one of his subjects.[9] In fact Henry was not the first person to have been offered Sicily. Before 1252 both Charles of Anjou and Richard, Earl of Cornwall, apparently turned it down, perhaps as early as 1250.[10] On being offered the throne, Richard is said to have replied, 'You might as well say, I will sell or give you the moon; climb up and take it.'[11]

Nevertheless the proposition was not without value. Even since the Norman Conquest of England the kingdom of Sicily had enjoyed special links with the Plantagenet dynasty. Frederick's death had left England with less of an attachment to the empire, and since the death that year of Henry, son of Frederick and Henry III's sister Isabella, the links between the Plantagenet and Hohenstaufen dynasties were all but lost. At the time of Henry's reign Sicily was also arguably the most developed kingdom in Europe. Its location as an island off the coast of southern Italy placed it at the corner of four empires: Italy to the north, the Latin empire to the west, the Muslim world to the south and the Greeks to the east, while its medical school at Salerno was the Paris or Oxford of health education and was respected for its multicultural array of students and teachers.[12]

Henry accepted the throne on behalf of his youngest son, Prince Edmund. Writing in May 1254, Innocent sent two letters to Henry, claiming first that he had obtained a large amount of money to help Henry, half to be paid at Lyon and the other half when he was ready to embark, and second that Henry's right to take a tenth of ecclesiastical property could be extended to five years instead of three. On the instruction of the nuncio Henry sent what money he could raise, but this was not enough to cover all the costs.

Innocent's successor, Alexander IV, confirmed the Sicily agreement on becoming Pope, and conditions for assuming the throne were formally offered in April 1255.[13] In short Sicily was to be held as a fief of the Holy See and Edmund would rule as papal vassal on the condition that he pay 2,000 ounces of gold on the feast of St Peter and Paul every year and provide soldiers for three months every year to be used by the Papal States.

Edmund was also to remit the £100,000, which had already been promised to him by Innocent to ensure he could take the throne. The Pope accepted that Henry's crusading vow should be transferred to an expedition to Sicily, and he would have permission to use crusader funds for that purpose. More troublingly for the magnates of England, Pope Alexander demanded that Henry should take sole care of papal expenses for Sicily.[14] Henry asked Cornwall for 40,000 marks to aid the cause, which he refused. In April 1255 Alexander was pushing Henry for £4,000, while Henry's debts to the Jews were over 300,000 marks.[15]

Edmund's hopes of obtaining the Crown of Sicily were already under threat. War between Conrad and the papacy became almost inevitable in September, at which point Alexander wrote again to Henry requesting troops and money. By early autumn the papal nuncio and collector, Rustand Masson, the Bishop of Hereford and the Bishop of Bologna all came to England to invest Edmund in his kingdom. On 9 October Henry hurried to London for the Michaelmas celebrations devoted to St Edward the Confessor, and four days later, on St Edward's day, the prelates were summoned by the nuncio to gather in London. Once again the bishops were against giving money to the king, and on hearing of the conditions attached to the Sicilian crown their responses largely echoed Richard of Cornwall's. On 18 October Edmund was invested in his new kingdom by the envoy, vowing to go to Apulia in acknowledgement of his crusader vow. Nevertheless, the situation was far from resolved. In December Henry still owed the Pope £4,000 as a guarantee for the Sicilian Crown.[16]

Meanwhile, there was trouble north of the border early in 1255 over the regency of Alexander III. During that year the nobility of Scotland came to Alexander at Edinburgh, along with followers of Alan Durwood. Though he was acting under the guise of looking for peace with Alexander, Durwood's intention was to capture him. His supporters asked for a second meeting, this time at Stirling, but before the event could take place members of the opposition captured the king at Edinburgh Castle and garrisoned it with their own men.

At about this time the Earl of Gloucester was moving north with a large band of men; apparently it was on the advice of Gloucester that the Scottish king had been captured in the first place. Also on his way north were Henry and the queen. On hearing of events at Edinburgh, Henry announced his shock at such treason and vowed to assist the Scottish king. His forces continued north, and on 25 August he issued a proclamation in Newcastle that he would maintain the liberties of the kingdom. Alexander's captors took him and his queen (Henry's daughter Margaret) to Roxburgh and then on to Wark, where they met Henry and Eleanor. Following a short and apparently friendly discussion, Alexander returned home with his captors after only one day, but Margaret remained with Henry and Eleanor and fell ill while she was still with her mother.

Henry was granted permission by Alexander to enter Roxburgh on 15 August. The King of Scotland was later freed by the Scottish nobles, led by the Earl of Menteith, who feared that if the king remained a captive of men who had been excommunicated it was likely that the Pope would place the country under interdict. Fearing for his safety, Durwood fled to Henry, who took several Scottish lords under his protection. Henry and Alexander met at Jedburgh with strong armies; the result was a three-week conference, and a peace agreement was made.[17]

Before the end of the year Edward's new wife visited England for the first time. So great was the size of Eleanor's entourage that from a distance it was believed to be a Spanish invasion. After landing in Dover on 17 October the princess was brought to

London where it was decreed that she should receive a rapturous welcome. Orders were made for bells to be rung, the streets to be decorated and the people of London to come out in their best clothes to offer their appreciation for the woman who would one day be queen. Even her place of residence was furnished with fine silk hangings and tapestries. While this act may have pleased the Spanish, who were accustomed to such things, questions were raised over the king's willingness to please foreigners above his own people.[18]

Peace with Louis was extended until October 1258, allowing Henry to concentrate on another more pressing issue.[19] As mentioned, Dafydd's death in 1246 had drastically weakened the power of the princes of Gwynedd, following which the sons of the late Griffith, Owen (or Owain) the Red and the soon to be infamous Llewellyn ap Griffith (or Gruffydd), were forced to protect their lands from attack from the English seneschal at Carmarthen. The awkwardly arranged Treaty of Woodstock left the brothers on relatively firm ground with respect to Snowdon and Gwynedd, while the lands of Cardigan and Carmarthen, for so long areas that had at times been owned by the Welsh and at others the Earl of Pembroke, were firmly under the control of the king together with several other lands that had once been won by Llewellyn ap Iorwerth.

For the English the situation was promising. When open warfare broke out between Llewellyn and Owen, now allied with other sons of Griffith's in 1254, there is little reason to believe that Henry or Edward saw this as anything to be concerned about. Nevertheless Llewellyn succeeded in consolidating Gwynedd under a single banner, and by 1255 he had augmented his hold over Snowdonia. Had it not been for Henry's decision to hand Edward the grant of Cheshire the threat from Llewellyn might have been greater. For the present it remained in check.[20]

Of more concern to Henry was news that the rebuilding of Westminster Abbey had been halted from lack of finance. So bad was the situation that the workmen and stonemasons threatened to take their labour elsewhere. In response Philip Lovel, the king's treasurer, was instructed to examine any debts the king was owed and call them in. The target was £400 to cover initial costs.[21]

Henry's poor financial situation also jeopardized the Sicily agreement. In February 1256 the Pope wrote to England demanding payment. At the time Henry's debt for Sicily was an unprecedented 135,501 marks. In response to this crisis he summoned the prelates to London on 12 February 1256 and eventually agreed to confirm the Great Charter regarding freedom of election. As for Sicily, the nuncio pressed the prelates for aid but achieved little. The Archbishop of Messina also addressed the magnates, who discussed the terms for several days before refusing again. At around this time Rustand received a series of letters from the Pope, reinforcing him with largely unheard-of powers to extract funds. At Easter the bishops were called again on the orders of the nuncio, and refused to yield with the support of the barons.[22]

Henry wrote to Pope Alexander on 27 March on the subject of his lack of funds and the lack of enthusiasm among his magnates for a campaign in Sicily.[23] In June Alexander wrote a reply to Henry's request to delay payment of money for the Sicilian agreement and again urged an expedition to Sicily. In August he released two bulls: one allowing Henry the proceeds of benefices on their becoming vacant, and the second to Rustand confirming this. In September he released a further eleven bulls, including an extension of Henry's deadline for payment.[24]

Better news for Henry was an improvement in relations between Aymer and the monks of Winchester. Aymer's dealings with the monks had almost completely broken down in 1253 but had been resolved by June 1256.[25] The situation in Gascony was also better following Edward's marriage, while a vague suggestion that Simon would imminently return to Gascony finally silenced Gaston de Bearn.[26]

Problems raising money continued into the next year. Early 1257 saw a visit from the Archbishop of Messina regarding Sicily. Another nuncio, Herlot, came to England around Easter. Rustand had also returned after a brief visit to Rome to answer accusations about his acceptance of bribes.[27] Henry wrote to the Pope and his own agents in Rome on the subject and was prepared to announce to his agents his renunciation of the Crown of Sicily if necessary. Nevertheless at Parliament in mid-Lent Edmund appeared alongside his father dressed in Apulian costume, at which point Henry announced that Edmund was the new King of Sicily. He also secured a guarantee of 52,000 marks from the Church.[28] Throughout the year Alexander again implored Henry to obtain the money needed for an expedition to Sicily. Alexander also stipulated at this point that permanent peace between Henry and Louis was a prerequisite for Edmund obtaining the Sicilian throne.[29] Boniface returned to England and summoned a meeting at Canterbury on 22 August 1257. Despite grievances against Henry, he attempted to find him 42,000 marks for Sicily. Henry in return again agreed to uphold the liberties of the clergy, while the Pope allowed Henry to take another tenth for five years.[30]

Henry and Eleanor were grieved by the death of their young daughter, Katherine, on 3 May. No more than three years old, she was described as extremely pretty but intellectually impaired. For a time the event left Henry in poor health, suffering a heavy fever that forced him to rest in London.[31]

While he recovered Llewellyn laid siege to the borders. He conquered the four cantreds (a land division in use at the time) of Perfeddwlad (the area between the rivers Conwy and Dee) within a week and subsequently Cardigan. With the exception of the castles of Deganwy and Dyserth, he encountered little resistance. Roger Mortimer lost his marches in the centre of Wales, and as Llewellyn's confidence grew the English also lost the marches on the Bristol Channel.[32]

Llewellyn was now being seen as something of a champion of the Welsh. After recovering from his fever Henry was furious at Llewellyn's progress and on hearing his son's request for assistance against Llewellyn his initial response was that Wales had been entrusted to Edward and it was his job to deal with it. Despite this initial refusal, in September Henry marched to Chester and then to Gannoch. After waiting for some weeks on the banks of the Conwy, the army retired home. In truth, both Henry and Edward had bigger problems to deal with and not nearly enough financial backing. When a truce was made with Llewellyn the following year, it was financially sensible to allow Llewellyn control of the disputed territories that he had reconquered.[33] To meet his debts Henry levied a scutage for the conflict. Pope Alexander pressed him again to meet the cost for Sicily and threatened him with excommunication.[34]

Better news came with the announcement that his brother, Richard, had been elected King of the Germans in 1257. The dethronement and later death of Frederick II, followed by the deaths of his sons Henry and Conrad in 1253 and 1254, had a significant effect on the Hohenstaufen empire. With Conrad dead, his rival, William of Holland, ruled Germany until 1256, but now he, too, was dead and a new king had to be elected. Among the favourites was Richard. Since embarking on his crusade Richard had earned a reputation as a person of importance and wisdom, while his moderating influence on the king, coupled with his valour in battle, brought him respect in the eyes of the papacy and the monarchs of Europe. Nearly a year passed before the replacement for William was elected, during which time the German princes were divided in their support between the Hohenstaufen and the papacy. Henry himself watched events closely. With Edmund due to take Sicily it was undoubtedly in his mind that the new King of the Germans should not interfere with his plans.

News of Richard's candidacy became known by 26 November 1256 when the Count Palatine, with backing from the Archbishop of Cologne, signed the conditions for supporting Richard. It was also announced that Richard would formally renounce any claim to Sicily, while the count would marry a daughter of Henry III. On 26 December Henry watched proudly as Richard accepted all the necessary conditions in London.

The situation, however, was less straightforward than it could have been. Despite assurances from the Archbishop of Cologne, the High Chancellor of the Holy Roman Empire and several other magnates that Richard's election had been the clearest and most unanimous ever known, during that year Alphonso of Castile was also elected to the same role with the backing of the Archbishop of Trier.[35] In January 1257 Richard's supporters attempted to enter the town of Frankfurt but were stopped at the gates. Over the course of the following day Richard was elected by the people before the gates, with the vote of four of the seven electors. News of the event became known to Henry III on 17 January, and Richard accepted the Crown. He bade his fellow magnates farewell at the mid-lent Parliament and left Yarmouth for the continent at the end of April.[36]

Away from politics, another event that raised the interest of Matthew Paris occurred on 9 March 1257. While staying at St Albans, a deputation of nine masters of the arts of Oxford came before the king, petitioning against their chancellor, Henry Lexington, Grosseteste's successor as Bishop of Lincoln, for try-ing to weaken the rights of scholars. On that same day Matthew himself had a private conversation with the king regarding the situation. Paris spoke bluntly. The University of Paris, he claimed, was already in great turmoil, and should Oxford face a similar crisis the whole Church would suffer. The conversation clearly made a mark on the king, and it was decided that both parties should have their say at the next Parliament.[37]

In early 1258 the Pope once again wrote to Henry urging him to try to meet his creditors with regard to Sicily.[38] By this time any claim Edmund had to the throne of Sicily had all but vanished following the crowning of Manfred as King in Palermo.[39]

The Sicily fiasco ended a highly testing period for Henry. The magnates still criticized him for his wastefulness, the enrichment of aliens and his seemingly poor ability to resist the demands of the Pope; murmurs continued that papal agents were still travelling the country, preying on the defenceless.

Peace with France was closer, but Henry's lack of leadership in Gascony had frustrated the nobles, losing him the support of Simon de Montfort. The election of Richard as King of the Romans had gained him a powerful ally in Europe but lost one at home. Llewellyn's rise in power, coupled with Henry's lack of funds, forced him to negotiate several uneasy truces, further strengthening Llewellyn's position. As rumours spread that the Welsh had entered secret negotiations with the lords of the marches and the King of Scotland Llewellyn's threat to the borders continued to intensify.

The people were also suffering. The previous winter had witnessed many problems throughout the country. The successful harvest of 1255 was a distant memory, after two bad ones. Late frost and disease among the cattle led to rising food prices and famine for many of the common folk. The failure of 1258's harvest meant that in some areas the price of wheat was two and a half times what it had been two years earlier.[40] Matthew Paris painted a morbid picture: 'The dead lay about, swollen and rotting, on dunghills, and in the dirt of the streets, and there was scarcely anyone to bury them.'[41]

If the road from Bouvines to Runnymede had indeed been inevitable for John, for Henry the road was even clearer. All the barons needed was a plan.

14

ALL ROADS LEAD TO OXFORD

Henry met his frustrated nobles at Parliament on 9 April 1258. His request for aid was again refused, and hostility between allies of the king and some of the other lords saw the Parliament adjourned without progress. For Henry the situation was grim. Political strife had left him financially stricken and with few allies. So bad were the royal finances that Edward was forced to pawn his favourite estates to William of Valence.[1]

The next Parliament was summoned for Westminster on 28 April 1258. During the interim the king had attempted with limited success to persuade the abbots of some of the great houses to act as sureties for him, but he was still to convince the magnates. When Parliament met, Herlot demanded, in the Pope's name, a third of all movables and immovables, a demand against which even past papal requests seemed insignificant.

Even before this Parliament met dissent had been brewing. Earlier in April certain followers of Aymer, Bishop Elect of Winchester, attacked and murdered servants of the baron John FitzGeoffrey. When John sought legal redress Henry refused, a blatant disregard of the Charter.[2] In Parliament things were getting worse. Simon and William of Valence exchanged heated words, resulting in Valence branding Simon a traitor.[3]

Recent events had led to the formation of the first opposition party since the war of 1215–17, with the Earls of Gloucester, Norfolk, Hereford (Humphrey de Bohun) as well as Leicester taking a tough stance against the king and his closest advisers.[4]

Only two days after the Parliament the king was shocked by the appearance of barons in armour at Westminster Hall. Though their swords were left by the door, their manner confirmed an unwillingness to compromise. Among the leaders was the Earl of Norfolk, Roger Bigod, with whom Henry had clashed in 1254.[5] When the king asked, 'What is it, My Lords? Am I your prisoner?' Bigod replied that he was not, but no longer were the lords willing to accept Henry's disregard for the Charters and his poor financial planning.

Evidently this challenge had been planned at least three weeks in advance. According to a document dated 12 April 1258, a confederacy had been assembled, made up of the Earl Marshal, Bigod; Simon de Montfort; de Clare, the Earl of Gloucester; Marshal's younger brother, Hugh Bigod; Peter of Savoy; Peter de Montfort, the Lord of Beaudesert; and John FitzGeoffrey. The document survives only in modern transcript, but its content is consistent with the events that followed. The men swore an aid for each other in the cause of justice and loyalty to the Crown.

Two documents were drawn up for the king's acceptance on 2 May. The first announced the king's agreement to their demands, including official confirmation that an aid would be granted with respect to Sicily should the Pope lower his conditions. It was also agreed that constitutional reform would occur before Christmas, on the advice of good and faithful men loyal to the king and country, including a papal legate should there be one.

Henry agreed to the content of the first document; Edward, William de Valance and several others on the king's side attested to his acceptance of the terms. In the second document plans for reform were laid out in more detail. In addition to the dismissal of foreign advisers the king must agree to the formation of a council of twenty-four elected magnates – among whom twelve would be chosen by the king, the other half by the opposition – which would meet one month after Pentecost.[6] Left with little choice, Henry and his heir swore on the gospels to adhere to these new arrangements.

When Parliament next met in Oxford on 11 June the barons came prepared for war. The growing crisis on the Welsh border potentially brought things to a head, though any new expedition to Wales would have to be deferred. The barons were resolute in their demand for reform, and the king's strict adherence to the Magna Carta and Charter of the Forest. A schedule of grievances was drawn up. In total twenty-nine articles were formally presented, addressing past abuses.

As a consequence of the assembly, the council of twenty-four was appointed. Of Henry's twelve, six were churchmen: Boniface of Savoy, Fulk, Bishop of London, the Abbot of Westminster, Aymer, the Bishop Elect of Winchester, the Dominican friar John of Darlington and the Chancellor, Henry Wingham. Also selected were John Mansel, his nephew Henry of Almain, his half-brothers William and Guy, and two earls, John du Plessis, Earl of Warwick, and John of Warenne, who was married to Henry's Lusignan half-sister, Alicia.

It seems certain there was some reluctance on the part of the barons to seem too close to the king. In contrast to Henry's choices, for the opposition Simon de Montfort was the only foreigner and Walter de Cantilupe, Bishop of Worcester, the only cleric. The other ten included three earls: Gloucester, Norfolk and Hereford; and seven barons: Roger Mortimer, John FitzGeoffrey, Richard Grey, William Bardolf, Peter de Montfort, Hugh Despenser and Hugh Bigod.

During the Oxford Parliament several other reforms were put forward. Under the supervision of the twenty-four it was announced that a body of fifteen would act as the king's permanent council. The occasion was another landmark in English history. The Parliament, dubbed the 'Mad' Parliament by the royalists, was to be the first of three annual meetings, consisting of the fifteen and another committee of twelve, chosen by the barons, for the purpose of discussing the proceedings of the council. Furthermore, another body of twenty-four, also a temporary body, was to be chosen to arrange grants to the Crown.

In practice, the twenty-four worked together with surprising vigour. In order to ensure that no interference took place, envoys were sent to France requesting that Louis refrain from becoming involved, while orders were also put out that the gates of London must be closed at night and the seaports closely guarded. The new regime was now able to establish direct authority over the executive of England. A justiciar, treasurer and chancellor were chosen, all of which appointments were to be held for a year at a time. Similar reforms were also drawn up for the sheriffs.

Despite its successes, the idea that the new movement brought with it a huge increase in the rights of the common man was by no means correct. Power was still limited to the barons and the prelates, and the idea, prevalent in England even before the Runnymede Charter, that the government should consult representatives of the shire court on financial or political issues was probably more hindered than empowered by the new provisions. The expulsion of foreigners from office, though it was among the foremost reasons for reform, was not implemented straight away. Nevertheless a justiciar was finally appointed in Hugh Bigod, a capable noble of English birth.

As in 1218, one of the first tasks awaiting the new government was the reversion of the royal castles, many of which were in the hands of foreign favourites, to nineteen English castellans who would maintain them for twelve years and surrender them to the king only on the orders of the new council.[7] Predictably, the Poitevins reacted badly to the new reforms. The general level of hatred towards them made it almost impossible for them to continue to operate without resorting to force. Again Valence and de Montfort clashed fiercely, and after the royal order went out on 22 June for the establishment of the body of fifteen Valence fled to Wolvesey Castle in Winchester, held by the Bishop Elect of Winchester.

Military action quickly followed. The barons called on the forces that had been in readiness for the Welsh campaign and immediately headed for Winchester. Henry accompanied the barons in besieging the castle, which was surrendered on 5 July. Under the surrender terms, the besieged were allowed to keep much of their land and money on the condition that they withdrew from the kingdom. Within a fortnight they crossed the Channel. Among them was Aymer, with the See of Winchester already lined up for a new candidate.

The barons had achieved complete victory. Short of allies, Henry and Edward had little choice but to observe the 'Provisions of Oxford' and seek to work constructively within the new reforms.[8] Exactly what the role of the king was in this new government seems to have been something of a grey area. That Henry remained king is unquestionable, but he now suffered a severe restriction of his authority. Proof of where the power then lay can perhaps be illustrated by an event that occurred later in July. When out on the Thames, the king was caught in a terrible thunderstorm, forcing him to take refuge at the Bishop of Durham's house, then held by Simon de Montfort. On being reassured by the earl that the storm was nearly over the king is said to have replied, 'I fear thunder and lightning exceedingly.

But by God's head I fear thee more than all the thunder and lightning in the world.'⁹

On 5 August Henry acknowledged the twenty-four-man council, authorized to reform the realm, and on 18 October he renewed the agreement. The October Parliament also saw four knights from each shire appear before the council to present the grievances of the ordinary people against the sheriffs, all of whom were due to be replaced under the new reforms. Henry's assent to this provision was recorded in a proclamation written in English, in addition to the usual Latin and French. This was the only such use of the vernacular to occur during his reign.¹⁰

Recent events in England also brought unexpected peace with Wales. Despite his desire for conquest Llewellyn was satisfied by the number of marcher lords involved in de Montfort's government.¹¹ Relations with France, however, were complicated. Richard's election as King of the Romans, Henry's alliance with Castile and the re-emergence of English power in Gascony were potentially bad news for Louis. Talk of permanent peace between the two nations had begun in earnest in 1257, and a preliminary agreement was mentioned during the 'Mad Parliament'. Though any formal agreement was delayed by the events that were happening in England at the time, efforts were still ongoing in May 1258 when de Montfort and Hugh Bigod treated with two of the Lusignans and Peter of Savoy in Paris.

Peace with France was not straightforward. The Provisions of Oxford held no validity in the eyes of the papacy, while formal ratification of the treaty in France with Simon and Bigod but without Henry would also be impossible. Under no circumstances would the King of France treat with anybody other than the King of England himself. Another decisive factor was that Simon remained married to the sister of the king, herself entitled by family right to the lands of her forefathers. In theory the same claim was also valid for her offspring. Simon was clearly aware of this, and that in itself threatened the stability of the opposition party and agreement with peace. It was only due to a compromise involving a substantial pay-off that de Montfort was prepared to let the matter go.[12]

Peace terms between Henry and Louis were in essence agreed by 28 May 1258, thanks largely to the work of the legate, Mansuetus.[13] Herlot wrote to Alexander congratulating him on this. In the same letter he also highlighted Henry's wish for another legate.[14] Herlot left England in August, while the prelates were summoned to meet the Archbishop of Canterbury at Merton. The barons were determined to appeal to the Pope regarding the nuncio's recent demands relating to Sicily and the removal of foreigners.[15]

Richard returned to England in January 1259 after eighteen months settling into his new position as King of the Romans. Prior to his crossing he was met by a party of magnates at Saint-Omer where he was informed that only on accepting the Provisions would he be allowed back into England. On his landing, Henry met him at Dover and asked that he take an oath to abide by the Provisions of Oxford. On 2 February Richard took the oath while still in Dover.[16]

On 9 February a council met in London, attended by all the key magnates, including Simon de Montfort. Peace with France was now a priority, in particular the issues that had emerged from recent talks. On 14 February a peace treaty was drawn up.[17] Preliminary ratification was achieved later in the year, leaving little more to do than for the kings to agree in person. The main items of importance were Henry's agreement to relinquish his claim on the French dukedoms and his apparent willingness to hold Gascony as a fief of France rather than in its own right. In exchange, Henry was to be acknowledged as Duke of Aquitaine in addition to inheriting Périgueux, Limoges and Cahors, and in the future Saintonge, Quercy and Agenais would also revert to him.[18] Henry and Eleanor crossed the Channel on 14 November 1259 and reached Paris on 24 November. The treaty was ratified during their visit and formally published on 4 December.[19]

Despite giving up elements of his birthright, Henry had cemented a powerful friendship and strengthened his position in the eyes of the papacy and his council. The Sicily agreement, though dead, still lingered in his mind, and when he wrote to the Archbishop of Messina on 16 January 1260 he was optimistic that the agreement could still be revived.

For Louis, critics argued that he gave up more than he needed to. True, the demesnes in Quercy, Périgord and Limousin were not particularly large, while land owned by Alphonso was not likely to pass to Henry any time soon, but certain members of his council were adamant that Gascony could have been taken outright with the appropriate resources.[20]

Questions about Louis's decisions were aired by his council. On asking why he accepted the peace, his response was that the two kings' wives were sisters and hence their children cousins. It was with the best of intentions, and to Louis's own credit in the eyes of the people, that such problems could be solved through thoughtful diplomacy rather than prolonged hostilities.[21] The upshot was that the situation in France had reached both a constructive and a necessary conclusion. The continued English presence in Gascony would be of critical importance to the reigns of Edward I, II and III, and would lead to the Hundred Years' War, but for Henry and Louis there would be no further conflict during their lifetimes.

Henry and Eleanor spent Christmas in Paris and remained with Louis for a while thereafter. In January Henry attended the funeral of Prince Louis, son of Louis IX, and on 22 January he gave his daughter, Beatrice, in marriage to Duke John of Brittany.

After leaving Paris he spent Easter in Saint-Omer and returned to England in April 1260.[22]

In the king's absence splits had already occurred among the barons. In the October Parliament of 1259 Edward listened with interest to criticisms advanced by the younger nobles that, though the king had agreed to the Provisions of Oxford quite honourably and had still not broken any promises, the barons had not fulfilled any of theirs. There were also increasingly insistent accusations, notably from the Earl of Gloucester, that certain individuals had become lazy. Less than two years after reform was outlined there were serious doubts over whether the Provisions of Oxford had actually been implemented. Edward took note of these criticisms and was instrumental in the creation of a new charter of provisions, this one known as the Provisions of Westminster: a new agreement that enforced most of the provisions that had been agreed in 1258 in addition to new reforms regarding inheritance and taxation.[23]

By the end of 1259 it was becoming clear that the Earl of Gloucester, who had accompanied Henry to France, was far removed from the views of de Montfort, whereas Edward held beliefs that were somewhat closer to those of his uncle Simon.[24] As dissent among the opposition continued, rumours were also growing of a possible invasion by the ousted Lusignans. The monks of St Swithun's had also attempted to capitalize on the absence of Aymer and elected a new bishop, but just as they were finalizing the election his consecration was prevented because Alexander IV summoned Aymer and consecrated him as Bishop of Winchester – some ten years after his election.[25]

The Pope wrote to the barons in 1260, replying to their letters to him in the aftermath of the agreements at Oxford justifying their refusal of Herlot's requests. The barons had argued that the demands for one-third of all movables and immovables would bankrupt them; Alexander's reply was a long-winded moral discourse on the superiority of the papacy. It made no mention of other grievances, including the matter of foreigners taking English benefices, a practice that had not altogether ended. Around that time a potential problem arose in the diocese of London as both Henry and the Pope attempted to claim a vacant benefice, leading to the killing of the Pope's proctor by persons unknown. At the end of the year the Pope wrote to Prince Edward asking him to use his influence to convince the magnates of England of the need to aid the papacy against the Tartars, who potentially threatened to overrun Christendom.[26] Then, with the king still in France, the situation back home took a sudden twist as Llewellyn invaded the marches and laid siege to Edward's castle at Builth.[27]

Despite Henry's insistence that no Parliament should be convened while he was overseas, one did take place at Easter in London under Simon on his own return from France. The debate was heated. Taking advantage of the king's absence, Simon demanded the expulsion from the council of Peter of Savoy, while Edward almost came to blows with Gloucester. Fortunately mediation by Cornwall kept things in check.

Word now reached Henry that Edward and Simon were in league against him.[28] He hurried home, collected an army with Gloucester and took up residence at St Paul's, now on the alert for an attack, while Gloucester remained within the city, keeping a close eye on the gates. Meanwhile Edward and Simon had amassed their own forces at Clerkenwell.[29] For two weeks both sides readied themselves for war. Evidently Henry struggled with his estrangement from Edward, claiming at one point, 'Do not let my son appear before me, for if I see him, I shall not be able to refrain from kissing him.' As it happened, he got his wish. Edward was reconciled with his father, and Henry brought accusations of treason against Simon.[30]

The stage was set for war, and this time Henry was prepared. During the autumn of 1260 he fortified the Tower of London and received a visit from Alexander III and Queen Margaret, probably around December. In February 1261 the Queen of Scotland gave birth to a daughter, Margaret, remembered to history as Queen of Norway.[31]

Though the king kept a low profile, his patience was exhausted. There seems little doubt that privately both Henry and Eleanor were looking at ways to escape the reforms imposed on them since 1258. Hoping to be absolved from the Provisions, Henry sent agents to the papacy and wrote to Louis and Edward, who had travelled to Gascony after the Parliament in October.[32]

Knowledge of the king's scheme had somehow become known on the continent. In March 1261 the king, aware of these developments, issued a proclamation against those who spread such rumours. He summoned Parliament to meet at the Tower, but the lords refused to attend through fear of attack. Henry then moved on to Windsor and then Winchester.[33]

Recent events had taken their toll. In April Henry dismissed Hugh Despenser as Justiciar and replaced him with his own candidate, fuelling the feud between the king and the opposition. The quarrel between the king and the leaders of the opposition, notably de Montfort, was referred for arbitration to Henry's new ally, Louis IX, though the matter was actually handled by his wife; the issues were referred to two commissioners and two umpires nominated by the queen.

By 18 May Henry's position was relatively secure, leading him to issue a somewhat ironic proclamation that any aliens who entered the kingdom under the authority of Simon should be banished. He also managed to make Hugh Bigod give up Dover Castle, partly owing to its position but mainly to combat Bigod's loyalty to de Montfort.[34] Pope Alexander IV died on 25 May but not before granting Henry one final favour. Thanks to a papal bull issued on 13 April, Henry announced his absolution from the Provisions before Parliament at Winchester on 14 June.[35]

After dissolving the Parliament Henry returned to the Tower and immediately set about replacing the new sheriffs and forcing the surrender of the nineteen royal castles gained by the barons. In August he issued a proclamation explaining his return to control and recent conduct, blaming the troubles on the oppressive attitude of the opposition.

The Provisions had been repudiated, but still there was no imminent sign of an uprising. The general antipathy among the common folk towards the king in 1258 had subsided, largely because the population at large were enjoying better conditions. Among the barons the situation was more complex. Though the king's actions united the opposition, exactly who they were was now a difficult question. Of the original twenty-four-man council, only five still supported the rebels. Simon and the Earl of Gloucester put their differences aside at a meeting at St Albans, along with some of the other lords. As with other recent gatherings, three knights were summoned from each shire. On hearing this, Henry wrote, with little effect, to the sheriffs on 11 September ordering that the knights should come to him at Windsor on 18 September where he would discuss a peace treaty with all the nobles. The council ordered that Henry's newly in-stalled sheriffs must leave office, whereas Henry wrote to the sheriffs ordering the opposite.[36] In October, Henry sent proctors to the new Pope with letters concerning his issues with Canterbury and the barons and requested, unsuccessfully, that he annul certain statutes and provisions.[37]

Talks between the king and the opposition resumed on 28 October. The rebels' position was once again weakened, thanks in no small part to further quarrels between Gloucester and Simon, following which Simon departed for the continent. On 7 December a treaty was in the preparation, and Henry was happy to pardon all who accepted the new conditions.[38]

With his position strengthened, he wrote to Alexander's replacement, Urban IV, in January 1262 asking for confirmation of Alexander's bulls of annulment of the Provisions of Oxford. The issue of appointment of the sheriffs was referred to Cornwall, apparently with the blessings of Parliament, though unsurprisingly he sided with Henry. During Lent, on 25 February, Henry received word from Urban IV that the bulls were valid. Official publication occurred in London, and the bulls were laid before the next Parliament.[39]

Henry and Eleanor once again crossed to France in July, hoping to consolidate support from Louis. His plans were delayed, however, when he contracted a fever that for a time was potentially life-threatening. Writing to his brother in September, he stated that he could only walk a little around his room. He remained abroad to undertake a long pilgrimage to Rheims during October and November, and by Christmas he had returned to England.[40]

Simon was also back in England by October 1262, leading to conflict over Henry's letter of papal absolution. Parliament was held in London on St Edward's Day, presided over by the Justiciar, Philip Basset.[41] With him he had a letter, apparently written by the Pope, confirming the Provisions. The papal letter to the barons was published, and its words left their mark on many of those present.

For Henry the situation was once again deteriorating. Through illness he had not been able to achieve his objectives when visiting Louis, and he decided to abide by the Provisions once more in January 1263. He wrote to Louis, outlining his hope for peace with Simon, but this was complicated by Simon's claim that though the king meant well his counsellors did not.

Evidently Louis agreed with Simon, and a letter he sent on 16 February said as much.

Meanwhile Henry's absence in France coincided with further trouble on the Welsh borders. The Earl of Gloucester was dead, and his successor Gilbert de Clare followed in his father's footsteps by continuing the feud with Simon. Since the Provisions of Oxford relations with Wales had improved considerably, but Llewellyn never remained inactive. The lack of an English threat in Wales allowed him to advance on the marches, leading to further warfare.

Edward was clearly angered by the lack of respect Llewellyn showed in keeping his side of the latest truce. His plan to encourage David, Llewellyn's brother, to launch a successful revolt failed, leading to Llewellyn's conquering of the four cantreds and eventually the castles of Deganwy and Dyserth after long sieges. While Roger Mortimer had seen his castles fall to Llewellyn, de Montfort once again negotiated an alliance with Llewellyn. Meanwhile Edward returned from France intent on pursuing military action against the Welsh and their baronial allies.

Henry remained at Westminster, still struggling to recover his health. His life was potentially put at risk when Westminster suffered a fire, but fortunately the damage was repairable.[42] Evidently, recent events and his own poor health had forced Henry to plan for the future. In March Henry announced that a general oath of allegiance to Edward as his heir would be required. In the light of this development the barons declared that Edward should agree to swear by the Provisions, following which Henry once again sought refuge in the Tower. On hearing this Simon declared war on all who refused the Provisions.

Herlot was back in England in the middle of March, at which point he attempted to reach a definitive conclusion on the subject of Sicily.[43] Parliament met in London on 2 April, only to break up without matters reaching a conclusion. Another papal visitor, a friend named Mansuetus, also arrived in England, apparently at the king's request.[44] The right of Edmund to the throne of Sicily was formally renounced at the invitation of Urban IV. On 25 July Urban announced his intention to send over an envoy to conclude the matter once and for all. Two days later a second letter, this time of introduction for the visitor, was sent, declaring that any claim Henry had of obtaining the Crown for Edmund must be fulfilled within four months. The Pope's communication illustrated his great disappointment at the way things were, particularly that England had not aided the papacy better. On his arrival Mansuetus was apparently shocked that the situation in England was much more grave than he had anticipated.[45]

In Rome the Pope refused to ratify some statutes from the previous year's synod in January of that year as they lacked approval of the royal licence, casting further doubt over the validity of the Provisions of Oxford. During the following month Urban wrote to Boniface condemning the Provisions and the behaviour of the nobles in general. Direction was also given at this stage for the archbishop to use his powers against any who aided the Provisions of Oxford.[46]

By the summer of 1263 both Simon and Edward had raised strong armies. Simon had control of Hereford, taking many possessions from the bishop and expelling his foreign canons. Also in his possession were Gloucester and Bristol.

On the royalist side, after taking care of some of the issues with the Welsh, Edward positioned himself at Windsor and succeeded in establishing control of Isleworth. His strategy was simple. Should the enemy attack, control of these areas would help secure the position of his mother and father at the Tower of London.[47]

Simon retook several castles, marching under the royal

standard. As the summer progressed he took London, whose citizens showed their hatred for the king in the usual fashion. So bad was the mood that on one occasion Eleanor's barge was attacked on leaving the Tower, forcing a hasty return.[48]

On 29 June Richard of Cornwall mediated a truce between Henry and Simon, completion of which occurred on 15 July. Once again Henry agreed to the Provisions, foreigners were again banished and a new justiciar was appointed in the person of Hugh Despenser. As was typical in the case of such an appointment Despenser took possession of the Tower, following which Henry returned to Westminster.

Edward again took up arms. Aided by several followers, including his cousin Henry, the son of the King of the Romans, he attempted to increase his following and again capitalize on the indecisiveness of the opposition. Yet for now there was no war. Neither side had a force that could be assured of victory. The idea was mooted that the situation could be resolved through the mediation of Louis, though the barons were unconvinced. Suspicious that Henry was hoping to acquire the aid of the King of France, the barons refused Henry the right to leave the kingdom until Louis could guarantee his immediate return.[49] A final agreement was mooted at a Parliament on 9 September, which also gave approval to the terms agreed in July. Henry travelled to see Louis, landing on 19 September (or perhaps the 21st). He met Louis and Simon in Boulogne three days later. The attendance was large, including every duke and noble of Burgundy, Spain and Champagne.

Discussions included the pilgrimage of Louis and other crusaders. It was also around this time that Louis's son, Philip, was crowned joint king.[50] No firm arrangements were made about the future of England, and Henry crossed back on 7 October, leaving Eleanor in France. A week after his return the volatile situation finally erupted. Henry and his lords had a violent confrontation with Simon in Parliament over household appointments, following which he departed for Windsor accompanied by his closest supporters.[51]

Urban wrote to Henry on 12 November announcing that a new legate, Guy Foulques, recently Bishop of Sabina, would soon be sent to England. Henry held another Parliament at Reading in November, though Simon did not attend in case he was attacked.[52] At the beginning of December, with the help of Cornwall, Henry ventured to Dover Castle and after being refused admittance attempted to take London but failed to get past the city gates.

Once again the situation had reached a deadlock. On 16 December Henry agreed that Louis should arbitrate on matters concerned with the implementation of the Provisions of Oxford. Before the year was over Henry returned to France. As Simon de Montfort was unable to travel, his loyal ally, Peter de Montfort of Beaudesert Castle, made the journey to France on his behalf.

Henry and Edward sailed to Wissant and met the King of France at Amiens. On 23 January 1264 Louis's decision about the Provisions was made known in a document known as the Mise of Amiens. Perhaps swayed by the absence of Simon Louis endorsed the decision of the papacy and declared the Provisions null and void.[53]

15

THE SLAYING OF THE DRAGON

The outcome of the Mise of Amiens was made known back in England on 25 January. Under its direction, all of the royal castles were to be returned to the control of the king, appointment of officers was to be the king's choice, employment of aliens was to be permitted, and the governing of the kingdom was to remain in accordance with the terms of the Charter of Liberties, already granted by the king's predecessors.[1]

Henry returned to England on 8 February 1264, landing in Whitsand accompanied by a strong force.[2] He had anticipated that Louis's ruling would not be accepted by the opposition, and indeed that was the case. In reality, the French king was never likely to favour the barons – to do so could incite a similar rebellion in France – but the outcome was always going to be too one-sided to be accepted by all parties. Had Simon had the opportunity to attend the meetings with Henry and Louis things might have been different, but as the talks had taken place with so few from the opposition in attendance there was a general feeling that the outcome was not a fair one.

The Londoners were the first to show unrest. On hearing the news they elected a constable and a marshal before joining with the reinstated Justiciar, Despenser, and marching on Isleworth. A manor, owned by Richard, Earl of Cornwall, was razed to the ground; the chronicler of London noted that this 'was the beginning of trouble and the origin of the deadly war'.[3]

The barons' forces moved towards Kenilworth, Simon's stronghold. The castle had undergone extensive development over the previous thirty years since it had been gifted to Simon in recognition of his marriage. For Simon the time was ripe for rebellion. Though he was low on supporters, he did have allies in his two sons, Simon and Henry, who were causing a good deal of trouble in the Midlands. Henry de Montfort crossed the Severn and attempted to make another alliance with Llewellyn. Meanwhile Edward failed initially to take Gloucester, leading to a brief truce, but he soon turned the tables on the opposition and following his success he moved to join the king at Oxford.

In Rome the Mise of Amiens was confirmed by Urban IV. In March the Pope wrote to Henry to congratulate him.[4] Henry held a conference at Oxford on 18 March with the barons who had been stationed at nearby Brackley. An attempt to negotiate a truce came to nothing, and before he left the king closed the university because of a riot during Lent.

While Valence pillaged the countryside, Henry assembled his forces and marched for Northampton, then held by Simon the Younger. The castle fell on 5 April after a two-day siege, and Simon the Younger was imprisoned with several others. The king's forces proceeded to lay waste to the elder Simon's Leicestershire estates, and when the royalists reached Nottingham the gate was hastily opened to allow their entry.[5]

In the south Simon's forces were welcomed by the Londoners, who embarked on an orgy of extreme violence. Countless innocent Jews were murdered, their estates were plundered and royal treasure was seized. Simon himself was not altogether innocent of the plunder. After some time in the capital he moved on to the Cinque

Ports, but his progress was halted at Rochester Castle, occupied by the staunchly royalist Earl of Warenne.

News of the siege reached Henry. After a five-day march the king's forces successfully relieved Rochester Castle, following which Simon retreated to London. The royalists continued towards the coast. Henry took Tonbridge on 1 May and then headed to Winchelsea, looking to consolidate the loyalty of the Cinque Ports as his regents had done forty-seven years earlier. He succeeded in persuading three of the ports to side with him through sieges, but was once again unable to obtain continuing loyalty.

His forces now low on provisions, the king moved from Battle to Lewes and took shelter at the Priory of St Pancras on 12 May, while Prince Edward and his men stayed at the nearby castle.[6] Simon, meanwhile, marched south from London, accompanied by a large following of Londoners. His forces camped at a small village called Fletching approximately nine miles from Lewes.[7]

Though he was heading a large army, Simon's numbers were smaller than those of the royals. The chronicler Matthew Paris speculates that the size of the king's force was approximately 60,000 compared to 50,000 for the opposition. The large size of the king's force seems a clear indication that many of those involved in the proceedings of 1258 no longer favoured Simon's cause. Among Henry's number were the lords of the marches, the returned Poitevins and most of the barons of the North whose ancestors had become so famous during the first barons' war.

Simon clearly recognized the difficulties he faced. Some of the opposition suggested a peace treaty, and an offer of 50,000 marks was presented to the king in exchange for his agreement to abide by the legislation of 1258 and 1259. Confident in his chances of victory, Henry rejected the offer immediately.[8]

Battle was unavoidable, and the day would prove unforgettable. On the morning of 14 May 1264 Simon's forces marched south from

Fletching. By dawn they were located at the top of the South Downs overlooking Lewes. Edward and his forces had established their head-quarters in Lewes Castle, the property of the Earl of Warenne and located at the north end of the town. To the south was the priory of St Pancras, where Henry and the King of the Romans were staying.

Incredibly de Montfort's forces formed up for battle unnoticed. Some commentators have speculated that attack was carried out with remarkable precision, while others accuse the royalists of dozing. Whatever the truth, Simon discounted any possibility of catching the royalists in their beds. His plan was to attack the priory, not the castle. He was still impeded in his movement by the fall that pro-hibited his journey to France for the Mise of Amiens, but he used the injury to his advantage. Playing on the royalists' knowledge that he usually travelled in a closed carriage, a vehicle of that type was placed in plain view on the northern spur, defended by militiamen from London. The earl, meanwhile, directed his knights from the south, keeping himself out of sight behind his men.

By now the royalists were awake and ready to take to the field. They marched under Henry's royal ensign, a dragon, famed for its impressive design. Henry commanded the centre of his forces, while Richard, the King of the Romans, took the left and Edward the right. The prince took Simon's bait and wrought vengeance on the Londoners for their treatment of his mother. Though the carriage in which Edward believed that de Montfort was travelling was destroyed, Edward's impetuousness got the better of him, however. He pursued the Londoners mercilessly, which took him several miles from the field.

Elsewhere things went less well for the king's forces. Despite their numerical advantage, Edward's poor tactics left them vulnerable. The forces led by Simon and the young Earl of Gloucester over-whelmed the royalist troops on the left. Henry was courageous, but owing to the failings of his son and brother he was now in severe danger. Cornwall was forced to take shelter in a mill, and the king in the priory.

On completing his rout of the Londoners Edward returned to the battlefield. Thinking his charge had been successful, he came back brandishing the prize of Simon's banner, and on realizing his mistake joined combat in the streets of the town. The bodies of victims covered not only the battlefield but the town, too. The townsfolk of Lewes were consumed by panic and remained in fear for several days. The barons, failing initially to capture the royal leaders, attempted in vain to scale the walls of the castle, following which the garrison retaliated by unleashing Greek fire (incendiaries) on the town.

In the chaos many of the king's knights tried to seek refuge in the priory, changing their armour for tunics in a bid to outwit the opposition. The prince took sanctuary in the church of the Franciscans. Others loyal to the king attempted to escape, many losing their lives either in the fighting or through drowning as they attempted to cross the River Ouse.[9] The forces of the Earl of Warenne, allied with the Poitevins, retreated to Pevensey Castle, some twelve miles to the south. Mortimer and the lords of the marches had more success, and the following day they were still fighting.

However, the battle belonged to Simon. Against the odds, victory was his. For the king there was little to do but curse his bad luck and poor judgement. Surrender was unavoidable; the young Earl of Gloucester received his sword. Henry's reputation was dented, as was his son's. The King of the Romans was equally humiliated. As he nervously left the mill, his face blackened and his armour covered in flour, his captors marched him through the town. As the Song of Lewes went:

> Richard, tho thou be ever trichard [trickery]
> Tricken shalt thou never more!

16

The Long March to Evesham

With the King of England and the King of the Romans both in his custody, Simon had the upper hand. The day after the battle Henry acknowledged his formal agreement to new provisions. No copy of the Mise of Lewes has survived, but in principle the king was required to uphold the Magna Carta, the Charter of the Forest and the Provisions of Oxford.[1]

On the orders of the Earl of Leicester a body of arbitrators was established. Surprisingly it included only one Englishman, the Bishop of London, and only two other churchmen, the Archbishop of Rouen and the latest papal legate, Guy Foulques, who was yet to arrive in England. The new arbitrators were instructed that control of the realm was to be in the hands of English-born subjects. To confirm the peace, both Edward and the son of the King of the Romans, Henry of Almain, were handed over to Simon as hostages.

At the time of the battle the new legate was on his way to England with a large body of troops for Henry. Unfortunately for the king he was still in Boulogne at the critical moment. Interestingly, on hearing that he had been chosen as an arbitrator the new legate was dismissive of the new government; he ordered the bishops who supported Simon to appear before him in Boulogne and to return to England with orders of excommunication against the rebels. When the Bishops of Winchester and London, the only two allowed to leave the kingdom, returned to Dover, the interdict notice was torn up and thrown into the sea.[2]

Three days after his surrender the king was taken to Battle, the site of the 1066 conquest, and then via Canterbury and Rochester to London. In keeping with the knightly code he was treated with the greatest respect, but as a ruler he was little more than a puppet of Simon. They reached London around 27 May, taking up residence again at St Paul's. Parliament was announced for 22 June and was attended by four knights from each shire. A new scheme of government was set up, involving Simon, the Earl of Gloucester and the Bishop of Chichester. The most significant introduction was the establishment of a council of nine counsellors to advise the king, three of whom would remain at court at all times, while Hugh Despenser remained as Justiciar.[3]

Despite the reforms, Simon's attempt to take control of the country proved difficult. The marches remained violent, and the royalists who had fled to Pevensey were well defended behind the castle's heavily fortified walls. Almost unnoticed, the Earl of Warenne had escaped to the continent to join the queen, who had gathered an army at Damme. Evidently, news of the planned invasion had reached Simon. Under his instruction Henry wrote to Louis requesting that no relief force should be raised. Concerned by the possibility of military action by Louis or the Queen of England, Simon compelled Henry to raise a force in his own name to meet on a down near Canterbury. Simon arrived there in August and watched over the coastline throughout September. A combination of Henry's letters and adverse wind conditions ensured that no invasion took place.[4]

While the opposition ruled the country, the cloud that remained over the ecclesiastical status of England was starting to have a demoralizing effect on the clergy. A synod was held in October, the same month that Urban died. The clergy had drawn up a protest against the legate's notice of excommunication and interdict, and this was approved on 19 October.[5] Unknown to most people in England the legate Guy had failed to come to England, largely as a result of de Montfort's triumph. London and the Cinque Ports were placed under interdict, and those who favoured Simon were warned to return their allegiance to the king. Finally the legate pronounced excommunication upon Simon himself and the Earls of Gloucester and Norfolk in addition to the Londoners and the people of the Cinque Ports in general.[6]

Henry was at Westminster on 2 October and then at Windsor on 18 November. Under Simon's instruction he was again forced to write to the queen, on this occasion to tell her not to attempt to raise money for his cause through any of his French fiefs, presumably something that Henry was hoping for.

Nevertheless he was not without allies. Later in November an attempt by the marchers to defeat Llewellyn sidetracked Simon. Henry was commanded to summon a conference at Oxford on 30 November, following which the pair travelled to Gloucester, and by 13 December they had arrived in Worcester. After discussions with the marcher lords the Provisions of Worcester was agreed, and after this the lords agreed to leave for Ireland for a year and a day.[7]

Later that month the king was ordered to send out writs for a Parliament at Westminster on 20 January 1265. The gathering proved to be yet another landmark in the history of England. Following from the events of 1258, two knights were sent from every shire in addition to two representatives from every city and borough. Exactly what happened remains open to debate. It can be argued that Simon's actions went a long way towards setting in motion the events that would eventually lead to the House of Commons, but it is also notable that Simon received little support from the earls and barons. At the time of the Battle of Lewes the majority of the nobility fought for the royalists, and even at the January Parliament only five earls and eighteen barons were summoned. Simon's strength lay in the high turn-out among the clergy, but perhaps the most credible feature was that the writs to the cities and boroughs were direct, rather than being channelled through the sheriffs as usual.[8]

By the time of the Parliament Simon had made a partial alliance with Edward, whose willingness to comply was almost certainly heightened by the failure of his mother's invasion. With the exception of the king Edward was undoubtedly the biggest loser from the Mise of Lewes. He had little choice but to release the earldom of Chester and his lands in Wales to the leader of the party in power, and since his surrender to Simon as a hostage he remained under close observation.[9]

The relationship between Simon and the Earl of Gloucester had cooled somewhat since Lewes. Like his father, Gilbert often clashed with Simon over the implementation of reforms, and he was becoming concerned that Simon was abusing his power. Reconciliation was in the air around the time of the Parliament, but further troubles threatened owing to disagreement over Simon's policy on foreign advisers. Despite constant criticism of the king for keeping foreigners in the realm, Simon still had not banned all of them under his own rule. For Gilbert this was unacceptable. At the time of the January Parliament the garrisons at Dover, Windsor and Wallingford were still controlled by foreigners.[10]

Henry remained at Westminster until March and gave his approval to the new constitution on the 14th. Meanwhile all was not well within the party in power. Hot on the accusation that

Simon was abusing his power, a fierce quarrel erupted in Parliament between Simon and the Earl of Derby, who was imprisoned and his lands confiscated. De Montfort's actions, particularly his alliance with Edward, were a step too far for the Earl of Gloucester. Matters between them came to a head following the break-up of Parliament. Accusations flew, mainly concerning Simon's alleged taking in of fugitives. The Earl of Gloucester fled to the marches and was joined soon after by Valence and Warenne with a small band of crossbowmen.

The dispute with Gloucester was potentially disastrous for Simon. Just as in 1259 the baronial party was split, and the possibility of an alliance between Gilbert de Clare and the continuously hostile marcher lords threatened the truce of Worcester. Gloucester was still powerful in the marches; not only did he remain Lord of Glamorgan but he was now also in possession of the forfeit lands in Pembrokeshire of William of Valence.

Simon may have lost Gilbert, but he still had the king, Richard and Edward under his control. The king was taken to Northampton and then to Worcester and Gloucester. While they were in Gloucester Gilbert watched the movements of his new enemy from the Forest of Dean. Henry and Edward left with Simon for Hereford where something of a truce was made between Simon and Gilbert. The outcome was a hastily written proclamation stating that any dissension between them was 'fraudulently invented'.

While both were undoubtedly happy to be back on terms, the peace was still fragile. Henry and Edward remained in captivity, but having agreed to submit to the earl Edward was allowed to ride and hunt. This was a decision de Montfort would regret. While out hunting on 28 May Edward escaped. Whether the guard he was riding with was simply outfoxed or whether he was in league with the prince is unclear. Either way, Edward was able to meet up with Roger Mortimer in the nearby wood and was soon safely behind the walls of Wigmore Castle. The following day Edward met the Earl of Gloucester at Ludlow, following which Gilbert pledged fealty to the prince.[11]

Once again the scene was set for war. Within days of the new alliance Warenne and Valence also pledged their allegiance to Edward. The prince had agreed to uphold the Charters, and now it was he, not the foreign tyrant Simon, who upheld the righteous cause.

Henry was undoubtedly buoyed by Edward's escape. Though he certainly supported his son's cause he had little option but agree to a writ, issued in his name, for war against the prince.[12] Simon's progress was for the first time under threat, however. Despite the submission of the remaining loyalists to Simon's army at Gloucester, June belonged to Edward. Thanks to the defection of the Earl of Gloucester, both his lands and those of the Severn Valley were under the prince's command.

De Montfort's options were limited. His past alliance with Llewellyn allowed him to seek his support, and by 22 June a treaty was agreed between them in the name of the King of England.[13] For Henry this must have been infuriating. Not only was he in league with his long-time enemy against his son, but, worse still, he had been humiliated by Simon, who made large concessions in negotiations with the Welshman. No longer was the Prince of Wales in command of the territories he had held in the past. He was now Prince of all Wales.

Henry's hopes rested with Edward. With both the Earl of Gloucester and the city of Gloucester firmly backing him the marchers were on the warpath. They sought out Simon and the king at Hereford, forcing Simon to make a move.

For de Montfort war was the last resort. If he had remained in Hereford his forces would have been in no position to match his enemies. Heading west, they first fled to the Usk, where they met armed resistance at Newport Bridge, which forced them to retreat into the Usk Valley. Thanks to their alliance with Llewellyn they managed to find some refuge in the hills, but this did not suit their English soldiers. As conditions worsened, a lack of food forced Simon to return to England.[14]

He and Henry went to Monmouth at the end of June and from there back to Hereford.[15] At the end of July Simon and his royal prisoner were still making their way along the Severn Valley. On 2 August they crossed the river at a ford south of Worcester, heading in the direction of Kenilworth Castle. They spent the night of 2 August camped out at Kempsey at one of the manors of the Bishop of Worcester.

Little did either man know that the situation elsewhere had changed significantly. South of Lewes, many of the royalists continued to withstand the onslaught of Simon the younger at Pevensey. Though Simon urgently recalled his son, the young Simon wasted time in London and plundering the countryside. However, when his men set up camp on the last day of July in the shadow of Kenilworth, waiting for his father's troops, there was little obvious sign that Edward was planning an attack.

Simon the elder's forces continued towards their rendezvous. They stayed at the abbey at Evesham on the night of 3 August. What happened next decided the fate of a kingdom. Declaring his wish to eat breakfast before leaving the abbey Simon and the king remained longer than planned. As it grew lighter out-side word came that soldiers had been seen advancing on the town.[16] At first this sounded like good news for Simon: after several months the forces led by his son had at last caught up with them.

Soon, however, it became evident that this assumption was incorrect. Unlike that day in Lewes fifteen months previously, the royalists now had the advantage. When the forces of Edward and Simon the young clashed near Kenilworth, it was Edward who came out on top, dispersing the rebels and forcing Simon the young to take refuge at the castle.

Edward had planned the attack on Evesham carefully, paying particular attention to the geography of the area. As the town was located on the right bank of a bend of the Avon, approachable only by crossing the water or via a narrow stretch of land, almost an isthmus, he carefully positioned his men in such a way as to prevent Simon's forces from escaping. He also stationed Roger Mortimer and his forces across the only other escape route. Simon did not miss the irony of the prince's strategy; he was recorded as saying that Edward had learnt from him.[17]

The Battle of Evesham was fought on 4 August 1265. A storm dominated the skies at the moment of the engagement, thick cloud shrouding the field in darkness on what had begun as a warm summer's day. Edward's horsemen cut down Simon's infantry, consisting mainly of Welshmen present thanks to the treaty with Llewellyn. The earl's men at arms, however, were reported to have fought valiantly, though they were outnumbered.

The core of Simon's forces was overwhelmed. The earl himself was praised for his heroic defence, though this day would be his last. Many great men lost their lives that day. Among them was the capable Justiciar, Hugh Despenser, whose good work in the office has generally been praised ever since. Also meeting his end was Simon's namesake, Peter of Beaudesert. Further to his role at Amiens, history has described this man as the leader of the 'Mad Parliament', in his own way the first ever Speaker of the House of Commons.

Those who were not killed were captured. Among them was King Henry III. To the last he had been forced to remain by his brother-in-law's side, which nearly resulted in his own death.

Scant though the records are, it is believed that the king was wounded and nearly killed by one of Edward's men, only to be spared when he revealed his identity with a desperate cry. Roger of Leyburn allegedly saved him. Edward ensured that his father was taken to a place of safety.

Though the battle was won, the carnage continued. The marchers took out their rage on those who sought to flee, and the bodies of the slain, on both sides, were mutilated by the sword.

And what of Simon de Montfort, the man whose vision was so admired? As was typical of the time, the traitor was beheaded after his death and his head sent as a gift to the wife of Roger Mortimer. This gruesome gesture aside, it was to the king's credit that he did not wish the man who had been variously his brother-in-law, soldier, seneschal and captor to be completely dishonoured. Whether it was in respect for his sister, recognition of his virtues or grudging admiration for the man, he decreed that Simon's remains and those of his son, Henry, should be buried before the altar of the abbey church. In the years that followed it was said that miracles occurred at his place of rest. His memory was treasured, and his body remained at the abbey until the reign of Henry VIII, when what remained of his corpse was further mutilated in the madness of the dissolution of the monasteries.[18] History recognizes his role in the development of Parliament.

17

The Seven-Year Harvest

Edward's victory brought the royalists back to power. Three days after the Battle of Evesham Henry issued a proclamation announcing that he had once more assumed power over the kingdom, while writs were also put out at Worcester asserting that the grants made under Simon were null and void due to their being issued in captivity.[1]

On 8 September Henry held a council at Winchester where forfeiture of the lands belonging to the rebels was formally announced. Another council was held at Windsor on 29 September, attended by the majority of the magnates of State and Church. Henry gave orders that London should submit peacefully, and over the coming days a series of meetings took place among the people, culminating in forty of the city's most prominent citizens being escorted to Windsor. In charge of this was Roger of Leyburn, an associate of the prince. The Londoners submitted on 6 October, following which Henry imprisoned some of their leaders at Windsor and imposed a 20,000-mark fee on the city in return for peace.[2]

The king's actions aroused some discontent. Many of the forfeits were given to his followers or used to pay off debts. Money was also sent to France to pay off the debts incurred by the queen, notably for the army that had remained stationed on the coast in preparation for an invasion.[3]

Away from England, there is evidence to suggest the Pope was largely unaware of recent events. While Simon was still alive, word reached the papacy that he had taken a tithe of ecclesiastical property to aid the revolution. Urban's successor was none other than the legate, Guy, taking the name Clement IV. Clement was vocal in his criticisms, and all of his correspondence and bulls regarding England at this time favoured the king. In a bull put out in September to the new legate, Ottoboni, he directed all who supported the earl to change allegiance or be excommunicated.

News of Edward's success must have been known by mid-September. Clement wrote to Ottoboni to lift the excommunication of Gilbert, Earl of Gloucester, on 22 September. On the same day a bull was issued, granting Henry a tenth of all ecclesiastical property.[4]

Another Parliament met in London on 13 October, where those who had fought against the king were formally disinherited.[5] By now most of the opposition had fled, while others had taken refuge in the baronial strongholds. Though certain members of the defeated party had refused to accept defeat at Evesham, there was no longer a sense of any lasting war. Simon the young remained at Kenilworth, though he had agreed to return his long-time captive, Richard, King of the Romans, and his son Henry of Almain.[6]

Eleanor was back in England at the end of October. Her husband travelled to Canterbury to meet her on 1 November before escorting her back to the capital. Also in her company was the new papal legate, Ottoboni, sent over by Clement to punish the bishops who had sided with the barons, excommunicate disinherited rebels and help restore order. Among the victims were four prelates, including the Bishop of Chichester. Should he have survived, a similar fate would have awaited the Bishop of Worcester, but he died before the legate's arrival.[7]

With the rebels disinherited there now began a scramble for honours among the victors. Edward reclaimed his right to the Earldom of Chester, while the former king of Sicily, Edmund, received some consolation for the loss of the throne by replacing Simon as Earl of Leicester. Another beneficiary was Roger Mortimer, whose gain of lands and franchises had a notable impact on the House of Wigmore.[8]

Though some gained, others lost. Perhaps the biggest victim of Simon's actions was his wife Eleanor, Countess of Leicester. Her family links with the king were not enough to save her. On the orders of the king Eleanor was banished from England for life.[9]

Henry held a Parliament at Northampton at the end of the year, at which time he received the submission of Simon the younger. Negotiations also began to appease Llewellyn. Two years earlier Henry would undoubtedly have been less willing to accept Llewellyn's recent progress, but England in 1265 was a tired and battered country. At this point Henry might have hoped that peaceful submission would be agreeable after seven years of hardship.

Sadly for Henry this was not to be. His decision not to execute any rebels may have won him respect, but his hard-line policy of financially ruining those who survived inspired insurrection. While Kenilworth held out strongly, Simon the younger left the castle and joined rebels on the Isle of Axholme, among the marshes of the lower Trent. This ruthless band maintained themselves throughout the winter, until Edward eventually convinced them to come to terms.

The elements of dissent that remained occupied the king's attention for most of the next year. Henry summoned the military to Oxford on 15 March 1266, ordering their arrival within three weeks. That same month Simon the young had moved south and was causing mischief among the Cinque Ports. In March Edward finally forced entry to Winchelsea, one of the Cinque Ports under Simon's control, and after subduing the town he dealt with a nasty confrontation with a troublemaker named Adam Gordon.

In May further disturbance threatened the king when the Earl of Derby, released after his imprisonment by Simon, raised a revolt in frustration. Henry of Almain defeated him at Chester-field, and the earldom of Derby passed to Prince Edmund.[10]

Henry was in Northampton on 6 May where a Parliament agreed that the provisions of 1258 and 1259 would be implemented in future, though without any restrictions on appointments. At the same Parliament talks took place to bring an end to the situation at Kenilworth. Prior to his departure, Simon the young had stock-piled provisions for the long term. So confident were the troops under siege that when one of the king's messengers was sent there he returned minus a hand.

Since August of the previous year Roger Mortimer had been mercilessly prosecuting the siege of Kenilworth. As time wore on splits had occurred between Mortimer and Gilbert de Clare, requiring the king and Edward to enforce the peace. After leav-ing Northampton, Henry and Edward continued to Kenilworth and during the siege Henry held another Parliament. Terms leading to the Dictum of Kenilworth were made on 24 August. An ancient charter was to be granted to the barons, while the king would be awarded a grant for three years of a tenth from the clergy. The terms for Kenilworth were officially published on 31 October and were accepted by the disinherited on 20 December after they finally ran low on provisions.[11]

Yet the legacy of Simon lived on. Rebellion broke out at Ely in the last quarter of the year, under the direction of John d'Eyville. Norwich and Cambridge were the major casualties of his plundering of much of East Anglia. A similar rebellion occurred in Northumberland under the direction of John de Vescy, who later submitted to Edward.[12]

It was at this time, according to the Scottish chronicler Walter Bower, that among the disinherited flourished the legendary outlaw Robin Hood. Among the lengthy passages of Bower's famous *Scotichronicon* is this startling reference:

> Then arose the famous murderer, Robert Hood, as well as Little John, together with their accomplices from among the disinherited, whom the foolish populace are so inordinately fond of celebrating both in tragedies and comedies, and about whom they are delighted to hear the jesters and minstrels sing above all other ballads.

In 1266 Bower mentioned him again:

> In that year also the disinherited English barons and those loyal to the king clashed fiercely; amongst them Roger de Mortimer occupied the Welsh Marches and John-de-Eyville occupied the Isle of Ely; Robert Hood was an outlaw amongst the woodland briars and thorns. Between them they inflicted a vast amount of slaughter on the common and ordinary folk, cities and merchants.

Though Bower was accurate in saying that d'Eyville and Mortimer remained on the warpath, whether the legendary outlaw really was one of those disinherited is difficult to verify. Trouble in Ely continued throughout 1266 and remained the one area of unrest after Kenilworth.

Henry announced a council at Bury St Edmunds on 21 February 1267, at which forces were summoned to finish off the dissenters. The king continued on to Cambridge the following month. Conflict occurred throughout March and April, as d'Eyville put up a stubborn resistance. Then, in April, Henry heard the shocking news that Gilbert de Clare had taken London and besieged the Tower.

Gilbert's rebellion was once more inspired by the antagonism between himself and Mortimer. A violent spat had occurred at Bury, following which Gilbert had made preparations in the marches to wage war against Mortimer. He entered London through trickery on 8 April, claiming that he wished only to meet with the legate, who was currently shut up in the Tower, along with some of the disinherited who had flocked to him for protection.

The timing of the siege was perfect for Gilbert. Edward had been sidetracked by de Vescy in Northumberland, while Henry was in Cambridge, monitoring the rebellion at Ely. Once more the Londoners rallied. Shortly after, d'Eyville and the Ely fugitives joined in besieging the Tower. On hearing the news Edward marched south. Henry left Cambridge and continued to Windsor and then to London on 5 May with an army of 109 standards. After being denied entry, he took refuge at the Cistercian abbey of Stratford Langthorne, awaiting negotiations for the release of the legate.[13]

Gloucester's desire was perhaps more to make a point rather than to start a full insurrection. Terms were agreed on 6 June, thanks in part to the calming influence of the King of the Romans. Henry entered the city within three days and on this occasion issued no penalties. Gilbert succeeded in winning better terms for the disinherited, and over the following month both he and John d'Eyville regained royal favour. Rebels who remained in Ely were subdued by Edward through a combination of force and diplomacy; they accepted the same terms as had been offered at Kenilworth. With that the second barons' war came to an end.[14]

Quelling the revolt at Ely settled the troubles that had spilled over from Evesham and brought to a long-overdue conclusion the most troubled period of Henry III's reign. The country was back under control and remained so. It was said by one of the chroniclers that Henry 'never fell back into his old ways' of abusing his position and empowering foreigners.[15]

In November 1267 Henry held a Parliament at Marlborough. Reforms were announced in light of the recent troubles; with the exception of the king retaining the right to appoint his own ministers and sheriffs, practically all the amendments introduced in the 'Mad Parliament' remained. When Henry celebrated Christmas with the legate at Winchester he had a lot to be relieved about.[16]

The year 1267 also brought an end to the problems in the marches, at least during Henry's reign. Llewellyn was encouraged by the weakened state of the English. By 1267 he had conquered much of mid-Wales, and had done a lot of damage to Edward's land in Cheshire. As the year wore on Ottoboni and Edward, perhaps somewhat wiser than he had been before the war, were happy to conclude the struggle peacefully. In September Edward and the legate accompanied Henry to Shrewsbury, where negotiations went well. Llewellyn gained enormously from the tired state of England, and two weeks after the initial agreement on 25 September ratification was agreed at Montgomery.[17]

In spring 1268 Henry allowed the legate to hold a council at St Paul's, during which Ottoboni sanctioned what later became celebrated as his 'Constitutions', subsequently the canonical foundation of Church government. He also preached about the need for an eighth crusade. In midsummer Henry held a Parliament at

Northampton, marking the occasion on which Edward and several nobles took up the cross. The legate left England at the start of August 1268, three months before Clement IV died.[18] In November Henry held a Parliament at Westminster, where he bestowed countless honours on Edward. He spent Christmas there, as he did for the rest of his life.[19] The Easter Parliament of 1269 largely involved money-lending regulations to resolve issues left over from the Magna Carta, while in August Henry agreed a treaty with Magnus of Norway concerning trade and mutual protection.[20]

On 13 October Henry held an assembly at Westminster, attended by many, including delegates from the cities and boroughs, confirming that de Montfort's efforts were by no means in vain. Westminster Abbey was at last completed, and Henry was present to attend the magnificent consecration ceremony. Its creation was a work of architectural and engineering genius. As at Rheims, the glorious apse, surrounded by several beautiful chapels, incorporated Gothic features such as flying buttresses, pointed arches, rose windows and ribbed vaulting. Its Englishness was registered through the use of single aisles and a long nave, sadly never completed during Henry's lifetime. In keeping with Henry's usual style, Purbeck marble was used for the columns, as at Guildford. Of the former church, the Norman nave remained for a further century, but this was replaced when funds allowed. Only the round arches and supporting columns of the undercroft and cloisters survived from the time of the Saxon king. At this point the bones of the Confessor were brought into their new magnificent home. Westminster was a success, and it has survived ever since.

While Henry watched the ceremony with quiet satisfaction, the Holy Land was still at war. Henry's request for a twentieth of movables to aid the crusade was discussed and granted.

Nevertheless he was released from his crusading vow on condition that Edward went in his place.[21] A Parliament of magnates met in April 1270 and arranged its collection to aid the expedition led by Prince Edward.[22] The eighth crusade began in 1270, and the ninth followed in 1271. Edward left Henry for the final time at Winchester Castle in August 1270. On the 5th of that month he took leave of the clerics in the chapter house, asking that they pray for him in his absence. He left Dover on 19 August.

It was also in that year that the great King of France, Louis IX, died in Tunis. Like Henry III he had come to the throne as a minor, and he reigned for forty-four years. In many ways Louis stands alone as a triumphant figure in European history, a man who possessed not only great piety but rare strength of conviction. During his reign he had succeeded in overseeing administrative changes that developed his country and won over the King of England. Though his crusades had been a failure, his goodness was widely adored. He did not share the extravagance of his fellow kings, or even the popes, having more sober tastes in food, wine and dress, and he was often less fussy than most. He preferred conversation to the songs of the minstrels and was never known to say anything negative about anyone. He shared Henry's commitment to feeding the poor and gave alms regularly. Nothing better explains his personality than a conversation with his later biographer, John of Joinville. On one occasion the king asked him whether he washed the feet of the poor on Maundy Thursday. When the man replied no, what a terrible idea, Louis replied, 'That is a very wrong thing to say, for you should never scorn to do what our Lord himself did as an example to us.'[23]

In the same year as Louis's passing England acquired a holy relic. A phial of blood had been purchased by Richard from the Count of Flanders in 1267, its authenticity assured by the Patriarch of Jerusalem. In 1270 it made its way to England and was presented to Richard's abbey at Hayles by his son. Over the next few years a new section of the abbey was built to house the vessel, encouraging pilgrims from all around to see the Holy Blood.

As winter progressed, Henry became ill at Westminster. He wrote to Edward on 6 February 1271 saying that he was beyond hope of recovery, though things had improved by April. He was informed later that year that Clement had been replaced by Gregory X while still with Edward in the Holy Land. The remainder of the year passed relatively quietly, but after Christmas Henry suffered another bout of sickness.[24]

His health continued to fail as the new year progressed, forcing him to write to Philip III in May 1272 excusing himself from paying homage for Aquitaine.[25] He was grieved by the passing of his grandson, Edward's son, John, on 1 August 1271, and on 2 April 1272 Richard Earl of Cornwall also died. His lands had been fully restored to him after his release in 1265, following which he spent much of his last four years returning to manage affairs in Germany. In 1269 he married his third wife and was back in England for the translation ceremony of Edward the Confessor at Westminster Abbey and to mediate peace between Edward and Gloucester. His fragile health was further worsened by news of the murder of his son, Henry of Almain, by the younger de Montfort, and in December 1271 he was stricken with paralysis. He died in April and was buried at Hayles Abbey alongside his second wife, Sanchia. Like his brother he oversaw the foundation of many religious houses and remains the only Englishman to rule over the Holy Roman Empire.[26]

Richard's death had a profound effect on the king, who was now one of a few remaining figures of his era. He summoned the strength to see off a dangerous riot in Norwich in August and soon returned to Winchester, the city of his birth.[27]

While making preparations for Christmas at Winchester he died on Wednesday 16 November. He spent his last hours at Westminster in the company of a large number of magnates. He heard confession and requested that his debts be repaid and his remaining possessions distributed among the poor. On 20 November his body, richly dressed and wearing a crown, was buried in Westminster Abbey. It would have warmed him that his burial coincided with the day of St Edmund the Martyr, one of his favourite kings. His heart was presented to the Abbess of Fontevraud in 1292, as he had promised some years before, while his body was buried in the abbey. Perhaps it was equally fitting that the exact location of his tomb was the spot where once the remains of St Edward the Confessor had also lain. Throughout his life it was that king whose memory King Henry III had most striven to uphold.[28]

It was said that his body 'shone more gloriously in death than he did in life'.

18

IN HISTORY AND IN MEMORY

The death of King Henry III brought with it the beginning of the reign of Henry's 33-year-old son, Prince Edward. At the time Edward was unaware he was King of England. He had remained at Acre from May 1271 to September 1272, awaiting reinforcements, before being forced to return home. His voyage took him to Sicily where he learnt from Charles of Anjou, brother of the late Louis IX, of the treble tragedy that had befallen his family: first the death of his son, followed by those of his father and uncle. It was noted with great interest that Edward showed more sadness for his father than his son. When questioned on the matter, he replied to Charles that while a man can have many sons he has only one father.

As the New Year dawned, Edward continued through Italy, receiving warm greetings wherever he travelled. Over the Alps he passed into Savoy where he was greeted by a large number of English prelates before proceeding into France and then on to Gascony. By 2 August 1274 he was back in England, and on the 18th he entered London and was crowned the following day. With this, the 35-year reign of Edward I finally began, during which time the tall man known as 'Longshanks' would leave his mark on English history and imagination.

Henry III's death in a sense marked the final exodus of the old guard that began with the death of Louis and included the passing of the king's brother and Boniface of Savoy. Just as in France, the new decade would bring with it the start of a new era, not only a new queen and dukes but several new prelates, including the first Archbishop of Canterbury for more than a quarter of a century.

Henry III was sixty-five years old when he died. His death was widely mourned but met with mixed reviews among the chroniclers. It was the opinion of Matthew Paris that Henry 'loved foreigners above all Englishmen and enriched them with innumerable gifts'.[1] Others held an altogether different view. When the rumour of Henry's death reached the ears of the chronicler of Tewkesbury Abbey in 1263 he made no criticism. Instead he celebrated the king as 'a lover and adorner of the holy church; a protector and consoler of religious orders; a vigorous governor of the kingdom; a well-versed restorer of peace and quiet; a generous giver of alms to the poor; always a pious helper of widows and orphans'.

How, some might wonder, can a man inspire such seemingly irreconcilable perceptions? Though many of history's key figures can be variously viewed as good or bad, even after 700 years the long reign of Henry III is difficult to understand fully. Having come to the throne at an early age, when the nation was at war, it is difficult to know for sure how much of his early reign was conducted under his own influence. Equally important, as his reign was heavily pressurized by demands for reform, and their implementation, it is less easy to pinpoint exactly where responsibility lies in the failures and successes of his administration. Even more difficult is the task of gaining insight into the king's personality. For those who lived during the turbulence of the thirteenth century there were no easy psychological generalizations to fall back upon, nor were a man's supporters or critics obliged to think of their king as intelligent or stupid or make any other such judgement.

Had Henry enjoyed the typical life of a prince, brought up in seclusion to become gradually accustomed to the role of state-craft and kingship, his reign might have been easier to define. It is often no surprise when a prince or princess who takes the throne in adulthood subsequently reigns in a way that reflects the beliefs inculcated in them in childhood. When studying the life of James I of England, for example, it is not difficult to under-stand how his beliefs were often affected by the personality of his tutors. For Henry III, however, we can make no such compar-isons. His reign began as an orphan. He had lost his father to dysentery, and he lost a mother to greed. Worse still, his reign began in the middle of a war that he played no part in starting.

It is hard enough to know what it meant to be a king of Eng-land in 1216 but much harder when the king was a boy. That he was the first child king of the Plantagenet dynasty makes com-parisons impossible – even the similarly unfortunate Ethelred the Unready from the House of Wessex cannot be compared in this way. For this reason studying the reign of Henry III is a com-plex task.

Taking the years 1216–34, it is useful to break them down into three periods. During 1215–17 the kingdom was in the grip of war, and circumstances forced the legate and William Marshal to take control. Most would argue that the regents did their job well, and the king's position was secured by their triumph. By 1218 the papal legate Gualo had been replaced, and in his absence others interfered. The role of Marshal was still of paramount importance, but the meddlesome personalities of Hubert, des Roches and, briefly, Pandulf undoubtedly left the king more an outsider in running the government than an insider. Arguably,

Marshal's death without assigning a new regent exacerbated the problem. The legate's departure cost the young king a close ally and father figure; the death of William Marshal was perhaps an even greater loss. Influence passed to less worthy figures, and it was during this period that Henry's kingship really began. It seems likely that the uncertainty he experienced at this time left him with a streak of insecurity that he never overcame. His ignorance of state affairs, particularly during his minority, is more difficult to pinpoint, and some might argue that this was surprising given that he came to the throne so young and reigned for so long. Was he not a quick learner? From the accounts of contemporary commentators it seems that the young king did not lack intelligence, ambition or a sense of adventure.[2]

As one would expect, the Henry who reached his majority in 1227 had matured and developed in many respects compared with the young boy who ascended the throne. In 1216 his accession had been unexpected: as a king, he was untrained, unprepared and forced to accept the trust and guidance of others. In 1227 he had already been king for eleven years. As a military leader he showed good early ambition, particularly in Wales and in regaining the royal castles. He showed signs of skill at diplomacy, during which time he created an early rapport with Alexander II. As an administrator there is less to go on. From that perspective the actions and outcomes of the period 1216–27 can largely be explained by the king's youth, the impact of the recent war and the implementation of new legislation. The decisions made by the kingdom, rather than the king himself, reflect in large part the personalities of his regents and advisers, themselves a mixture of Englishmen and foreigners.

But somewhere along the line the boy became a man, capable of ruling in his own right. By 1223 papal authority granted him the opportunity to become his own king, but there is little evidence that anything significantly changed. The dismissal of his tutor, des Roches, in 1227 might be taken as a sign that Henry was moving forward, but the next five years belonged more to Hubert than to him. With the exception of Henry's military campaign in France, there is little to indicate that he took much initiative at that point. During the period 1227–32 was Henry overly relaxed in his approach to kingship, or was he intimidated and dominated by his more experienced counsellors? Complaints levelled against the Justiciar by the magnates might suggest the latter, but, if so, why did the king not dispose of him? His decision to oust the Justiciar in 1232, if not entirely owing to the influence of his former tutor, des Roches, perhaps finally displayed a willingness to assert himself.

But there are other clues about Henry's kingship. Among the first things he did on dismissing Hubert was to order an inquiry into the amount of royal treasure that had been paid into the exchequer during Hubert's tenure, debts that were still owed to the king and any other matter subject to the Justiciar's authority. Was this investigation evidence of his earlier laxity in controlling affairs of state or of Hubert's powerful hold over him? The fact that Henry almost completely changed the government that year might suggest he had at last decided to make his own appointments, yet the continuing influence of des Roches calls this into question. If these changes were the work of des Roches, his subsequent decision to sack des Roches would show he had learnt his lesson. Whatever the reason, events during 1232–4 confirm that Henry lost his appetite for employing a senior magnate. No longer would any of Henry's old advisers or mentors have a significant effect on government.

It is difficult to accept that a king approaching twenty-five years of age could have been so ill-informed of what was happening in his own realm. If we accept the chroniclers' attribution to him of 'simplicity', we might be able to explain his behaviour as ineptitude. Yet other aspects of his life demonstrate a more gifted nature. As a young boy he was praised for his potential. He was described as intelligent; some even went as far as precocious. If this were true, we might have expected the young Henry III to be a 'chosen boy' – a king in the Arthurian mould. Looking back on his reign, particularly his role in the creation of Westminster Abbey and other achievements in the field of architecture, it is difficult to rule out the suggestion that he was indeed gifted, in some areas at least.

As a boy he certainly showed the potential for greatness. His childhood promise blossomed in adulthood into a wide range of interests, particularly artistic. As an adult he possessed many fine qualities. He was personally affable and courteous, and his meetings with Matthew Paris and Louis IX demonstrate that he was easy to talk to, often taking a great interest in the matters under discussion. His sudden and fierce temper showed him to be a true Plantagenet, but he was also easily appeased. If he is compared to his ancestors, the similarities are less note-worthy than the differences. He was indifferent to hunting and did not share Richard I's love of tournaments. Though he displayed some military audacity in the early years of his majority, and again in 1242 and 1253, he was less ambitious on the conti-nent than some of his predecessors and preferred to be at peace with France and Wales rather than extended military cam-paigns. He travelled and enjoyed sightseeing but, unlike his father, preferred to return to his favourite palaces at Woodstock, Winchester, Westminster, Windsor, Clarendon and Marlborough or to visit the religious houses that he adored. His travels spanned long periods and relatively small distances. In times of peace he remained for several weeks or months in the same place.

It is one thing to study a man but another to study a king. Under no circumstances can the study of a monarch be complete without understanding those who came before and immediately after him. Few historians who have studied the reign of Henry's father have denied the importance of John's submission to Innocent III in 1213. Many, particularly his critics, would even argue that this event went a long way towards defining his reign. Something similar may be said of Henry III. Thanks to the papacy John nearly lost a kingdom, but in 1215 he kept one. In Henry's case the importance of Gualo cannot be underestimated, and his letters to the popes, particularly Innocent III and Honorius III, reveal a special bond between mother Church and 'beloved son'. A pope writing to a king might see this relationship as solely spiritual. To a child who had become an orphan there was perhaps more to the role of the legate than merely a spiritual or temporal adviser. Indeed, the writings of Honorius III to Gualo reflect as much. More intriguing still was how this relationship went on to affect the king's personality and rule. Whereas his father's affiliation with the papacy was a combination of diplomacy and fear, for Henry III it was altogether more meaningful. Unlike his father, Henry was deeply religious. He took great delight in religious festivities, none more so than the translation of the relics of St Thomas or the acquisition of the Holy Blood. He often took the sacraments and sometimes attended Mass three or four times in a day. He enjoyed the practice of pressing or kissing the hand of the celebrant and was often noted for walking in quietly should a Mass already be taking place. During the 1240s he saw to it that over a hundred paupers were fed daily, sometimes even a thousand. When he travelled to France he left orders for the poor to remain fed in his absence and showed similar generosity to the French when in Paris. On the death of his sister, Isabella, he ordered 100,000 people to be fed in her honour.

It could be argued that this is unsurprising. Do those raised in a heavily religious environment not themselves follow a similar path? But if that were necessarily so, surely the Vatican-raised Frederick II would have been a stout supporter of the papacy rather than waging war against it. Equally strange is how Henry's own religious bearing differed considerably from his ancestors'. Unlike his father he was not an atheist; unlike his uncle he did not go on a crusade. He was often outstandingly generous; indeed, much of his spending was inspired by religious motives. He donated a great deal of money to shrines and gave generously when on pilgrimage. He founded religious houses, including Netley Abbey in Hampshire in 1239, endorsing with it the mission of the Cistercians, and Ravenstone in Buckinghamshire in 1255. His riches also brought the Dominicans to Canterbury and Bamburgh, and similar gifts attracted the Franciscans to Winchester and Nottingham. He gave generously to hospitals and other religious houses, including Whitby and Chertsey, both of which he visited more than once.

In other areas his characteristics are less easy to define. His squandering of wealth, particularly to enrich personal favourites, was seen as a sign of generosity by those who loved him but wastefulness by his enemies. Unlike earlier kings he spent all of his life in England, except for the occasional excursion to Wales, Scotland or France, yet to his critics he was more of a Poitevin than an Englishman.

What it meant to be an Englishman at that time is not easy to define. Unlike now, there was no clear notion of patriotism. If the question had been put to Henry II or one of his sons, they would probably have been confused. Every king since William the Conqueror was of Norman descent, and they ruled not only over England but duchies and counties in many parts of modern-day France. Henry II was the most ambitious of the English kings, commanding an Angevin empire that extended as far as the Pyrenees. Was it also not said by Richard I that he cared 'not an egg' for England? John was perhaps an even better example of what it meant to be a King of England at the time. He was described as the most purely Poitevin of Henry II's children: he was of medium height with dark hair, and his features were unmistakably southern. He had been brought up in Fontevraud in the care of the clergy and, aside from his birth, did not see England until the age of seven.[3] As the youngest son of a king he was destined for a different life. His father's original intention was for John to be a great lord in Wales and Normandy.[4] In 1183 Henry also demanded that Richard, heir to the throne, relinquish Aquitaine in John's favour. Within a year John invaded Aquitaine, laying waste to Poitou, before becoming King of Ireland in 1185. There is no clear evidence from any of this that he felt much affinity with England.

During the early years of Henry III's reign, also, little that is English can be found. The dominant language of the court was French, and it was a matter of small consequence that the rebel barons called on a Frenchman, Louis, to be the saviour of England. But within a couple of years this had perhaps begun to change. By the time Falkes de Breauté had surrendered his mighty castle at Bedford, the last of the great foreigners had been defeated. For an assessment of the reign of Henry III this was significant. The rebel barons, particularly the northerners in 1214, had shown clear opposition to John's policies abroad. It has often been argued that the Great Charter was itself an attempt to curb the Angevin empire. During Henry III's rule the magnates' lack of enthusiasm for spending English resources on foreign campaigns indicates that similar sentiments persisted even two generations after Bouvines.

The rise in national identity made a mark on the events of 1232–4, culminating in the dismissal of des Roches. By that time Henry was well into his majority. Between 1234 and 1258 his foreign policy was guided predominantly by French domestic policy and the continuing crusade in the south, especially the undertaking, and subsequent failure, of the Poitou endeavour in 1242. In Wales Henry's early attempts at subduing the hostile uprisings of Llewellyn ap Iorwerth were constrained by poor finances and military weakness, though he later showed better judgement in placating Llewellyn and winning over his sons. During this period relations between England and Wales improved notably compared with the earlier years.

The other significant influence on foreign policy was England's position as a papal vassal. Support from the papacy brought stability to England during Henry's minority, but in his majority it posed his greatest challenges. The Popes' desire for further crusades, and their collections of tithes in the 1230s, 1240s and 1250s, placed previously unheard-of demands on the clergy, and consequently England suffered. Throughout the twelfth century the papacy was beginning to develop something of a theocratic influence over Europe, and by the time of Henry III this had reached its zenith. It is either a blessing or a curse that Henry came to power after the brilliant papacy of Innocent III. With power came influence and great cost. Many of the religious houses of Europe suffered financial exploitation. They were certainly not poor, but the continued burden on their resources severely compromised their ability to function, and worse still it swayed the allegiance of the clerics. It was perhaps for this reason that Henry found it easier to confer clerical offices on foreigners rather than the shrewder English, who would have tried to resist the new wave of papal demands. Undoubtedly the worst problem for the English Church was the papal tax on churchmen's revenues. This levy, originally a one-off, became firmly entrenched during Henry's reign and a source of increasing friction.

The biggest problem for the king, however, was the provision that the Pope could install his own candidates in key appointments. True, many of these involved only cathedral offices, and many went to Englishmen, but they still demonstrated who was in control, and they infuriated the magnates. Yet Henry's reign had survived with papal support; without it a French invasion would have been inevitable in 1213. It is no coincidence that Henry's ill-advised invasion of Poitou in 1242 came at the only time when the Holy See was vacant. His attempts to withstand the Pope's demands in the late 1240s brought him brief support from Parliament, but it nearly caused England to be put under interdict. When Henry backed down he lost allies, but he arguably saved the country from a greater threat. The best example of that threat comes from the later years of Frederick II, who risked losing his empire without papal support.

As to Henry's appearance, we have little to go on. If the account given by Nicholas Trevet can be accepted he was a man of some 5 feet 6 inches or 1.68 metres in height, with a lean build and potentially strong of stature, but without the physical presence of his son or uncle. A drooping eyelid perhaps limited his ability to focus and may have affected his confidence. His effigy is marked by several lines across the forehead, as can be expected of a man who lived to sixty-five. That he was of sound constitution is evident from his long reign, and he was of generally pleasant appearance from what is known of his family history.

If Henry's temperament and piety won him respect, his prowess on the battlefield has been the subject of more critical scrutiny. For Henry's critics, this is where most of his failings lay. If he had been a better warrior, victory against the Welsh,

French, Gascons, Poitevins and Anjouvins could have been his, and he might even have led a successful crusade.

Exactly how important military calibre was to the making of a good king is worthy of investigation. It is true that in those times military courage was a requirement. Though seemingly not short of ambition, Henry appears to have lacked the bravado of many of his forebears. Less easy to determine is the impact that his physical characteristics had on his abilities in battle and as a military leader. Both his son and his uncle outdid Henry in physical presence and bravery, but that alone did not make them good or bad kings. Even tyrants rarely lack courage or intelligence. The successes enjoyed by his son Edward I, his uncle Richard I and even his brother-in-law Simon de Montfort were achieved less as a result of their physical prowess than the sound planning that preceded them. Indeed it was said of those men that they could see their opponents' weaknesses before they could themselves. By comparison, Henry's campaign of 1230 lacked direction, and the 1242 mission lacked both direction and drive. It was the view of the historian T.F. Tout that Henry's mission to Gascony before Edward's marriage also began in the same misguided way. His endeavours in Wales suffered from different problems; battle was often joined in the hills or in areas where the English were deprived of food. His war with Richard Marshal was perhaps an even greater illustration of how bad things could get when Henry was unprepared.

The two greatest battles of his time reflect more credit on his opponents than on the king. Lewes, lying on a peninsula, was lost through the failings of Prince Edward but also the tactical brilliance of Simon de Montfort. The king's own strategy and fighting prowess deserve little criticism. Personally he fought bravely, and his strategy stood a good chance of working, but the great weakness at Lewes was the royalists' inability to learn from

Simon. The royalists' victory at Evesham was praiseworthy, but Edward, rather than Henry, was the victor on that occasion.

Henry's best feature as a warrior was his knowledge of siege-craft. His experience at London, Newark and Lincoln during his early years taught him, perhaps, more than he realized. His greatest conquests as a king were at Bedford in 1224, Mirebeau in 1230 and Kenilworth in 1267. Bedford in particular is worthy of special mention. During the siege Henry ordered a belfry, a wooden siege tower, to be constructed and manned by archers and crossbowmen. According to Roger of Wendover this was so effective that no defender would dare remove his armour for fear of being shot. Similar tactics eventually conquered Kenilworth, though in that case his own knowledge had also cost him – his prudent spending on reinforcements turned a good castle into a great castle, which he then gave away. Henry's fortifications at the Tower of London, Dover and Kenilworth were unquestionably among the finest engineering accomplishments of his reign. As discussed in Chapter 11, Henry took a great interest in fortifications and spent as much as a tenth of his own money wisely strengthening his castles' defences.

So why did he fortify so many castles? A military historian might praise the brilliant engineering of many of his castles, which left a lasting legacy. But on another level one might speculate on Henry's keenness that his castles should be able to withstand outsiders. His early childhood revolved around conquest and the invasion of his father's kingdom, and his own early reign was dominated by the rise of the rebel barons and attacks from overseas. His throne was the target of a usurper before he had even attended his coronation. In some ways these experiences served him well. During his reign England did not suffer a single successful invasion from abroad. Moreover Henry would have been only too aware that almost every Plantagenet king before him had been the target of rebellion, usually by a family member. Henry II had famously faced revolts by all of his sons, while Henry III's uncle, Richard I, was plagued by the ambitions of his brother John. It is strange to think that, of all the Plantagenet kings, John was the only one who never faced such an attack. In 1215 reform was the only practical cause the rebel barons could turn to, but even in the darkest days of 1215 there was no serious call for the king to lose his crown.

Thankfully for England, Henry learnt from some of John's mistakes. But, whereas his father kept his friends close and his enemies closer, Henry's stance was altogether more detached. He kept his friends close and his enemies outside the walls. It is no coincidence that his eleven trips to the Tower of London were all when he was under the most pressure, particularly in 1238 and the 1260s. If his attempts to fortify his castle were as much to protect himself as his kingdom, the effects were largely the same.

Some kings rule through fear, and others do not. Lacking the ruthless streak of some of his forebears, perhaps the biggest challenge that faced Henry III was knowing exactly who his friends were. The first barons' war sought to address his father's wrongs by strengthening his enemies, but it ended with a better solution implemented under the guidance of his friends. Gualo and the ageing Earl Marshal did their jobs admirably; however, those who followed had more to gain personally. Hubert was capable but defensive; Pandulf was inquisitive but ultimately a Roman; des Roches was equally capable but always potentially treacherous. The years 1219–32 were a difficult time for Henry, but those that followed proved a great education in kingship. For the first time Henry was making his own choices. These first ventures led to failure, and at this point he probably never doubted himself more.

The events of 1236–39 were also extremely important to his later reign. The adverse consequences of his alliance with Frederick were not his fault, but through his submission to the papacy he was forced to endure them. His marriage in 1236 was an altogether different affair. Aside from his links with the King of France, invaluable in the latter part of his reign, he gained no material benefits from the marriage.

After 1234 he had few allies. Having seen those he loved capable of treason he was nervous about who was with him and who was not. There was no better example than the man who married his sister. The breakdown of relations with Simon in 1239, and again in 1252, must have had a major impact on Henry. How could he have trusted this man and got it so wrong? Assessing Simon's character is equally difficult. In the past Simon has been hailed as a great hero or, alternatively, castigated as a man who sought only personal gain. Perhaps both views are valid up to a point. As one historian of recent times has remarked, it is in the inconsistencies of a person, not the bland generalizations, that one is really able to get to know their character. Simon's brilliant inconsistencies certainly defined him, and whether he was pursuing selfless reform or personal benefit the effects he had on England were lasting.

The reforms introduced in 1258 are difficult to characterize. Were they the outcome of a natural progression or a result of the king's failings? According to the anonymous tribute of 1263, Henry was 'a lover and adorner of the holy church; a protector and consoler of religious orders; a vigorous governor of the kingdom; a well-versed restorer of peace and quiet; a generous giver of alms to the poor; always a pious helper of widows and orphans'. He was certainly a good friend of the Church and a generous benefactor, but whether he was a vigorous governor or even a restorer of peace and quiet is more debatable. That he was easily appeased and preferred truces to war is apparent. If he was a vigorous governor, he certainly lacked an iron fist. Had he not been forced to endure the oppressive demands of the papacy the period 1239–57 might have passed in a more tranquil fashion. Since the later years of John's reign a lack of money had impeded his progress against the Welsh and overseas, and this certainly continued well into Henry III's reign.

There were times when Henry proved himself to be a capable administrator. The period between 1234 and 1257, when he ruled without a justiciar, passed largely successfully. Problems with the currency illustrated the financial pressures on him and perhaps a lack of control, but at least the government prevented mutilation of the coinage.

It must not be forgotten that in important ways Henry's was the first reign of its type. Never before 1215 had a monarch been so dependent on his own people. The effects of the charter at Bristol began a process of change, both in the practicalities and in the mindset of the people. The new legislation of 1217 brought with it a new Magna Carta and Forest Charter, and their reissue in 1225 set the tone for Henry's majority. By 1225 the myth of the Magna Carta had already taken hold, and its reissue in 1237 and 1253 made the changes irreversible. By 1234 the role of the King of England was already very different from twenty years earlier. Effective cooperation with the barons and senior churchmen was essential rather than merely important. Yet, despite Henry's financial troubles, no extraordinary taxation was implemented in England between 1237 and 1270.[5] If he had adhered more closely to the Charters he might have succeeded in obtaining more aid and more swiftly, but there is little reason to see his behaviour as being responsible for what was to come.

Despite de Montfort's defeat at Evesham on that stormy day in August 1265, the fires of the previous decade left a lasting impression on England. The terms of the Dictum and the events that followed ensured that the legacy of the Provisions and the Great Charter would not be consigned to history. At his first Parliament, dated two weeks after Easter 1275 at Westminster and attended by all the leaders of the kingdom, Edward set out his intentions from the beginning. The key principle was that any law that had become ineffective through either disorder or past mistakes should be rectified. Henry had learnt from his past mistakes and ruled peacefully in his final years, and Edward aimed to do likewise.

The failures of the past inspired Edward, but so did the successes. He believed his rule would be stronger if his subjects loved him, and this approach guided his reign. He inherited not only the restraints imposed on his father's government but its debts. As a consequence, war with Wales remained a constant threat, and peace with France and Scotland was difficult to maintain. In 1295 war with France and Scotland were both pressing issues. For success in either Edward needed the support of his magnates, and in November of that year he called what historians have dubbed the 'model' Parliament. Among those who attended were two knights from every shire and two burgesses from every borough. His behaviour on this occasion bore more than a passing resemblance to de Montfort's Parliaments of 1259 and 1265, and experiments with the constitution continued throughout his reign.[6]

The impact of the changes during Henry III's reign on the development of the political system and the life of the country is difficult to quantify. It is perhaps appropriate to describe them as part of a process of gradual evolution towards democratic government, but this is of course a judgement made with hindsight rather than the attitude of the king himself. The progression from the coronation charter of Henry I through to the model Parliament of 1295 did not come about through the actions of any one king, nor were they necessarily intended: the personal grievances of de Montfort, the conditions of the common people and papal demands concerning Sicily also played their part in shaping the eventual outcome.

By the end of the reign of Henry II a shift was discernible in the way England's magnates saw themselves. Richard's long absence allowed the magnates to expand their influence at the king's expense, and John's attempts to redress the situation only brought conflict. Change was already under way, though the immediate outcome might have been different had Henry III been a more dominant individual. He liked peace, and for much of his reign he lived in peace. His attempts to rule in the manner of his forebears, or for that matter his brothers-in-law, were perhaps a sign of his capacity to be swayed rather than his own ambition. At times his willingness to relinquish control did more harm for peace than his attempts to repudiate the Charters.

Perhaps the period between the battles of Lewes and Evesham best illustrate what it meant to be a king of England. While Henry was in captivity the Crown effectively belonged to Simon, and as the latter assumed power he, too, aroused discontent: the champion of all that was good himself came to be seen as a tyrant. If the great Simon de Montfort could not rule in peace, who could? This question puts the issue of Henry's capacities as a king into perspective.

Despite the conflicts the thirteenth century was generally a good time to be an Englishman. During Henry's reign England prospered. This was a period not only of political evolution but of cultural development. Henry's artistic eye had a profound effect on the development of the cathedrals and abbeys and altered the face of England's towns and cities. He embraced ideas and cultures from the continent and commissioned numerous paintings, including those at the Tower of London, and his favourite palaces at Woodstock, Westminster and Windsor. Those in the castle at Windsor, in particular, helped transform it into one of the finest in Europe. His tendency to listen to the advice of his new favourites, though perhaps a political weakness, was also a sign of his openness to new things.

This was a time of rapid development in literature, too. It was customary for the knightly class to be well versed in French and Latin, the majority speaking what was later called Anglo-French. Relations with France brought a steady influx of ideas and culture to England, despite a pronounced antipathy towards the French. Self-improvement was seen as a virtue, and Englishmen frequently left their country to study in Paris. Latin was, and remained, the language of the Church, while the French 'romances' were a popular form of entertainment among the upper classes. Among the most famous was the *Roman de la Rose*, a poetic allegory on the subject of courtly love. In 1225 a biography of William Marshal was written – a rags-to-riches tale. This was also the time that the Arthurian fables captured hearts in both France and England.

University life prospered. The gifted sons of Europe flocked to Paris or Bologna and increasingly to Oxford. The university, founded during the reign of Henry II, flourished under Henry III, and by 1255 it rivalled the great universities on the continent. The teachings of great scholars such as Grosseteste and Roger Bacon won the university great fame. Cambridge University also dates from this period. Also around that time, though sadly in little more than a passing footnote, students from Cambridge made a short-lived attempt to start a university at Northampton.[7]

Nothing gives a greater insight into Henry's character than his relationships with his family. In spite of his faults, he never wavered in his devotion. He loved his wife and his family, and no air of scandal ever touched his marriage. For the first time since William the Conqueror nothing blameworthy could be said against a King of England. He was kind to his friends, and kinder still to his family. During his life he enjoyed a special relationship with both his sons, and with his daughters, and wept copiously on the death of his daughter, Katherine.

Examples of his devotion are easily found. Writing to the Constable of Windsor in 1242, Henry instructed that Edward must not be deprived of the best wines, while the king also initiated the capture of a baby goat for the sickly Katherine to play with at Swallowfield.

He faced many challenges, the most telling of which have already been analysed in detail. During his reign Llewellyn ap Iorwerth demanded formal recognition as Prince of Wales. This was also a time when the object of the crusades changed. The disunity over the Cinque Ports at the end of John's reign left the coast susceptible to attack, but during Henry's reign this changed. Over the next century the ports from Sussex to Kent played a large role in the defence of the realm and dominance over the high seas. As history would later recall, after 1217 England ruled the waves.[8]

As for the chroniclers, it is unsurprising that their opinions differed depending on whether their allegiance lay with or against him. Matthew Paris and Roger of Wendover did not enjoy the luxury of viewing Henry III's reign with the benefit of hindsight. However, they made no effort to disguise his good qualities. Had he not been a king he might have been remembered as a good man. His piety was as sincere as any man's in his time, even rivalling some of the popes and archbishops. Had his life been concerned solely with improvements to his castles and the promotion of architecture there is equally little reason to find fault.

But a good man does not necessarily make a great king, and it is in this capacity Henry III will inevitably be judged first and foremost. For 700 years his failings have been his greatest claim to fame, and his attempt to win the throne of Sicily was particularly egregious. His extravagance and poor planning came at the worst possible time, and the failings of his closest advisers brought more harm than good. Nevertheless the reforms that limited his kingship were not the only important features of his reign. For the majority of his rule England made peaceful progress. The barons, though at times restless, were largely placated through quiet negotiation. He avoided many of the difficulties of his forebears, particularly long-term conflict abroad. If he is to shoulder blame for the financial burdens placed on the country by the papacy, it is equally right that he should receive credit for the benefits. England's relations with the papacy brought links with Europe and stability. As a great historian once said, Christianity 'connected mankind by higher and more universal ties of nationality. It taught men of every race and language that religion ought to bind them together by ties which no political prejudices ought to have strength to sever, and thus revealed how the progress of human civilization is practically connected with the observance of the divine precepts of Christ.'[9] At no time was such a claim more relevant than during the thirteenth century.

But perhaps in understanding the reign of Henry III yet another important factor must be taken into account. As another great historian, Henry Luard, said on researching the period, 'there can be no worse error than to judge one age by the ideas prevalent in another . . . of no age is this more true than of the thirteenth century'. In the seventeenth century comparisons were drawn between the reigns of Henry III and Charles I at the time of the civil war of 1644–9, but it is now apparent how different the circumstances were.[10] If there was indeed anything to be learnt from 1258–65 during the reign of Charles I, then sadly Charles I was also guilty of missing it.

If we are to find common ground between Henry III and another king of England we have to go all the way back to the monarch Henry esteemed more than any other. Like Henry, Edward the Confessor attempted to rule in peace but refused to move heaven and earth to ensure it. He was revered for his piety, generosity and beneficent rule, though his laxity allowed others, including foreign favourites, to empower themselves. Both kings gave generously to monasteries, at home and abroad, and during their reigns foreign churchmen gained greatly. As Henry had an obsession with Westminster Abbey, Edward had one with rebuilding the monastery at Thorney beyond the western gate of London – in fact he spent a tenth of all his possessions on it. The building was the earliest English example of Romanesque architecture in England.[11]

Perhaps it should be no surprise that Henry's favourite saint had such a profound effect on his own life and rule. After his death a cult of Henry emerged, and there were pilgrimages to his tomb. Miracles were said to have been witnessed there, and there were calls for him to be beatified. Like his antagonist interred at Evesham, there were strong beliefs about him, for better and worse. Is it a coincidence that Henry ordered the rebuilding of the abbey that had originally been constructed by Edward. Was it also a coincidence that at his second coronation he was crowned with the diadem of St Edward? Or that his final place of rest should be the very spot where the famous saint once lay?

Well. If the diadem fits . . .

Notes and References

Prelude

1   Hunt (1900e); Hallam (2002a), pp. 23–6.

2   Henry II's legitimate offspring were William, Count of
    Poitiers (1153–6), Henry the Young (1155–83), Matilda,
    Duchess of Saxony (1156–89), Richard the Lionheart
    (1157–89), Geoffrey, Duke of Brittany (1158–86),
    Eleanor, Queen of Castile (1162–1214), Joan, Queen of
    Sicily (1165–99), and John, King of England
    (1166–1216).

3   Giles (1849), Vol. 2, pp. 175–80; Hallam (2002b), p. 192;
    Hallam, pp. 24–5

4   McLynn, pp. 22–3.

5   Hunt (1900e).

6   Danziger and Gillingham, pp. 153–4.

7   Hunt (1900e); Giles (1849), Vol. 2, pp. 179–81.

8   Danziger and Gillingham, pp. 153–67; McLynn, pp. 282–3;
    Giles (1849), Vol. 2, pp. 182–3, 186–7; `Luard (1865), p. 74;
    Luard (1869), p. 50.

9   He had fathered at least seven bastards elsewhere. Luard
    (1864), p. 56.

10 McLynn, p. 294; Giles (1849), Vol. 2, pp. 187–8, 193; Luard (1869), p. 50.

11 McLynn, pp. 294–9.

12 The death of Henry I, the youngest son of William the Conqueror, in 1135 plunged England into civil war. His successor was his widowed daughter Matilda, later married to Geoffrey Plantagenet, son of the Count of Anjou. In 1148 she returned to France and renounced her claim to the English throne, instead focusing on establishing it for her son, Henry. The following year he inherited the Duchy of Normandy and then his father's title Count of Anjou. McLynn, pp. 1–2.

13 McLynn, pp. 302–3.

14 Danziger and Gillingham, pp. 153–67; McLynn, pp. 304–5; Giles (1849), Vol. 2, pp. 203–4; Luard (1869), p. 392.

15 Danziger and Gillingham, pp. 153–67; Giles (1849), Vol. 2, p. 205; Luard (1864), p. 56; Luard (1865), p. 78.

16 Giles (1849), Vol. 2, p. 215.

17 Danziger and Gillingham, pp. 153–67; McLynn, pp. 280–82; Giles (1849), Vol. 2, pp. 215–17.

18 Giles (1849), Vol. 2, pp. 197–200; Danziger and Gillingham, pp. 143, 153–67.

19 Giles (1849), Vol. 2, p. 215. Danziger and Gillingham, pp. 143–4

20 McLynn, pp. 372–4; Giles (1849), Vol. 2, pp. 239–40.

21 Giles (1849), Vol. 2, p. 246; Luard (1869), p 53.

22 Danziger and Gillingham, pp. 153–67; McLynn, pp. 376–8; Giles (1849), Vol. 2, pp. 246–51.

23 Giles (1849), Vol. 2, pp. 258–60; McLynn, pp. 380–82; Hunt (1900e).

24 Danziger and Gillingham, p. 165; McLynn, pp. 380–82; Holt (1961), p. 79; Holt (1965), p. 106; Giles (1849), Vol. 2,

pp. 257–8; Luard (1865), p. 268.

25 Danziger and Gillingham, pp. 144-9, 153–67; McLynn,
     pp. 380–82; Gasquet (1910), pp. 3–4; Holt (1961), p. 87;
     Holt (1965), pp. 129–30; Giles (1849), Vol. 2, pp. 263–71;
     Hardy (1869), p. 17; Luard (1864), p. 60; Luard (1865),
     p. 82.

26 Danziger and Gillingham, pp. 166–7, 257–8; Holt (1965),
     pp. 119, 130.

27 Luard (1877), pp. 8–9.

28 Giles (1849), Vol. 2, pp. 271–4, 293–5, 300–303; Hardy
     (1869), p. 18.

29 Giles (1849), Vol. 2, pp. 303–4; Danziger and Gillingham,
     pp. 255–8.

30 Danziger and Gillingham, pp. 255–8.

31 Luard (1877), p. 9.

32 Holt (1965), p. 22.

33 Danziger and Gillingham, pp. 255–8; Holt (1961), p. 102;
     Holt (1965), pp. 135, 139; Carpenter (2003), pp. 85–7, 135,
     159.

34 Danziger and Gillingham, pp. 257–8; Holt (1965), p. 142;
     Giles (1849), Vol. 2, pp. 305–6.

35 Danziger and Gillingham, pp. 255–60; Holt (1961), p. 107;
     Holt (1965), p. 153; Giles (1849), Vol. 2, pp. 305–8; Hardy
     (1869), p. 20.

36 Holt (1961), pp. 111–13.

37 Danziger and Gillingham, pp. 255–76; Holt (1965), p. 155;
     Giles (1849), Vol. 2, pp. 309–23; Hardy (1869), p. 20.

38 Danziger and Gillingham, pp. 255–76; Holt (1965), p. 266;
     Giles (1849), Vol. 2, pp. 326–33.

39 Gasquet, p. 17; McLynn, pp. 432–4; Giles (1849), Vol. 2,
     pp. 333–4; Hardy (1869), p. 21.

40 Gasquet, pp. 20–21; McLynn, pp. 445–8; Giles (1849),

Vol. 2, pp. 342–7.

41 Holt (1965), p. 243; Giles (1849), Vol. 2, pp. 357–9; Luard (1865), p. 283.

42 Danziger and Gillingham, pp. 261–7; Hunt (1900e); Giles (1849), Vol. 2, pp. 335–9; Luard (1864), p. 62.

43 Danziger and Gillingham, pp. 261–7; McLynn, pp. 338–41; Holt (1961), pp. 131–2; Holt (1965), p. 258.

44 Giles (1849), Vol. 2, pp. 345–7; Hunt (1900e); Danziger and Gillingham, pp. 266–7.

45 Gasquet, p. 23; Hunt (1900e); Holt (1961), p. 1; Giles (1849), Vol. 2, pp. 340–41; Hardy (1869), p. 21.

46 Gasquet, pp. 24–5; Giles (1849), Vol. 2, pp. 362–3.

47 Giles (1849), Vol. 2, pp. 365–7; Luard (1865), p. 285.

48 Holt (1961), p. 53.

49 Danziger and Gillingham, pp. 265–9; Holt (1961), p. 132.

50 Gasquet, p. 26.

51 Danziger and Gillingham, pp. 6–7; McBrien (1995), p. 667.

52 Luard (1877), p. 11.

53 Holt (1961), p. 138.

54 Giles (1849), Vol. 2, pp. 377–9.

55 Powicke (1947), p. 1; Luard (1869), p. 407.

Chapter 1

1 Tout (1906), p. 19; Powicke (1947), pp. 1–2.

2 Powicke (1947), p. 1.

3 Hunt (1900d); Luard (1869), p. 54.

4 Powicke (1962), p. 1; Powicke (1947), pp. 1–2.

5 Hallam, p. 23.

6 Holt (1965), pp. 100–101; Hennings, p. 1; Powicke (1947), pp. 3–4; Giles (1849), Vol. 2, pp. 379–81; Powicke (1962), pp. 1–2.

7   Hunt (1900d).

8   Tout (1906), p. 19; Powicke (1947), p. 1; Powicke (1962), pp. 1–3.

9   Hallam, p. 26.

10   Hennings, pp. 1–3; Hunt (1900d); Tout (1906), pp. 20–21; Hallam, pp. 23–6; Gasquet, pp. 28–9; Powicke (1962), p. 1; Powicke (1947), pp. 3–4.

11   Hallam, pp. 28–9; Powicke (1962), pp. 1–3.

12   *Dictionary of National Biography*, 'William Marshal'.

13   Powicke (1947), pp. 4–7.

14   Powicke (1962), pp. 2–3; Hennings, p. 3.

15   Hallam, pp. 26–7.

16   Powicke (1947), pp. 6–7; Powicke (1962), pp. 4–5; Holt (1965), pp. 269–92.

17   Tout (1906), pp. 22–3; Powicke (1947), pp. 4–8; Powicke (1962), pp. 4–5.

18   Powicke (1962), p. 8.

19   Powicke (1947), pp. 7–8; Giles (1849), Vol. 2, pp. 381–2.

20   Luard (1877), p. 12; Gasquet, p. 30.

21   Luard (1877), p. 12; Gasquet, pp. 30–33.

22   Hunt (1900d); Tout (1906), pp. 21–3; Gasquet, pp. 29–31; Powicke (1947), pp. 2, 6–9; Hennings, p. 4; Giles (1849), Vol. 2, pp. 385–6.

23   Powicke (1947), pp. 7–8; Hennings, pp. 3–4; Giles (1849), Vol. 2, pp. 382–3.

24   Tout (1906), pp. 22–3.

25   Powicke (1947), p. 5; Luard (1877), p. 12; Gasquet, p. 30.

26   Luard (1877), pp. 12–13.

27   Luard (1877), pp. 13–14; Gasquet, pp. 31–3.

28   Gasquet, pp. 33–4.

29   Tout (1906), pp. 23–4; Giles (1849), Vol. 2, pp. 387–8; Powicke (1962), pp. 9–11.

30 Tout (1906), pp. 22–7; Powicke (1947), p. 10.

31 Powicke (1947), p. 28.

32 Powicke (1947), pp. 8–9; Tout (1906), pp. 22–7.

33 Tout (1906), p. 22–7; Hennings pp. 4–5, 8–9; Powicke
    (1947), pp. 10–11; Powicke (1962), pp. 8–9; Luard (1865),
    p. 408.

34 Luard (1877), p. 14; Gasquet, pp. 33–7.

35 Powicke (1947), pp. 10–11.

36 Tout (1906), pp. 21–4; Hallam, pp. 28–9; Gasquet,
    pp. 29–31.

37 Tout (1906), pp. 22–7; Giles (1849), Vol. 2, pp. 389–90.

38 Tout (1906), pp. 22–7; Hallam, pp. 28–9; Powicke (1947),
    pp. 10–11; Giles (1849), Vol. 2, pp. 391–3.

39 Powicke (1947), pp. 11–12; Powicke (1962), pp. 10–12.

40 Tout (1906), pp. 25–6; Giles (1849), Vol. 2, pp. 392–7.

41 Hunt (1900d).

42 Powicke (1947), p. 13; Powicke (1962), pp. 12–13.

43 Tout (1906), pp. 25–6; Hardy (1869), p. 23.

44 Luard (1877), pp. 14–15; Powicke (1947), p. 13.

45 Powicke (1947), pp. 13–17; Powicke (1962), pp. 12–13;
    Tout (1906), pp. 22–7; Giles (1849), Vol. 2, pp. 398–400;
    Luard (1865), p. 287.

46 Powicke (1947), pp. 16–17, 23; Powicke (1962), pp. 13–14;
    Giles (1849), Vol. 2, pp. 400–402; Hardy (1869), p. 23.

47 Hunt (1900d); Hennings, pp. 4–5, 8–9; Tout (1906),
    pp. 22–7; Hallam, pp. 28–9; Powicke (1962), pp. 12–14.

48 Hunt (1900d); Hennings, pp. 4–5, 8–9; Tout (1906),
    pp. 22–7; Hallam, pp. 28–30; Powicke (1962), pp. 12–15.

49 Powicke (1947), pp. 19–21.

Chapter 2

1 Giles (1848), p. 69; Hume, p. 57; Luard (1865), p. 80; Luard (1866), p. 450.

2 Giles (1849), Vol. 2, p. 61; McLynn, p. 394; Colvin, pp. 90–158.

3 Powicke (1947), pp. 18–19, 21–3.

4 Tout (1906), pp. 27–8; Holt (1965), pp. 272–3.

5 Danziger and Gillingham, pp. 123–35.

6 Also mentioned was the payment of dower to Berengaria, widow of Richard I, as requested by Honorius. Luard (1877), p. 15.

7 Luard (1877), p. 15; Gasquet, pp. 37–40; Powicke (1947), p. 30; Hennings, p. 12.

8 Powicke (1947), p. 27.

9 Hunt (1900d); Powicke (1962), pp. 16–17; Tout (1906), pp. 28–9; Giles (1849), Vol. 2, p. 404.

10 Hunt (1900d); Luard (1877), p. 15; Hennings, pp. 9–10; Hardy (1869), p. 23.

11 Tout (1906), pp. 27–8.

12 Giles (1849), Vol. 2, pp. 404–5.

13 Hunt (1900d).

14 Tout (1906), pp. 30–31; Powicke (1962), pp. 16–17.

15 Hunt (1900d); Luard (1877), pp. 16–17; Powicke (1962), pp. 16–17; Luard (1864), p. 63; Luard (1865), p. 289.

16 Luard (1877), pp. 16–17.

17 Gasquet, pp. 41–2; Powicke (1962), pp. 16–17; Luard (1877), p. 17; Hardy (1869), p. 24.

18 Hunt (1900d); Powicke (1962), pp. 16–17; Giles (1849), Vol. 2, pp. 413–14; Powicke (1947), p. 27; Carpenter (2003), p. 303.

19 Gasquet, pp. 44–5; Tout (1906), pp. 28–30; Hunt (1900d);

Giles (1849), Vol. 2, pp. 413–14; Powicke (1962), p. 17.

20 Hunt (1900d); Tout (1906), pp. 28–30; Hallam, p. 30; Gasquet, pp. 44–5.

21 Tout (1906), pp. 30–31.

22 Luard (1877), pp. 18–19.

23 Hunt (1900d); Luard (1877), p. 20; Hardy (1869), p. 25.

24 Giles (1849), Vol. 2, pp. 426–7.

25 Powicke (1962), pp. 18–19; Giles (1849), Vol. 2, p. 428; Luard (1866), p. 455.

26 The diadem was the first in a hereditary collection of regalia. It was destroyed in the English Civil War.

27 Hunt (1900d); Tout (1906), p. 31; Hallam, pp. 30–34; Gasquet, p. 53.

28 Powicke (1962), pp. 18–19.

29 There seems some doubt over the actual dates of these letters. Gasquet suggests they were sent on 14 May, while Hunt suggests 26 May, implying a delay after the coronation. It is possible that there were two letters, one on each date. Luard (1877), p. 21; Gasquet, pp. 48–9; Stubbs, p. 32.

30 Dower is the right of a woman to receive income from her late husband's estate. Dowry is the property brought to a marriage by the wife. Luard (1865), p. 291.

31 Hunt (1900d); Tout (1906), p. 31; Gasquet, p. 53; Luard (1877), p. 23; Hardy (1869), p. 25.

32 Hunt (1900d); Giles (1849), Vol. 2, p. 427.

33 Hunt (1900d); Giles (1849), Vol. 2, pp. 427–8.

34 Powicke (1962), p. 24; Luard (1877), p. 23; Gasquet, pp. 53–5; Giles (1849), Vol. 2, pp. 427–8; Luard (1865), p. 293.

35 Hunt (1900d); Tout (1906), pp. 31–3; Powicke (1947), pp. 52–3; Powicke (1962), pp. 22–3; Giles (1849), Vol. 2, pp. 428–9; Luard (1866), p. 64.

NOTES AND REFERENCES

36 Tout (1906), pp. 32–4; Luard (1877), p. 23.

37 Luard (1877), p. 23.

38 Luard (1877), p. 24; Hunt (1900d); Gasquet, pp. 53–5.

39 Luard (1877), pp. 24–5.

40 Powicke (1962), pp. 22–3; Hunt (1900d); Tout (1906), pp. 32–4; Gasquet, pp. 53–5; Luard (1866), p. 69; Hardy (1869), p. 26.

41 Tout (1906), pp. 32–4; Giles (1849), Vol. 2, pp. 439–41; Powicke (1947), pp. 56–7; Luard (1865), p. 297.

42 Gasquet, pp. 59–62; Luard (1869), pp. 62–3.

43 Hunt (1900d); Hennings, pp. 147–8; Giles (1849), Vol. 2, pp. 443–4; Luard (1877), p. 26; Luard (1866), p. 83.

44 Luard (1877), p. 26.

45 Tout (1906), pp. 34–5; Giles (1849), Vol. 2, pp. 443–4.

46 Luard (1877), pp. 26–7; Gasquet, pp. 70–72, 73–5; Luard (1866), p. 83.

47 Tout (1906), pp. 33–4; Luard (1877), p. 29; Luard (1865), p. 299.

48 Powicke (1947), pp. 58–9; Hunt (1900d); Hennings, pp. 17–19; Tout (1906), pp. 33–4; Giles (1849), Vol. 2, pp. 432–3.

49 Hunt (1900d); Luard (1866), pp. 67, 81, 85; Luard (1864), p. 67.

50 Luard (1877), p. 26; Gasquet, pp. 73–5; Powicke (1947), pp. 43–5, 56–7.

51 Hunt (1900d); Hennings, pp. 19–20; Tout (1906), pp. 33–5; Powicke (1947), pp. 50–51; Giles (1849), Vol. 2, pp. 449–50; Luard (1866), p. 84.

52 Powicke (1947), p. 59; Powicke (1962), pp. 24–6.

53 Luard (1877), p. 27; Gasquet, pp. 75–6; Powicke (1947),
    pp. 43–5; Powicke (1962), pp. 24–6; Giles (1849), Vol. 2,
    pp. 449–50.
54 Luard (1877), p. 27; Gasquet, p. 77–9; Powicke (1947),
    pp. 43–5, 58–60; Powicke (1962), pp. 24–6; Luard (1866),
    p. 84.

Chapter 3

1   Gasquet, pp. 76–81; Luard (1877), p. 27.
2   Luard (1877), p. 26; Giles (1849), Vol. 2, pp. 444–5; Luard
    (1866), p. 81.
3   Hunt (1900d); Powicke (1947), pp. 170–71; Luard (1866),
    pp. 81–2.
4   Gasquet, p. 72; Luard (1877), pp. 25–6; Hardy (1869), p. 27.
5   Luard (1877), p. 28; Powicke (1947), pp. 170–71.
6   Tout (1906), pp. 38–41.
7   Tout (1906), pp. 38–41; Powicke (1962), pp. 88–91.
8   Tout (1906), pp. 38–41; Giles (1849), Vol. 2, p. 450.
9   Gasquet, pp. 79–81; Giles (1849), Vol. 2, pp. 451–3; Powicke
    (1962), pp. 26–7.
10 Powicke (1947), pp. 63–5; Giles (1849), Vol. 2, pp. 451–3;
    Powicke (1962), pp. 26–7; Hennings, pp. 22–5; Luard
    (1865), p. 300.
11 Gasquet, pp. 79–81.
12 Tout (1906), pp. 35–6.
13 Luard (1877), pp. 28–9; Gasquet, pp. 79–81.
14 Hallam, p. 27.
15 Hunt (1900d); Hennings, pp. 22–5; Tout (1906), pp. 35–6;
    Hallam, p. 34.
16 Hunt (1900d); Hennings, pp. 22–5; Tout (1906), pp. 35–6;
    Hallam, p. 34.

17 Luard (1877), p. 28.

18 Luard (1877), p. 29.

19 Hunt (1900d); Hennings, pp. 28–9, 148–57; Tout (1906), pp. 36–7, 40–41; Hallam, p. 34; Luard (1877), pp. 29–31.

20 Later that year there was an inspection into the forests, concerning which would be exempt from forest laws. Giles (1849), Vol. 2, pp. 458–9.

21 Gasquet, pp. 82–4; Giles (1849), Vol. 2, pp. 455–6; Luard (1877), p. 29.

22 Hunt (1900d); Hennings, p. 30; Luard (1877), pp. 29–32; Gasquet, Ch. 5.

23 Giles (1849), Vol. 2, pp. 456–7.

24 Tout (1900).

25 Tout (1900); Powicke (1962), pp. 40–42, 90–92; Luard (1866), p. 94; Hardy (1869), p. 28.

26 Tout (1906), pp. 39–41; Tout (1900).

27 Hunt (1900d); Tout (1906), pp. 36–7, 40–41; Luard (1877), pp. 29–31; Powicke (1947), pp. 174–5.

28 Powicke (1947), p. 159.

29 Luard (1877), p. 29–30; Hardy (1869), p. 28.

30 Luard (1877), pp. 29–32; Giles (1849), Vol. 2, pp. 461–3.

31 Hunt (1900d); Luard (1877), pp. 29–31; Gasquet, pp. 82, 89–90, 94–6; Giles (1849), Vol. 2, pp. 461–3, 466–7.

32 Hallam, p. 34; Giles (1849), Vol. 2, pp. 459–60.

33 Hunt (1900d); Gasquet, pp. 92–4.

34 Luard (1877), p. 33; Gasquet, pp. 92–4; Giles (1849), Vol. 2, pp. 466–74.

35 Luard (1877), p. 33; Gasquet, p. 102.

36 Hunt; Luard (1877), pp. 29–34; Giles (1849), Vol. 2, pp. 473–7.

37 Luard (1877), pp. 29–38; Gasquet, pp. 82, 103–5, 112–14; Powicke (1947), pp. 346–7.

38 Luard (1877), pp. 29–38; Gasquet, pp. 82, 103–5, 112–14.

39 Powicke (1947), p. 175; Giles (1849), Vol. 2, pp. 480–81.

40 Tout (1906), pp. 40–41; Giles (1849), Vol. 2, pp. 483–5; Tout (1900).

41 Giles (1849), Vol. 2, pp. 485–7.

42 Powicke (1947), pp. 43–5.

43 Hunt (1900d); Luard (1877), pp. 29–38; Gasquet, pp. 82, 103–5, 112–14; Giles (1849), Vol. 2, pp. 486–7. There is an interesting note here, picked up by the historians William Hunt and William Stubbs, that during the minority of the king the permanent council of his advisers had developed as a separate body from the king's court. So there now existed the precursor to the Privy Council and later still the Cabinet.

44 Hunt (1900d); Tout (1906), pp. 36–41.

45 Tout (1906), pp. 36–41; McBrien, p. 638.

46 Hunt (1900d).

47 Hunt (1900d); Powicke (1962), pp. 93–4; Giles (1849), Vol. 2, pp. 486–7.

48 Gasquet, pp. 109–13; Tout (1900); Powicke (1947), pp. 71–2; Powicke (1962), pp. 40–42; Carpenter (1996), p. 59.

49 Hunt (1900d); Giles (1849), Vol. 2, pp. 488–9.

50 Hunt (1900d); Hennings, p. 30; Hallam, p. 38; Luard (1877), pp. 29–38; Gasquet, pp. 82, 103–5, 112–14.

51 Hallam, p. 47; Giles (1849), Vol. 2, pp. 508–11; Tout (1906), pp. 42–3.

52 Hunt (1900d); Powicke (1962), pp. 44–5; Luard (1869), p. 70.

Chapter 4

1 Powicke (1947), p. 176; Powicke (1962), pp. 92–3.
2 Gasquet, p. 116.
3 Hunt (1900d); Luard (1877), pp. 38–9; Gasquet, pp. 117–23; Giles (1849), Vol. 2, pp. 499–505, 508–9; Luard (1866), pp. 65, 107, 109.
4 Hunt (1900d); Luard (1877), pp. 39–41; Gasquet, pp. 121–7; Giles (1849), Vol. 2, pp. 519–21; Luard (1864), p. 71.
5 Luard (1877), pp. 40–41; Gasquet, pp. 121–7; Giles (1849), Vol. 2, pp. 498–9; Luard (1866), p. 109.
6 Powicke (1947), pp. 129–31.
7 Luard (1877), pp. 40–41; Gasquet, pp. 124–7.
8 Hallam, p. 38; Giles (1849), Vol. 2, pp. 527–31.
9 Hallam, pp. 38, 42; Luard (1877), pp. 40–41; Gasquet, pp. 124–7.
10 Luard (1877), p. 40; Gasquet, pp. 127–8; Giles (1849), Vol. 2, pp. 514–17.
11 Powicke (1947), pp. 176–7.
12 Hunt (1900d).
13 Tout (1906), pp. 36–41; Powicke (1947), p. 72; Powicke (1962), pp. 94–5; Giles (1849), Vol. 2, pp. 531–2.
14 Hunt (1900d); Giles (1849), Vol. 2, p. 533.
15 Powicke (1947), pp. 167–9, 176–83; Giles (1849), Vol. 2, pp. 534–7; Powicke (1962), pp. 94–5.
16 Tout (1906), pp. 40–41; Powicke (1962), pp. 94–5.
17 Hunt (1900d).
18 Giles (1849), Vol. 2, pp. 536–7; Powicke (1962), pp. 94–5.
19 Hunt (1900d); Hennings, pp. 33–4.

20 Hunt (1900d); Hennings, pp. 31, 157–9; Tout (1906),
   pp. 41–2; Hallam, pp. 24–5; Powicke (1947), pp. 167–8,
   182–3; Giles (1849), Vol. 2, pp. 538–9.
21 Hallam, p. 44.
22 Tout (1906), pp. 42–4; Luard (1864), p. 74.

Chapter 5

1 Powicke (1947), pp. 88–9; Powicke (1962), pp. 18–19;
   Giles (1849), Vol. 2, pp. 538–9.
2 Hunt (1900d); Giles (1849), Vol. 2, p. 538.
3 Luard (1877), pp. 41–2.
4 Luard (1877), pp. 41–2.
5 Luard (1877), pp. 42–3; Gasquet, p. 130; Giles (1849),
   Vol. 2, pp. 539–40.
6 Hunt (1900d); Powicke (1947), p. 126; Giles (1849), Vol. 2,
   pp. 538–40.
7 Hallam, pp. 44–6; Giles (1849), Vol. 2, p. 540.
8 Hallam, p. 46; Giles (1849), Vol. 2, p. 540.
9 Hunt (1900d); Hallam, pp. 44–6; Giles (1849), Vol. 2,
   p. 541; Luard (1866), p. 127.
10 Hunt (1900d).
11 Giles (1849), Vol. 2, pp. 543–4; Luard (1866), p. 127.
12 Hunt (1900d); Hennings, pp. 242–3.
13 Tout (1906), pp. 43–4; Giles (1849), Vol. 2, pp. 542–3.
14 Luard (1866), p. 128.
15 Hunt (1900d); Hallam, p. 48; Giles (1849), Vol. 2,
   p. 546.
16 Twenge was again present in Rome in 1239,
representing the grievances of many of the barons. On
this occasion his mission was a success (Gasquet,
pp. 135–9).

17 Luard (1877), pp. 44–7; Gasquet, pp. 133–7; Powicke (1947), p. 279.

18 Hunt (1900d); Hennings, p. 36; Hallam, pp. 46–52; Gasquet, pp. 130–32; Powicke (1947), p. 79; Carpenter (1996), p. 52; Giles (1849), Vol. 2, pp. 552–3.

19 Tout (1906), pp. 47–8.

20 Hunt (1900d); Tout (1906), pp. 44–5; Hallam, pp. 46–52; Powicke (1947), pp. 80–83; Powicke (1962), pp. 50–51; Giles (1849), Vol. 2, pp. 553–6.

21 Hunt (1900d); Giles (1849), Vol. 2, pp. 555–7.

22 Giles (1849), Vol. 2, pp. 561–2; Luard (1864), p. 87.

23 Hunt (1900d).

24 Powicke (1947), p. 138; Giles (1849), Vol. 2, pp. 557–8, 561–3; Luard (1864), p. 34.

25 Hallam, pp. 46–52.

26 Hunt (1900d); Hennings, pp. 39–44; Tout (1906), p. 47; Giles (1849), Vol. 2, pp. 565–6.

27 Powicke (1947), pp. 124–5.

28 Luard (1877), p. 46.

29 Powicke (1947), pp. 126–7; Pollock and Maitland, p. 565.

30 Hallam, pp. 52–3.

31 Powicke (1947), pp. 126–7; Powicke (1962), pp. 54–6; Tout (1906), pp. 48–9.

32 Luard (1877), pp. 46–7.

33 Powicke (1947), pp. 126–7.

34 Hunt (1900d); Hennings, pp. 39–44; Tout (1906), pp. 47–8; Hallam, pp. 52–3; Powicke (1947), pp. 128–9, 132–3.

35 Hunt (1900d); Hennings, pp. 39–44; Tout (1906), p. 47; Hallam, pp. 52–3; Powicke (1947), pp. 128–9, 132–3.

36 Hennings, pp. 39–44; Hallam, pp. 52–3; Powicke (1947), pp. 138–40; Giles (1849), Vol. 2, pp. 571–2.

Chapter 6

1   Gasquet, pp. 137–43.
2   Hunt (1900d); Giles (1849), Vol. 2, pp. 569–70.
3   Powicke (1947), pp. 129–31.
4   Tout (1906), pp. 48–9.
5   Hunt (1900d); Powicke (1947), p. 131.
6   Powicke (1947), p. 131; Powicke (1962), pp. 54–5; Giles
    (1849), Vol. 2, p. 572.
7   Powicke (1947), p. 131.
8   Tout (1906), pp. 48–9; Powicke (1962), pp. 56–7; Giles
    (1849), Vol. 2, p. 572.
9   Hunt (1900d).
10 Tout (1906), pp. 49–51; Giles (1849), Vol. 2, p. 573.
11 Hunt (1900d); Giles (1849), Vol. 2, pp. 574–5.
12 Powicke (1947), pp. 132–3; Giles (1849), Vol. 2, pp. 580–82.
13 Hunt (1900d); Tout (1906), pp. 48–50.
14 Hunt (1900d); Powicke (1947), pp. 134–5; Giles (1849),
    Vol. 2, pp. 580–82.
15 Powicke (1947), p. 136; Powicke (1962), pp. 48–9; Carpenter
    (1996), p. 50.
16 Hunt (1900d); Giles (1849), Vol. 2, p. 586.
17 Powicke (1947), p. 136; Powicke (1962), pp. 57–9; Giles
    (1849), Vol. 2, pp. 587–9; Luard (1869), p. 79.
18 Tout (1906), pp. 48–51; Powicke (1962), pp. 57–9; Giles
    (1849), Vol. 2, pp. 589–91; Luard (1864), p. 93; Luard
    (1865), pp. 86, 314.

Chapter 7

1   Langton also advised Gregory against the election of
    Neville. Luard (1869), pp. 73–4.

2 Gasquet, pp. 137–45; Powicke (1962), pp. 56–7.

3 Gasquet, pp. 137–45; Powicke (1962), pp. 56–7; Luard (1865), p. 312.

4 Powicke (1947), p. 140; Hallam, p. 53.

5 Powicke (1947), pp. 136–7.

6 Powicke (1947), pp. 137–9; Powicke (1962), pp. 59–61.

7 Tout (1906), pp. 51–2.

8 Powicke (1947), pp. 136–7.

9 Hunt (1900d); Giles (1849), Vol. 2, p. 596.

10 Hallam, p. 53.

11 Powicke (1947), pp. 136–7.

12 Luard (1877), p. 48; Gasquet, pp. 143–8.

13 Luard (1877), p. 49.

14 Gasquet, Ch. 9.

15 Luard (1877), p. 49; Gasquet, Ch. 9.

16 Luard (1877), p. 49; Giles (1849), Vol. 2, p. 607; Hardy (1869), p. 35.

17 Hallam, pp. 53, 54, 56; Howell, p. 10; Giles (1852–4), Vol. 1, p. 1; Maddicott, p. 19.

18 Hallam, pp. 53, 54, 56; Giles (1849), Vol. 2, pp. 607–9; Luard (1864), p. 96.

19 Giles (1849), Vol. 2, pp. 609–10.

20 Hallam, pp. 53, 54, 56.

21 Luard (1877), p. 50.

22 Luard (1877), pp. 49–50.

23 Hunt (1900d).

24 Luard (1877), p. 50.

25 Powicke (1947), pp. 307–8.

26 Hallam, pp. 84–5.

Chapter 8

1   Howell, pp. 10–11; Gasquet, pp. 160–70; Hardy (1869),
    p. 36.
2   Howell, pp. 1, 12; Hardy (1869), p. 36.
3   Howell, pp. 1–2.
4   Hunt (1900d); Howell, p. 12.
5   Hunt (1900d); Hennings pp. 48–50.
6   Howell, pp. 13–14; Giles (1852–4), Vol. 1, pp. 7–8; Hardy
    (1869), p. 36.
7   Hallam, pp. 56, 58; Giles (1852–4), Vol. 1, pp. 8–9; Howell,
    p. 14.
8   Giles (1852–4), Vol. 1, p. 8.
9   Hallam, pp. 56, 58.
10 Hallam, pp. 56, 58; Giles (1852–4), Vol. 1, pp. 9–10.
11 Hallam, pp. 56, 58; Giles (1852–4), Vol. 1, pp. 9–10;
    Howell, pp. 17–18.
12 Howell, p. 7.
13 Hallam, pp. 56, 58.
14 Powicke (1947), pp. 148–50; Powicke (1962), pp. 68–9;
    Giles (1852–4), Vol. 1, pp. 12–14; Luard (1864),
    pp. 249–50.
15 Powicke (1947), pp. 150–52; Powicke (1962), pp. 68–71.
16 Luard (1877), p. 51; Hallam, p. 79.
17 Hunt (1900d); Tout (1906), pp. 54–5; Powicke (1947),
    pp. 148–53; Giles (1852–4), Vol. 1, pp. 29–30.
18 Hunt (1900d); Powicke (1947), p. 290; Giles (1852–4),
    Vol. 1, pp. 35, 42–5; Luard (1869), p. 84.
19 Powicke (1947), pp. 352–3; Powicke (1962), pp. 74–5;
    Hennings pp. 50–51.
20 Hunt (1900d); Hennings pp. 50–51; Tout (1906), p. 55;
    Giles (1852–4), Vol. 1, p. 68.

21 Gasquet, Ch. 10; Giles (1852–4), Vol. 1, pp. 54–5.
    Presumably this did not include John's right to submit
    England to the papacy in 1213.

22 Hunt; Giles (1852–4), Vol. 1, pp. 36–7.

23 Powicke (1947), pp. 140–41; Giles (1852–4), Vol. 1, pp. 47–8.

24 Hunt (1900d); Hennings, pp. 52–4; Gasquet, Ch. 10;
    Powicke, p. 159; Whatley, p. 464; Giles (1852–4), Vol. 1, p. 70.

25 Gasquet, Ch. 10; Giles (1852–4), Vol. 1, pp. 62–3, 71–93;
    Luard (1864), p. 105.

26 Gasquet, Ch. 10.

Chapter 9

1   Giles (1852–4), Vol. 1, p. 117.

2   Maddicott, pp. 1–7; Hallam, p. 75. The death without issue
    of the Earl of Huntingdon, Chester's heir following the
    death of Ranulph de Blondevilles, saw the Earldom of
    Chester pass to the Crown (Powicke, p. 142).

3   Giles (1852–4), Vol. 1, p. 117.

4   Away from court, Richard was developing a close affinity
    with Frederick, his brother-in-law since 1235. The pair
    often wrote to one another, as when Frederick told Richard
    of the crusade and the recent birth of his son.
    Giles (1852–4), Vol. 1, pp. 117–20.

5   Hunt (1900d); Hennings, pp. 54–5; Powicke (1947),
    pp. 290–91.

6   Powicke (1947), pp. 290–91; Giles (1852–4), Vol. 1,
    pp. 122–3; Maddicott, p. 21.

7   Gasquet, Ch. 10; Powicke (1947), pp. 204–5. Giles (1852–4),
    Vol. 1, p. 124.

8   Hunt (1900d); Giles (1852–4), Vol. 1, p. 119. (Tout refers to
    23 April as the date of this meeting.)

9   Tout (1906), pp. 56–7; Powicke (1947), pp. 352–3; Giles
    (1852–4), Vol. 1, pp. 126–8.

10 Gasquet, pp. 178–80; Powicke (1947), pp. 186–7; Giles
    (1852–4), Vol. 1, p. 125; Luard (1865), p. 318.

11 Hunt (1900d); Powicke (1947), pp. 186–7; Hardy (1869),
    p. 39.

12 Hallam, pp. 60–61; Danziger and Gillingham, p. 7.

13 Giles (1852–4), Vol. 1, pp. 132–3.

14 Hunt; Gasquet, pp. 178–80; Tout (1906), pp. 55–6; Giles
    (1852–4), Vol. 1, pp. 135–6.

15 Powicke, pp. 270–71; Carpenter (1996), p. 62; Giles
    (1852–4), Vol. 1, pp. 136–7, 164–5.

16 Hunt (1900d); Hallam, p. 59.

17 Giles (1852–4), Vol. 1, p. 139.

18 Hunt (1900d); Giles (1852–4), Vol. 1, pp. 158–60. Henry
    and Gilbert made up in 1240 thanks to the mediation of
    Richard, Earl of Cornwall.

19 Powicke (1947), pp. 204–5; Giles (1852–4), Vol. 1,
    p. 172.

20 Giles (1852–4), Vol. 1, p. 172.

21 Giles (1852–4), Vol. 1, pp. 193–4; Hunt (1900d); Maddicott,
    p. 25.

22 Powicke (1947), pp. 354–5; Giles (1852–4), Vol. 1,
    p. 261.

23 Gasquet, pp. 184–7.

24 Giles (1852–4), Vol. 1, p. 254.

25 Gasquet, pp. 184–7; Giles (1852–4), Vol. 1,
    pp. 266–8.

26 Gasquet, pp. 178–85.

27 Hunt (1900d); Giles (1852–4), Vol. 1, pp. 278, 309–11.

28 Gasquet, pp. 175–9.

29 Giles (1852–4), Vol. 1, pp. 262–3, 283–7.

30 Gasquet, pp. 187–8; Giles (1852–4), Vol. 1, pp. 295, 299–300, 318–21.

31 Powicke (1947), pp. 314–15.

32 Tout (1906), pp. 55–6; Carpenter (1996), p. 190; Giles (1852–4), Vol. 1, pp. 268–70, 290, 320.

Chapter 10

1 Isabella died in childbirth in December 1241.

2 Gasquet, pp. 179–81; Hunt (1900d); Giles (1852–4), Vol. 1, pp. 241, 246, 319; Luard (1865), p. 323.

3 Giles (1852–4), Vol. 1, p. 290.

4 Hunt (1900d); Tout (1906), p. 58; Gasquet, pp. 195–9; Giles (1852–4), Vol. 1, pp. 352–6, 382–3.

5 Hunt (1900d); Giles (1852–4), Vol. 1, pp. 163, 334–6.

6 Powicke (1947), pp. 188–9; Giles (1852–4), Vol. 1, pp. 394–5.

7 Hunt (1900d); Giles (1852–4), Vol. 1, pp. 371–3.

8 Gasquet, pp. 195–8; Giles (1852–4), Vol. 1, p. 373–6.

9 Hallam, pp. 62–3; Giles (1852–4), Vol. 1, p. 311.

10 Hunt (1900d); Hallam, pp. 62–3; Giles (1852–4), Vol. 1, p. 378.

11 Hunt (1900d); Giles (1852–4), Vol. 1, pp. 395–6.

12 Powicke (1947), pp. 188–9; Powicke (1962), pp. 102–3; Giles (1852–4), Vol. 1, pp. 396–400.

13 Hunt (1900d); Gasquet, pp. 202–4; Powicke (1947), pp. 298–9, 306–7.

14 Powicke (1947), pp. 190–91.

15 Giles (1852–4), Vol. 1, pp. 405–6.

16 Hunt (1900d); Giles (1852–4), Vol. 1, p. 406.

17 Giles (1852–4), Vol. 1, pp. 413–17.

18 Shirley, pp. 21–2; Powicke (1962), pp. 102–3.

19 Hunt (1900d); Giles (1852–4), Vol. 1, pp. 418–20.

20 Giles (1852–4), Vol. 1, pp. 418–22; Powicke (1962), pp. 102–3.

21 Shirley, pp. 25–9; Hunt (1900d); Hennings, pp. 56–9; Tout (1906), pp. 59–62; Hallam, pp. 24–5; Gasquet, pp. 202–4; Powicke (1947), pp. 190–91, 194–5; Powicke (1962), pp. 102–3; Giles (1852–4), Vol. 1, pp. 423–31; Luard (1866), p. 162.

22 Hunt (1900d); Powicke (1947), pp. 290–91; Powicke (1962), p. 105; Giles (1852–4), Vol. 1, pp. 445–6, 459–60; Luard (1866), p. 162; Luard (1865), p. 330.

23 Powicke (1947), p. 141.

24 Gasquet, pp. 207–9.

25 Gasquet, pp. 205–6; Giles (1852–4), Vol. 1, pp. 448–50.

26 Gasquet, pp. 209–14; Powicke (1947), pp. 272–3; Giles (1852–4), Vol. 1, pp. 460–64, 480–81, 487; Giles (1852–4), Vol. 2, pp. 6–7, 17–19.

27 Gasquet, pp. 213–15; Giles (1852–4), Vol. 1, pp. 479–80; Giles (1852–4), Vol. 2, 13–14.

28 Powicke (1947), pp. 300–301; Carpenter (1996), p. 62; Giles (1852–4), Vol. 2, pp. 7–9.

29 Gasquet, pp. 213–18; Giles (1852–4), Vol. 2, pp. 8–9.

30 Powicke (1947), pp. 298–9.

31 Gasquet, pp. 213–18; Giles (1852–4), Vol. 2, pp. 14–16.

32 Hunt (1900d); Hennings, pp. 59–60; Tout (1906), pp. 59–63; Powicke (1947), pp. 354–5; Gasquet, pp. 220–22; Luard (1866), p. 164; Giles (1852–4), Vol. 2, pp. 32–4; Hardy (1869), p. 43; Luard (1869), p. 92.

33 Hunt (1900d); Powicke (1947), pp. 292–3, 299.

34 Gasquet, pp. 218–20.

35 Tout (1906), p. 63; Giles (1852–4), Vol. 2, pp. 1–3, 4–5, 38–41.

36 Gasquet, pp. 220–24.

37 McBrien, p. 802; Giles (1852–4), Vol. 2, pp. 45, 48–9.

38 Gasquet, pp. 223–5; Giles (1852–4), Vol. 2, 49–50.

39 Gasquet, pp 228–9, 235–45; Powicke (1947), pp. 346–9; Luard (1877), p. 8.

40 Hunt (1900d); Hennings, pp. 60–63; Tout (1906), p. 62; Gasquet, pp. 226–7; Powicke (1947), pp. 356–7; Giles (1852–4), Vol. 2, 56–8.

41 Gasquet, pp. 246–7; Powicke (1947), pp. 280–81; Hennings, pp. 63–5; Luard (1864), p. 279.

42 Powicke (1947), pp. 357–61; Gasquet, pp. 251–4.

43 Hunt (1900d); Giles (1852–4), Vol. 2, pp. 36–7.

Chapter 11

1   Powicke (1962), p. 18.

2   Hallam, pp. 30–31, 100.

3   Hallam, pp. 30–31, 100.

4   Noake, p. 53; Harvey, p. 244.

5   Harvey, p. 227; Gasquet (1908), p. 116.

6   Milman, p. 159; Henry, p. 5; Harvey, p. 232.

7   Anon, p. 108; Harvey, pp. 230–31.

8   Harvey, p. 220.

9   Harvey, p. 236.

10 Harvey, p. 229.

11 Harvey, pp. 221, 224.

12 Winkles and Moule, pp. 1–4; Harvey, p. 239.

13 Moule, p. 42; Harvey, p. 246; Luard (1864), p. 146.

14 Winkles and Moule, pp. 82–4. Harvey, p. 241; Hallam, pp. 48–9.

15 Gasquet (1908), pp. 30–34.

16 Cook; Harvey, p. 237.

17 Harvey, p. 243.

18 Giles (1852–4), p. 435; Luard (1864), p. 146; Luard (1865), p. 302 .

19 Carpenter (1996), pp. 199–201.
20 Carpenter (1996), p. 200.
21 Lockwood and Cates, p. 22; Hull, p. 99; Gascoigne and Gascoigne, p. 58.
22 Pettifer, p. 99.
23 Gascoigne and Gascoigne, p. 72; Colvin, pp. 20–82.
24 Brown.
25 Pettifer, p. 253.
26 Gascoigne and Gascoigne, pp. 88–9.
27 Gascoigne and Gascoigne, p. 140.
28 Ditchfield, pp. 29–56.

Chapter 12

1   Hunt (1900d); Hallam, p. 47; Giles (1852–4), Vol. 2, pp. 115–16, 140–41; Luard (1869), p. 94.
2   Powicke (1947), pp. 364–5; Gasquet, pp. 257–9; Giles (1852–4), Vol. 2, pp. 164–5.
3   Tout (1906), p. 61.
4   Gasquet, pp. 255–9.
5   The Province of Canterbury or the Southern Province remains one of two provinces of the Church of England, the other being York. At the time it consisted of thirty dioceses.
5   Gasquet, pp. 258–63.
6   Powicke (1947), pp. 360–61.
7   Gasquet, pp. 261–5.
8   Gasquet, pp. 265–9; Hennings, pp. 65–9; Giles (1852–4), Vol. 3, pp. 16–17; Giles (1852–4), Vol. 2, pp. 203–4.
9   Gasquet, pp. 263–79.
10 Gasquet, Ch. 15, pp. 273–5; Giles (1852–4), Vol. 2, pp. 209–11, 254–7.
11 Gasquet, Ch. 15, pp. 273–9.

12 Tout (1906), pp. 67–8.

13 Maddicott, pp. 29–31; Tout (1906), pp. 64–5.

14 Powicke (1947), pp. 214–15; Maddicott, pp. 106–8.

15 Tout (1906), pp. 64–5; Maddicott, pp. 110–11.

16 Powicke (1947), p. 217.

17 Hunt (1900d); Gasquet, pp. 261–5. Paris II, pp. 229-30

18 Powicke (1947), pp. 318–19; Hunt (1900d); Giles (1852–4), Vol. 2, pp. 233–4.

19 There is a conflict of sources here. According to some, this happened in 1248.

20 Hunt (1900d).

21 Gasquet, pp. 281–5.

22 Powicke (1947), pp. 227–31, 230–31; Luard (1865), p. 91.

23 Hunt (1900d); Hallam, p. 74; Powicke (1947), pp. 208, 318–19.

24 Hunt (1900d); Powicke (1947), pp. 230–31.

25 Gasquet, pp. 285–7; Giles (1852–4), Vol. 2, pp. 329–31.

26 Hallam, pp. 72–4.

27 Gasquet, pp. 285–7.

28 Gasquet, pp. 291–5.

29 Gasquet, pp. 301–5.

30 Powicke (1947), pp. 194–5.

31 Hunt (1900d); Powicke (1947), p. 217.

32 Powicke (1947), pp. 216–17.

33 Tout (1906), pp. 65–6; Hallam, pp. 68–72.

34 Hunt (1900d); Powicke (1947), pp. 230–31; Luard (1866), p. 184; Luard (1864), pp. 290–92.

35 Hunt (1900d); Hallam, p. 74, 76–7; Powicke (1947), pp. 216–17; Powicke (1962), p. 112.

36 Hennings, pp. 72–7, 78–9; Hallam, pp. 74, 76–7; Maddicott, p. 118; Morris, p. 17.

37 Hallam, p. 76.

38 Gasquet, pp. 339–41; Powicke (1947), p. 231; Powicke (1962), pp. 106–7.

39 Hunt (1900d); Hallam, pp. 74, 76–7; Powicke (1947), pp. 366–70.

40 Gasquet, pp. 305–11; Hunt (1900d).

41 Powicke (1947), pp. 194–5.

42 Hallam, pp. 76–7; Hardy (1869), p. 48.

43 Hunt (1900d); Hallam, pp. 74, 76–7.

44 Hunt (1900d); Giles (1852–4), Vol. 3, p. 14–16.

45 Gasquet, pp. 295–9, 311–13.

46 Gasquet, pp. 313–15; Giles (1852–4), Vol. 3, pp. 1–3; Carpenter (1996), p. 191.

47 Giles (1852–4), Vol. 3, pp. 10–13; Luard (1864), p. 151.

48 Hunt (1900d); Gasquet, pp. 315–19; Giles (1852–4), Vol. 3, pp. 23–7.

49 Hunt (1900d); Gasquet, pp. 315–19.

50 Hallam, p. 79.

51 Hallam, pp. 76–7; Gasquet, pp. 315–19; Giles (1852–4), Vol. 3, p. 38.

52 Tout (1906), pp. 64–6; Luard (1864), pp. 311–15.

53 Hunt (1900d); Hennings, pp. 72–9.

54 Hunt (1900d); Powicke (1947), pp. 230–33.

55 Hunt (1900d); Giles (1852–4), Vol. 3, pp. 27–32, 34–7.

56 Hunt (1900d); Shirley, pp. 101–2; Luard (1865), pp. 345–6.

57 Powicke (1947), pp. 234–7.

58 Powicke (1947), pp. 233–4; Carpenter (1996), p. 186; Hunt (1900d); Tout (1906), pp. 66–7, 69; Hardy (1869), p. 51.

59 Powicke (1947), pp. 232–3; Tout (1906), pp. 66–7, 69.

60 Hunt (1900d); Hennings, pp. 176–7; Tout (1906), pp. 66–7, 69; Powicke (1947), pp. 232–3; Giles (1852–4), Vol. 3, pp. 80–84; Luard (1865), p. 94.

61 Powicke (1947), pp. 230–33; Powicke (1962), pp. 118–19.

62 Tout (1906), pp. 66–7, 69; Hardy (1869), p. 50.

63 Powicke (1947), p. 239; Giles (1852–4), Vol. 3, pp. 97–8, 100–106; Hallam, p. 78.

64 Powicke (1947), pp. 239–41; Hallam, p. 78; Giles (1852–4), Vol. 3, pp. 98, 106–9; Luard (1864), pp. 327–8; Luard (1865), p. 95.

65 Hallam, pp. 80–82; Giles (1852–4), Vol. 3, pp. 106–10.

66 Giles (1852–4), Vol. 3, p. 110.

Chapter 13

1 Matthew Paris was still critical of Henry's manner in receiving the second gift. Hallam, pp. 80–82; Giles (1852–4), Vol. 3, p. 112.

2 Hallam, p. 78; Gasquet, pp. 325–7; Giles (1852–4), Vol. 3, pp. 66–7.

3 McBrien, pp. 667–8.

4 Hallam, p. 65.

5 Powicke (1947), p. 241.

6 Hallam, pp. 80–82; Giles (1852–4), Vol. 3, p. 115; Luard (1864), p. 329.

7 Powicke (1947), pp. 308–9; Giles (1852–4), Vol. 3, p. 114.

8 Around this time Henry spent six days at St Albans. On this occasion he was praised by Matthew Paris for his generosity to the abbey, which exceeded that of any other king, including its founder. Giles (1852–4), Vol. 3, p. 116; Hunt (1900d).

9 Powicke (1947), pp. 236–7; Giles (1852–4), Vol. 3, pp. 89–93.

10 Gasquet, pp. 341–5.

11 Powicke (1947), pp. 238–9.

12 Hallam, pp. 42–3.

13 Hunt (1900d); Tout (1906), pp. 70–71; Hardy (1869), pp. 51–2.

14 Gasquet, pp. 345–9; Hardy (1869), pp. 51–2.

15 Gasquet, pp. 351–5; Tout (1900).

16 Gasquet, pp. 345–7; Powicke (1947), pp. 372–3.

17 Hunt (1900d); Hennings, pp. 80–82; Hardy (1869), pp. 54–5.

18 Hunt (1900d); Hallam, pp. 80–82; Hunt (1900b); Giles (1852–4), Vol. 3, pp. 135–6.

19 Powicke (1947), pp. 194–5.

20 Hallam, p. 47; Tout (1906), pp. 67–9; Luard (1869), pp. 384–5.

21 Hallam, pp. 82–4; Colvin, pp. 190–436.

22 Gasquet, pp. 340–55; Powicke (1962), pp. 121–3; Giles (1852–4), Vol. 3, p. 168; Luard (1864), pp. 384–5.

23 Hunt (1900d); Gasquet, pp. 359–63.

24 Gasquet, pp. 345–7; Hardy (1869), pp. 57–8.

25 Gasquet, pp. 319–21.

26 Powicke (1947), pp. 223–5.

27 Gasquet, pp. 369–73; Giles (1852–4), Vol. 3, pp. 244–5, 65–9.

28 Hunt (1900d); Giles (1852–4), Vol. 3, p. 225.

29 Powicke (1947), pp. 242–3; Hunt (1900d); Giles (1852–4), Vol. 3, p. 225.

330 Giles (1852–4), Vol. 3, p. 236–7; Gasquet, pp. 373–5.

31 Giles (1852–4), Vol. 3, p. 241.

32 Tout (1906), p. 68.

33 Tout (1906), pp. 68–9; Giles (1852–4), Vol. 3, p. 245.

34 Hunt (1900d).

35 Hallam, pp. 82–4; Tout (1900).

36 Tout (1900); Powicke (1962), p. 121; Giles (1852–4), Vol. 3, pp. 217–24.

37 Hallam, pp. 84–6; Giles (1852–4), Vol. 3, p. 223.

38 Gasquet, pp. 373–7.

39 Tout (1906), p. 70.

40 Carpenter (2003), p. 57.

41 Carpenter (2003), p. 57; Luard (1866), p. 462.

Chapter 14

1   Hunt (1900d); Tout (1906), pp. 83–4; Giles (1852–4), Vol. 3, pp. 270–71.

2   Hallam, p. 88; Maddicott, p. 152.

3   Hennings, pp. 88–91, suggests that this occurred in 1257.

4   Tout (1906), pp. 83–4; Maddicott, pp. 152–4.

5   Henry is reputed to have said, 'I will send and have your corn threshed out and sold, and so humble your pride', to which the witty earl replied, 'And I will send you the heads of the threshers.' Hunt (1900d).

6   Powicke (1947), pp. 377–9; Carpenter (1996), pp. 194–5.

7   Powicke (1947), pp. 378–9; Powicke (1962), pp. 136–7.

8   Tout (1906), pp. 83–6; Hardy (1869), p. 62; Luard (1865), p. 97.

9   Hunt (1900d); Giles (1852–4), Vol. 3, pp. 294–5.

10 Hunt (1900d); Tout (1906), pp. 83–4; Hallam, pp. 86–90; Gasquet, pp. 321–5; Powicke (1962), pp. 144–6.

11 Tout (1906), pp. 86–8.

12 Maddicott, pp. 155–7, 172–7, 179; Powicke (1947), pp. 247–9; Powicke (1962), pp. 124–5.

13 Powicke (1947), pp. 247–9.

14 Gasquet, pp. 375–81.

15 Gasquet, pp. 375–7; Giles (1852–4), Vol. 3, p. 300.

16 Giles (1852–4), Vol. 3, pp. 316–18; Shirley, p. 132; Hardy (1869), p. 63.

17 Hunt (1900d); Hallam, pp. 88–92; Gasquet,
pp. 377–81.

18 Hallam, pp. 24–5; Tout (1906), p. 88; Powicke (1962),
pp. 126–7.

19 Powicke (1947), pp. 253–5; Powicke (1962), pp. 126–7.

20 Tout (1906), p. 88.

21 Hallam, pp. 90–92.

22 Powicke (1947), pp. 169–70; Powicke (1962), pp. 154–5;
Hunt (1900d).

23 Hunt; Carpenter (1996), Ch. 12; Tout (1906), pp. 88–9;
Gasquet, pp. 377–81; Maddicott, p. 185; Powicke (1962),
pp. 146–7.

24 Tout (1906), pp. 88–91; Hunt (1900d).

25 Tout (1906), pp. 88–91; Luard (1869), p. 125.

26 Gasquet, pp. 383–5.

27 Morris, p. 46.

28 Hunt (1900d); Carpenter (1996), pp. 220–22.

29 Tout (1906), pp. 88–91.

30 Most of the blame for Edward's anger has been placed
at his mother's door.

31 Hunt (1900d); Luard (1866), p. 217.

32 Hunt (1900d); Tout (1906), pp. 88–91; Hallam, p. 96;
Gasquet, pp. 385–9; Morris, p. 47.

33 Hunt (1900d); Powicke (1962), pp. 162–3.

34 Hunt (1900d).

35 Hunt (1900d); Powicke (1962), pp. 162–3; Tout (1906),
pp. 88–91; Gasquet, pp. 385–9.

36 Hunt (1900d); Powicke (1962), pp. 162–7; Tout (1906),
pp. 90–91; Gasquet, pp. 385–9.

37 Gasquet, pp. 385–9.

38 Hunt (1900d); Powicke (1962), pp. 166–7; Tout (1906),
pp. 90–91.

39 Hunt (1900d); Powicke (1962), pp. 168–9; Tout (1906), pp. 90–91; Gasquet, pp. 385–9.

40 Hunt (1900d); Powicke (1962), p. 170; Maddicott, p. 221.

41 Hunt (1900d); Gasquet, pp. 385–9.

42 Hunt (1900d); Powicke (1962), pp. 171–4.

43 Gasquet, pp. 375–9, 387–95.

44 Gasquet, pp. 375–9, 387–95.

45 Gasquet, pp. 375–9, 387–95.

46 Hunt (1900d); Gasquet, pp. 395–8.

47 Tout (1906), pp. 91–3.

48 Hunt (1900d); Powicke (1962), pp. 176–7; Hennings, pp. 105–11; Tout (1906), pp. 91–3; Gasquet, pp. 395–8.

49 Hunt (1900d); Tout (1906), pp. 91–3.

50 Hunt (1900d); Powicke (1962), pp. 178–80; Hallam, p. 96; Maddicott, pp. 242–3; Luard (1864), p. 176.

51 Hunt (1900d); Luard (1869), p. 136.

52 Hennings, pp. 105–11; Gasquet, pp. 395–8.

53 Hunt (1900d); Powicke (1962), pp. 182–4; Hennings, pp. 105–11; Tout (1906), pp. 91–3; Hallam, p. 96; Luard (1869), pp. 137–9.

Chapter 15

1 Hallam, pp. 96–7; Hardy (1869), p. 71.

2 Hunt (1900d); Gasquet, pp. 375–9, 387–95.

3 Tout (1906), p. 93; Powicke (1962), pp. 184–5.

4 Gasquet, pp. 375–9, 387–95; Powicke (1962), pp. 184–5; Hardy (1869), p. 71.

5 Hunt (1900d); Powicke (1962), pp. 186–7; Carpenter (1996), pp. 224–5; Hennings, pp. 113–19; Tout (1906), pp. 93–6; Gasquet, pp. 375–9, 387–95; Luard (1869),

pp. 141–3.

6 Evidently Henry became aware that de Montfort had left London while he was still at Battle. Maddicott, p. 270; Luard (1869), pp. 145–8.

7 Tout (1906), pp. 93–7; Powicke (1962), pp. 186–9.

8 Hunt (1900d); Tout (1906), pp. 93–6.

9 Hallam, pp. 96–7; Tout (1906), pp. 95–7; Luard (1869), pp. 150–52.

Chapter 16

1 Hunt (1900d); Tout (1906), p. 97.

2 Gasquet, pp. 375–9, 387–95; Powicke (1962), pp. 194–5; Luard (1869), pp. 152–3.

3 Hunt (1900d); Hennings, pp. 179–80; Powicke (1962), pp. 191–2.

4 Hunt (1900d); Powicke (1962), pp. 192–3; Hardy (1869), p. 74.

5 Gasquet, p. 399.

6 Gasquet, pp. 398–404.

7 Tout (1906), pp. 98–9; Hunt (1900d); Luard (1869), pp. 158–9.

8 Hunt (1900d); Hennings, pp. 123–5.

9 Tout (1906), pp. 98–9.

10 Hallam, pp. 96–8.

11 Tout (1906), pp. 100–101; Powicke (1962), pp. 200–201.

12 Hunt (1900d); Powicke (1962), pp. 200–201.

13 Tout (1906), pp. 100–101; Powicke (1962), pp. 200–203.

14 Tout (1906), pp. 100–101.

15 Hunt (1900d); Powicke (1962), pp. 202–4.

16 Hunt (1900d); Powicke (1962), pp. 203–5; Carpenter (1996), p. 224–5; Hennings, pp. 123–8; Luard (1865), pp. 364–5;

Luard (1869), pp. 168–9.

17 Tout (1906), pp. 102–3; Powicke (1962), pp. 203–5.

18 Hunt (1900d); Hennings, pp. 130–34; Tout (1906), pp. 102–3;
Luard (1869), pp. 170–74.

Chapter 17

1 Hunt (1900d).

2 Hallam, pp. 98–100; Hunt (1900d); Tout (1906), pp. 102–3;
Luard (1865), pp. 102–3; Luard (1869), pp. 175–7.

3 Hunt (1900d).

4 Hunt (1900d); Hallam, pp. 98–100; Gasquet, pp. 403–7.

5 Hallam, pp. 98–100; Powicke (1962), pp. 204–5; Luard
(1865), p. 366.

6 Tout (1906), p. 103.

7 Hunt (1900d); Gasquet, pp. 403–7; Luard (1869),
pp. 183–4.

8 Tout (1906), pp. 102–3.

9 Tout (1906), pp. 102–3; Powicke (1962), pp. 206–7.

10 Tout (1906), pp. 103–4; Luard (1865), p. 368; Luard (1866),
p. 463.

11 Hunt (1900d); Hennings, pp. 139–44; Powicke (1962),
pp. 208–9; Tout (1906), pp. 103–5; Luard (1865),
pp. 366–70.

12 Tout (1906), pp. 104–5; Powicke (1962), pp. 212–14; Luard
(1869), pp. 193–5.

13 Hunt (1900d); Hallam, p. 100; Powicke (1962), pp. 213–15;
Luard (1865), p. 105; Luard (1869), p. 374.

14 Hunt (1900d); Hallam, p. 100; Tout (1906), pp. 104–5;
Luard (1869), pp. 201–7.

15 Gasquet, pp. 413–18.

16 Hunt (1900d); Powicke (1962), pp. 214–18.

17 Hallam, p. 47; Tout (1906), pp. 105–6; Powicke (1962), pp. 214–18.
18 Gasquet, p. 411 Powicke (1962), pp. 218–19; Luard (1865), pp. 106–7.
19 Hunt (1900d).
20 Hunt (1900d).
21 Gasquet, p. 411; Hunt (1900d); Hallam, p. 104; Powicke (1962), pp. 220–21.
22 Hunt (1900d).
23 Hunt (1900d); Hallam, pp. 90–93, 104.
24 Hunt (1900d); Gasquet, p. 417.
25 Hunt (1900d).
26 Hallam, p. 104; Luard (1865), p. 243.
27 Hunt (1900d); Luard (1865), p. 111.
28 Hunt (1900d); Hennings, p. 146; Hallam, p. 105.

Chapter 18

1   Hallam, p. 105.
2   Powicke (1947), pp. 70–71.
3   McLynn, pp. 27–8.
4   McLynn, pp. 27–8.
5   Powicke (1947), p. 162.
6   Tout (1906), pp. 145–7.
7   Hennings, p. 246.
8   Powicke (1947), pp. 8–9.
9   Luard (1877), pp. 4–5.
10 Powicke (1962), p. 8.
11 Hunt (1900a).

BIBLIOGRAPHY

Anonymous (1865), *History and Antiquities of Lincoln: Lincoln Cathedral*, Brookes and Vibert

Bartlett, Robert (1993) *The Making of Europe: Conquest, Colonization and Cultural Change, 950–1350*, Harmondsworth: Allen Lane

— (2000), *England Under the Angevin Kings 1075–1225*, Oxford: Oxford University Press

Bennett, James (1830), *The History of Tewkesbury*, Tewkesbury: Longman, Rees, Orme, Brown and Green

Blaauw, William Henry (1871), *The Barons' War Including the Battles of Lewes and Evesham*, London: Bell and Daldy

Bradbury, Jim (1998), *Philip Augustus, King of France, 1180–1223*, London: Longman

Britton, John, and Brayley, Edward Wedlake (1830), *Memoirs of the Tower of London*, London: Hurst, Chance and Co.

Brown, R. Allen (1977), *Allen Brown's English Castles*, London: B.T. Batsford

Bumpus, T. Francis (1921), *The Cathedrals of England and Wales*, T. Wener Laurie

Carpenter, D.A. (1990), *The Minority of Henry III*, Los Angeles, California: University of California Press

— (1996) *The Reign of Henry III*, London: Hambleton Press

— (2003) *The Struggle for Mastery: Britain 1066–1284*, Oxford: Oxford University Press

Carter, John (1824), *Specimens of Gothic Architecture and Ancient Buildings in England*, Vols 1–4, London: Edward Jeffrey and Son

Church, S.D. (ed.) (1999) *King John: New Interpretations*, Woodbridge: Boyd and Brewer

Colvin, H.M. (1971) *Building Accounts of King Henry III*, Oxford: Clarendon Press

Cook, George Henry (1957), *The English Cathedral Through the Centuries*, London: Phoenix House

Costain, Thomas B. (1973), *The Pageant of England 1216–1272: The Magnificent Century*, London: Tandem

Danziger, Danny, and Gillingham, John (2003), *1215: The Year of Magna Carta*, London: Hodder and Stoughton

Davis, John Paul (2009), *Robin Hood: The Unknown Templar*, London: Peter Owen

De Ros, Lord (1866), *Memorials of the Tower of London*, London: John Murray

Ditchfield, Peter Hampton (1907), *History of the County of Berkshire*, Vol. 3, London: Constable

Ellis, Alexander J. (1868), *The Only English Proclamation of Henry III, 18 October 1258*, London: Asher and Co.

Gascoigne, Christina, and Gascoigne, Bamber (1976), *Castles of Britain*, London: Book Club Associates

Gasquet, Francis Aidan (1908), *The Greater Abbeys of England*, London: Chatto and Windus

— (1910), *Henry the Third and the Church: A Study of Ecclesiastical Policy and of the Relations between England and Rome*, London: G. Bell and Sons

Giles, J.A. (1848), *The Life and Times of Alfred the Great*,

London: George Bell

— (1849), *Roger of Wendover's Flowers of History, Comprising the History of England from the Descent of the Saxons to AD 1235*, Vols 1–2, London: Henry G. Bohn

— (1852–4), *Matthew Paris's English History from the Year 1235 to 1273*, Vols 1–3, London: Henry G. Bohn

Gillingham, John (1999), *Richard I*, New Haven, Connecticut: Yale University Press

Hallam, Elizabeth (2002a), *Chronicles of the Age of Chivalry: The Plantagenet Dynasty from 1216 to 1377*, London: Salamander Books

— (2002b), *The Plantagenet Chronicles: Medieval Europe's Most Tempestuous Family*, London: Salamander Books

Halliwell, James Orchard (1846), *Letters of the Kings of England*, Vols 1–2, London: Henry Colburn

— (1860), *The Chronicle of William de Rishanger, of the Barons' War: The Miracles of Simon de Montfort*, London: Camden Society

Hamilton, J.S. (2010), *The Plantagenets: History of a Dynasty*, London and New York: Continuum

Hardy, Thomas Duffus (1869), *Syllabus (in English) of the Documents Relating to England and Other Kingdoms Contained in the Collection Known as 'Rymer's Foedera'*, Vol. 1, London: Longmans, Green and Co.

Harvey, John (1956), *The English Cathedrals*, London: B.T. Batsford

Hawkins, John Sidney (1813), *An History of the Origin and Establishment of Gothic Architecture*, London: J. Taylor

Hearne, Thomas (1810), *Robert of Gloucester's Chronicle*, London: Mercier and Chervet

Hennings, Margaret (1924), *England Under Henry III*,
   New York: Longmans, Green

Henisch, Bridget Ann (1999), *The Medieval Calendar Year*,
   Philadelphia, Pennsylvania: Pennsylvania University Press

Henry, David (1753), *An Historical Description of the Tower
   of London and Its Curiousities*, London: J. Newbery

Henry, John, and Parker, James (1856), *Annals of England:
   An Epitome of English History*, Vols 1–2, Oxford and
   London: John Henry and James Parker

Holt, J.C. (1961), *The Northerners: A Study in the Reign of
   King John*, Oxford: Clarendon Press

— (1965), *Magna Carta*, Cambridge: Cambridge University
   Press

Hopkins, John Henry (1836), *Essay on Gothic Architecture*,
   Burlington, Vermont: Smith and Harrington, 1836

Howell, Margaret (2001), *Eleanor of Provence: Queenship in
   Thirteenth-Century England*, Oxford: Blackwell

Hume, David (1858), *History of England from the Invasion
   of Julius Caesar to the Abdication of James the Second*,
   Vol. III, Boston, Massachusetts: Phillips, Sampson and Co.

Hunt, William (1888), *The English Church in the Middle Ages*,
   London: Longmans, Green and Co.

— (1900a), *King Edward the Confessor: A Short Biography*,
   Oxford: Oxford University Press

— (1900b), *Eleanor of Castile, Queen of Edward I: A Short
   Biography*, Oxford: Oxford University Press

(1900c), *King Henry I of England: A Short Biography*, Oxford:
   Oxford University Press

(1900d), *King Henry III of England: A Short Biography*,
   Oxford: Oxford University Press

(1900e) *King John of England: A Short Biography*, Oxford:
   Oxford University Press

Jeake, Samuel (1728), *Charters of the Cinque Ports: Two Ancient Towns and Their Members*, London: Bernard Lintot

Keen, Maurice (ed.) (1999), *Medieval Warfare: A History*, Oxford: Oxford University Press

Knight, Stephen, and Ohlgren, Thomas (1997), *Robin Hood and Other Outlaw Tales*, Kalamazoo, Michigan: Medieval Institute Publications

Lapper, Ivan, and Parnell, Geoffrey (2000), *Landmarks in History: The Tower of London*, Oxford: Osprey Publishing

Lewis, Suzanne (1987), *The Art of Matthew Paris in the Chronica Majora*, Berkeley, California: University of California Press

Lockwood, Henry Francis, and Cates, Adolphus H. (1834), *The History and Antiquities of the Fortifications to the City of York*, London: J. Weale, Charles White, J. Lee, J. Noble, J. and G. Todd

Luard, Henry Richards (1864–9), *Annales Monastici*, Vols 1–5, London: Longmans, Green, Reader and Dyer

— (1872–83), *Matthaei Parisiensis, Monachi Sancti Albani, Chronica Majora*, Vols 1–7, London: Longmans and Co.

— (1877), *On The Relations Between England and Rome During the Earlier Portion of the Reign of Henry III*, London: Longmans, Green, Reader and Dyer

Maddicott, J.R. (1994), *Simon de Montfort*, Cambridge: Cambridge University Press

McBrien, Richard (1995), *The HarperCollins Encyclopaedia of Catholicism*, San Francisco, California: HarperCollins

McLynn, Frank (2006), *Lionheart and Lackland: King Richard, King John and the Wars of Conquest*, London: Vintage

Milman, Henry Hart (1868), *Annals of St Paul's Cathedral*, London: John Murray

Mitchell, Sydney Knox (1914), *Studies in Taxation under John and Henry III*, New Haven, Connecticut: Yale University Press

Morris, Marc (2009), *A Great and Terrible King: Edward I and the Forging of Britain*, London: Windmill Books

Mortimer, Ian (2009), *The Time Traveller's Guide to Medieval England*, London: Vintage

Mortimer, Richard (1994), *Angevin England 1154–1258*, Oxford: Blackwell

Moule, Thomas (1860), *Descriptive Account of the Cathedral Church of York*, London: David Borgue

Nicolle, David (2002), *Medieval Siege Weapons: Western Europe AD 585–1385*, Oxford: Osprey Publishing

Noake, John (1866), *The Monastery and Cathedral at Worcester*, London: Longman and Co.

Ohlgren, Thomas (1998), *Medieval Outlaws*, Stroud: Sutton Publishing

Parker, John Henry (1859), *An Introduction to the Study of Gothic Architecture*, Oxford: John Henry Parker

Pettifer, Adam (1995), *English Castles: A Guide by Counties*, Woodbridge, Suffolk: Boydell Press

Polluck, Frederick, and Maitland, F.W. (2007), *The History of English Law before the Time of Edward I*, Clark, New Jersey: Lawbook Exchange

Powicke, Maurice (1947), *King Henry III and the Lord Edward*, Vols 1–2, Oxford: Clarendon Press

— (1962) *The Oxford History of England: The Thirteenth Century 1216–1377*, Oxford: Clarendon Press

Prestwich, Michael (1997), *Edward I*, New Haven, Connecticut: Yale University Press

Prestwich, Michael, Britnell, Richard, and Frame, Robin (2005), *Thirteenth Century England X*, Woodbridge, Suffolk: Boydell Press

Prothero, George Walter (1877), *The Life of Simon de Montfort Earl of Leicester with Special Reference to the Parliamentary History of His Time*, London: Longmans

Pugin, A. (1838), *Antient Edifices in England*, Vols 1–2, London: Henry G. Bohn

Rapin-Thoyras, Paul de (1726), Whatley, Stephen (tr.) Le Clerc, Jean *et al. Acta Regia, or an Account of the Treaties, Letters, and Instruments between the Monarchs of England and Foreign Powers, publish'd in Mr. Rymer's Foedera, which are the basis of the English history, and contain those authorities which rectify the mistakes that most of our writers have committed for want of such a collection of records.* London: J. Darby, A. Bettesworth, F. Fayram *et al.*

Reeve, Matthew M. (2008), *Thirteenth-Century Wall Painting of Salisbury Cathedral*, Woodbridge, Suffolk: Boydell Press

Ruskin, John (1854), *On the Nature of Gothic Architecture*, London: Smith, Elder and Co.

Shirley, Walter Waddington (1862–6), *Royal and Other Historical Letters Illustrative of the Reign of Henry III*, Vols 1–2, London: Longmans, Green, Reader and Dyer

Steane, John (1993), *The Archeology of the Medieval English Monarchy*, New York: B.T. Batsford

Stone, John Benjamin (1870), *A History of Lichfield Cathedral with a Description of Its Architecture and Monuments*, London: Longmans, Green, Reader and Dyer

Stoughton, John (1862), *Windsor: A History and Description of the Castle and the Town*, London: Ward and Co.

Stubbs, William (1870), *Select Charters and Other Illustrations of English Constitutional History*, Oxford: Clarendon Press

Tout, Thomas Frederick (1900), *Richard, Earl of Cornwall: A Short Biography*, Oxford: Oxford University Press

— (1906) *The History of England: From the Accession of Henry III to the Death of Edward III (1216–1377)*, London: Longmans, Green and Co.

— (1933), *Chapters in the Administrative History of Medieval England*, Manchester: Manchester University Press

Vincent, Nicholas (2001), *The Holy Blood, King Henry III and the Westminster Blood Relic*, Cambridge: Cambridge University Press

Warton, T., Bentham, J., Grose, F., Milner, J. *et al.* (1808), *Essays on Gothic Architecture*, London: J. Taylor

Wheeler, J. (1842), *A Short History of the Tower of London with a List of the Interesting Curiousities Contained in the Armories and Regalia*, London: T. Hodgson

Winkles, Benjamin, and Moule, Thomas (1838), *Winkles's Architectural and Picturesque Illustrations of the Cathedral Churches of England and Wales*, Vols 1–2, London: Effingham Wilson, Royal Exchange and Charles Tilt

Woolgar, C.M. (2006), *The Senses in Late Medieval England*, New Haven, Connecticut: Yale University Press

PICTURE CREDITS

All photographs of buildings and sculptures are reproduced courtesy of Mike Davis unless otherwise indicated. The images of Eleanor of Aquitaine's tomb at Fontevraud, King John's tomb at Worcester Cathedral and William Marshal's effigy at London's Temple Church are from Christopher Knight's *The Popular History of England*, Bradbury and Evans, London, 1856. The drawings of King John murdering his nephew Arthur and of Edward saving his father, Henry III, at the Battle of Evesham are from Samuel Goodrich's *Pictorial History of England*, E.H. Butler and Co., Philadelphia, 1871. Depictions of King John's defeat at Bouvines, the arrival of Prince Louis in England and the Battle of Lincoln are from Matthew Paris's thirteenth-century *Chronica Majora*. The drawing of John signing the Magna Carta and the portraits of Henry III and Edward I are from *Cassell's Illustrated History of England*, Cassell, London, 1902. The portrait of Henry III is from Charles Knight's and Harriet Martineau's *Pictorial History of England*, W. and R. Chambers, London, 1855. The nineteenth-century engraving of Eleanor of Provence by B. Eyles is after a portrait by J.W. Wright in Sydney Wilmot's *The Queens of England*, Volume I, J.S. Virtue, London, 1868. The photograph of the west front of Wells Cathedral is reproduced courtesy of Pat Sayles. The stained-glass window showing Simon de Montfort's men being blessed before the Battle of Evesham is in St Lawrence's Church, Evesham (photograph: Mike Davis; with kind permission of the Church Conservation Trust). The illustrations of Westminster Abbey from the south-east and of the nave and choir from the west are by Warwick Goble from Francis Aidan Gasquet's *The Greater Abbeys of England*, Chatto and Windus, London, 1908. Henry III's tomb at Westminster Abbey is from Samuel Rawson Gardiner's *Students' History of England: From Earliest Times to the Death of Edward VII*, Longmans, Green and Co., 1915.

INDEX

Aberconwy, 139
Abergavenny, 95
Abingdon, 100, 119, 178
Abingdon, Edmund of, *see* Canterbury,
  Edmund Rich, Archbishop of
Adour, valley of the, 163
Agenais, 202
Aigueblanche, Peter of, 125; *see also*
  Hereford, Bishop of
Albigensian Crusade, 69, 73, 78, 117,
  163, 182
Albini, Philip of, 37
Alexander II, King of Scotland, 25,
  27–9, 48, 52, 54, 78, 86, 102, 114, 137,
  148, 244
Alexander III, King of Scotland, 148,
  169, 186–7, 193, 205
Alexander IV, Pope, 185–6,
  189–91, 201, 203–5, 207
Almain, Henry of, 197, 210, 219, 230,
  232, 238
Alphonse, Count of Poitiers, 78, 129,
  164
Alphonso VIII, King of Castile, 17, 19
Alphonso X, King of Castile,
  175–7, 183, 192, 202
Amiens, 144, 226
Amiens, Mise of, 211, 213–14, 216
Andrew, Prior of St Swithun's,
  Winchester, 127
Angers, 18, 79
Angevin Empire, 8, 16–17, 21, 32, 61,
  70, 86, 249
Anglesey, 159
Anjou, 16, 18–19, 22, 61, 65, 70, 79, 86,
  178, 184, 241, 252, 264
Apostolic See, 38, 65, 70, 83
Apulia, 186, 190
Aquitaine, 15–16, 18, 61, 63, 65, 172,
  177, 201, 238, 249
Aquitaine, Eleanor of, *see* Eleanor of
  Aquitaine
Arthur, Duke of Brittany, 16–18, 22, 26
Artois, Robert, Count of, 167
Aumale, William of, 35, 52–3, 57, 80

Auvergne, 66–7, 70
Avon, river, 226
Axholme, Isle of, 231

Bacon, Robert, 90
Bacon, Roger, 259
Baldwin II, Emperor of the Latin
  Empire of Constantinople,
  119–20
Baltics, 71, 120
Bamburgh, 248
Banstead, 134
Barbezieux, 133
Bardney Abbey, 134
Bardolf, William, 197
Barres, William des, 42
Basset, Gilbert, 92, 95, 99
Basset, Philip, 207
Bath, 105, 149
Bath, Jocelin, Bishop of, 31
Bazas, 66, 104, 176
Bearn, Gaston de, 163–4, 170, 175–6,
  190
Beatrice, daughter of Henry III, 176,
  202
Beatrice, Queen of Sicily, 160, 178
Beatrice of Savoy, Countess of
  Provence, 133–4, 178
Beaulieu, 28, 76, 148
Beaudesert, 7–8, 12, 196, 211, 226
Becket, St Thomas, 10, 52, 84, 104,
  146, 149–50, 247
Bedford Castle, 32, 63–5, 249, 253
Beeston Castle, 155
Benauges, 176
Berenger, Raymond, Count of
  Provence, 107–8, 134, 138,
  159–60
Bergerac, Lord of, 66
Berkhamsted Castle, 36–7, 156
Berwick, 25
Beverley Minster, 147
Bigod, Hugh, 196–8, 200, 205
Bigod, Roger, 4th Earl of Norfolk, 140,
  196–7, 221

306

INDEX

INDEX

Ludgershall, 154
Ludlow, 32, 224
Lusignan, Geoffrey, 80, 172
Lusignan, Guy de, 197
Lusignan, Hugh de (IX), 18, 22
Lusignan, Hugh de (X), 51, 60–62,
  65, 69–70, 72, 75, 79–80, 102, 104,
  129–33, 164
Lyon, 139–41, 160–61, 174, 182, 185

Magna Carta, 9, 11, 65, 83, 197, 219,
  236, 256; *see also* Charter of
  Liberties *and* Great Charter
Maidstone, 173
Maine, 16, 18
Malmesbury, 30
Mansel, John, 129–30, 197
Mansuetus, 201, 209
Marche, Count of, *see* Lusignan, Hugh
  de (X)
marcher, 32, 73, 200, 221, 223–4, 227
marches, 32, 35, 84, 191, 193, 204, 208,
  215, 217, 220, 223, 233–5
Margaret of Kent, 134
Margaret, Queen of France, 108–9,
  131, 178, 184, 205
Margaret, Queen of Norway, 205
Margaret, Queen of Scotland, 128,
  148, 158, 169, 187, 205
Marinus, 161
Marisco, William de, 121
Marlborough, 39, 50, 69, 105, 235, 246
Marsh, Geoffrey, 97–8
Marshal, Gilbert, 4th Earl of
  Pembroke, 100, 110, 122, 280
Marshal, Richard, 3rd Earl of
  Pembroke, 86, 89, 93–101, 188, 252
Marshal, William, 1st Earl of
  Pembroke, 30–35, 37, 39–43,
  47–50, 56, 154, 243–4, 254, 259
Marshal, William, 2nd Earl of
  Pembroke, 56, 65, 72, 80–81, 84, 117
Martin, papal collector, 136–7, 140–41,
  161
Mary, Duchess of Brabant, daughter of
  Philip II, 18
Maud's Castle or Painscastle, 86
Mauleon, Savary de, Seneschal of
  Poitou, 62, 70
Mauley, Peter de, 66

Menteith, Walter Bailloch, Earl of, 187
Merton, 88, 111–12, 184, 201
Merton, statute of, 111–12
Messina, Archbishop of, 189–90, 202
Mirebeau, 18, 80, 253
Monmouth, 95–6, 149, 225
Monmouth, John of, 32
Montfort family, de, 117–19, 163
Montfort de, Henry, 214, 227
Montfort, Peter de, 8, 196–7, 211, 226
Montfort, Simon de, 6th Earl of
  Leicester
  background and arrival in England,
    87, 110, 114, 117–19
  marriage, dispute and exile, 117,
    119–20, 122–3, 155, 163, 255
  Seneschal of Gascony, 163–6,
    168–71, 175–6, 190, 193
  opposition to the king, 177, 193,
    195–6
  Provisions of Oxford, 13, 197,
    199–201, 203–11, 213–16, 236
  second barons' war, 8–9, 13,
    215–17, 219–27, 230, 291–2
  defeat at Evesham, 227, 229–32,
    256
  legacy, 8–9, 13, 227, 236, 252–3,
    255–8
Montfort, Simon de, the Younger, 214,
  225–6, 230–32, 238
Montgomery, 57, 73, 84–5, 154, 235
Mortimer family, 32
Mortimer, Roger, 191, 197, 208, 217,
  224, 226, 231–4
Mountsorrel, 39–40

Nantes, 79–80
Netley Abbey, 248
Nevers, Count of, 38
Neville, Ralph, Bishop of Chichester
  and Chancellor of England, 55, 79,
  100–101, 121, 136, 277
Newark, 15, 28, 30–31, 33, 40, 48, 152,
  253
Newbury Castle, 34
Newcastle, 137, 155, 187
Niort, 62
Normandy, 16–19, 35, 60–61, 65, 70,
  78–9, 86, 172, 249, 264
Northampton, 23–4, 40, 48, 58, 61, 63,